EP Second Reader

EP Reader Series

Volume 2

First Edition

CONTENTS

Poetry   6
The City Zoo   31
The Adventures of Old Mr. Toad   37
Short Stories   81
The Adventures of Jimmy Skunk   100
Short Stories   142
Fifty Famous Stories   150
The Bobbsey Twins at Snow Lodge   227
Thirty More Famous Stories, selections   342

Answers   369
About   379

ACKNOWLEDGEMENTS

Thank you to Abigail Baia for her beautiful cover art.
Thank you for George Comninos for permission to print his story, *The City Zoo*.

Welcome to Easy Peasy All-in-One Homeschool's Second Reader

We hope you enjoy curling up with this book of books.

This is Easy Peasy's offline version of its assignments for Reading 2. The novels and poetry included are found in the public domain and have been gathered here along with each day's assignment directions. There are differences between this course and the online version because some reading assignments are not found in the public domain and had to be replaced.

Online activities from Easy Peasy's website, apart from reading, have been replaced with offline readings and activities found in this book.

It is noted when children could use online vocabulary games for review, but options for vocabulary review are included in the book.

Day 1

1. Read this famous poem. It's a Mother Goose nursery rhyme.
2. The first verse says that the sheep will come home on their own. Is that what happened? (Answers)

LITTLE BO-PEEP
Little Bo-Peep has lost her sheep,
And can't tell where to find them;
Leave them alone, and they'll come home,
And bring their tails behind them.

Little Bo-Peep fell fast asleep,
And dreamt she heard them bleating;
But when she awoke, she found it a joke,
For still they all were fleeting.

Then up she took her little crook,
Determined for to find them;
She found them indeed, but it made her heart bleed,
For they'd left all their tails behind 'em!

It happened one day, as Bo-peep did stray
Unto a meadow hard by--
There she espied their tails, side by side,
All hung on a tree to dry.

She heaved a sigh and wiped her eye,
And over the hillocks she raced;
And tried what she could, as a shepherdess should,
That each tail should be properly placed.

Day 2

1. Read these poems by Mother Goose.
2. What was Little Boy Blue doing instead of looking after the animals? (Answers)
3. Why does Johnny want the rain to go away? (Answers)
4. How should we be like a clock? (Answers)

LITTLE BOY BLUE

Little Boy Blue, come, blow your horn!
The sheep's in the meadow, the cow's in the corn.
Where's the little boy that looks after the sheep?
Under the haystack, fast asleep!

RAIN

Rain, rain, go away,
Come again another day;
Little Johnny wants to play.

THE CLOCK

There's a neat little clock,--
In the schoolroom it stands,--
And it points to the time
With its two little hands.

And may we, like the clock,
Keep a face clean and bright,
With hands ever ready
To do what is right.

WINTER

Cold and raw the north wind doth blow,
Bleak in the morning early;
All the hills are covered with snow,
And winter's now come fairly.

Day 3

1. Read these poems by Mother Goose.
2. Do you have twenty nails on each hand and twenty-five all together?
3. Is the poet telling the truth or is there deceit, lying, in the poem? (Answers)

FINGERS AND TOES
Every lady in this land
Has twenty nails, upon each hand
Five, and twenty on hands and feet:
All this is true, without deceit.

A SEASONABLE SONG
Piping hot, smoking hot.
What I've got
You have not.
Hot gray pease, hot, hot, hot;
Hot gray pease, hot.

DAME TROT AND HER CAT
Dame Trot and her cat
Led a peaceable life,
When they were not troubled
With other folks' strife.

When Dame had her dinner
Pussy would wait,
And was sure to receive
A nice piece from her plate.

Day 4

1. Read these poems by Mother Goose.
2. If the old woman hasn't left, then where is she living? (Answers)
3. Why did Tweedle-Dum and Tweedle-Dee forget to fight? (Answers)

CROSS PATCH
Cross patch, draw the latch,
Sit by the fire and spin;
Take a cup and drink it up,
Then call your neighbors in.

THE OLD WOMAN UNDER A HILL

There was an old woman
Lived under a hill;
And if she's not gone,
She lives there still.

TWEEDLE-DUM AND TWEEDLE-DEE

Tweedle-dum and Tweedle-dee
Resolved to have a battle,
For Tweedle-dum said Tweedle-dee
Had spoiled his nice new rattle.

Just then flew by a monstrous crow,
As big as a tar barrel,
Which frightened both the heroes so,
They quite forgot their quarrel.

Day 5

1. Read these Mother Goose rhymes.
2. When is Joan alone? (Answers)
3. Draw a picture about one of these poems or tell someone about what happens in them all.

OH, DEAR!

Dear, dear! what can the matter be?
Two old women got up in an appletree;
One came down, and the other stayed till Saturday.

LITTLE JUMPING JOAN

Here am I, little jumping Joan,
When nobody's with me
I'm always alone.

PAT-A-CAKE
Pat-a-cake, pat-a-cake,
Baker's man!
So I do, master,
As fast as I can.

Pat it, and prick it,
And mark it with T,
Put it in the oven
For Tommy and me.

Day 6

1. Read these poems by Walter De La Mare.
2. Why is Tim so tired? (Answers)
3. What does he think is so ugly in *I can't Abear*? (Answers)
4. What do you think it means that he can't "abear" the butcher shop? (Answers)
5. What about a butcher shop do you think he can't stand?

6. What do you think happened in *Some One*?

<u>Tired Tim</u>

Poor Tired Tim! It's sad for him.
He lags the long bright morning through,
Ever so tired of nothing to do;

He moons and mopes the livelong day,
Nothing to think about, nothing to say;
Up to bed with his candle to creep,
Too tired to yawn, too tired to sleep:
Poor Tired Tim! It's sad for him.

I Can't Abear

I can't abear a Butcher,
I can't abide his meat,
The ugliest shop of all is his,
The ugliest in the street;
Bakers are warm, cobblers dark,
Chemists burn watery lights;
But oh, the sawdust butcher's shop,
That ugliest of sights!

Some One

Some one came knocking
At my wee, small door;
Some one came knocking,
I'm sure – sure – sure;
I listened, I opened,
I looked to left and right,
But naught there was a-stirring
In the still dark night;
Only the busy beetle
Tap-tapping in the wall,
Only from the forest
The screech-owl's call,
Only the cricket whistling
While the dewdrops fall,
So I know not who came knocking,
At all, at all, at all.

Day 7

1. Read these poems by Walter De La Mare.
2. What is *The Cupboard* about? What does the boy want? How can he get it? (Answers)
3. What is *The Window* about? Why can he see people but they can't see him? (Answers)
4. The widow may not have a lot of money, but why is she not really poor? (hint: second to last line) (Answers)
5. There is a long list in this poem of different kinds of weeds. Usually you think that weeds are for pulling and throwing away, but weeds can have a lot of uses and can even be eaten.

The Cupboard

I know a little cupboard,
With a teeny tiny key,
And there's a jar of Lollypops
For me, me, me.
It has a little shelf, my dear,
As dark as dark can be,
And there's a dish of Banbury Cakes
For me, me, me.
I have a small fat grandmamma,
With a very slippery knee,
And she's the Keeper of the Cupboard
With the key, key, key.
And when I'm very good, my dear,
As good as good can be,
There's Banbury Cakes, and Lollypops
For me, me, me.

The Window

Behind the blinds I sit and watch
The people passing – passing by;
And not a single one can see
My tiny watching eye.

They cannot see my little room,
All yellowed with the shaded sun;
They do not even know I'm here;
Nor'll guess when I am gone.

A Widow's Weeds

A poor old Widow in her weeds
Sowed her garden with wild-flower seeds;
Not too shallow, and not too deep,
And down came April – drip – drip – drip.
Up shone May, like gold, and soon
Green as an arbour grew leafy June.

And now all summer she sits and sews
Where willow herb, comfrey, bugloss blows,
Teasle and pansy, meadowsweet,
Campion, toadflax, and rough hawksbit;
Brown bee orchis, and Peals of Bells;
Clover, burnet, and thyme she smells;

Like Oberon's meadows her garden is
Drowsy from dawn to dusk with bees.
Weeps she never, but sometimes sighs,
And peeps at her garden with bright brown eyes;
And all she has is all she needs—
A poor Old Widow in her weeds.

Day 8

1. Read these poems by Walter De La Mare.
2. What animals does he say can't see him?
3. In fact moles can see, they just see very poorly. Bats can see, but they can't see well in the dark which is when they like to fly. Owls can see by day, but they are usually asleep because they like to be out at night as well.
4. *Summer Evening* paints a word picture. Can you picture the scene? Draw the picture he describes in this poem.

All But Blind

All but blind
In his chambered hole
Gropes for worms
The four-clawed Mole.

All but blind
In the evening sky
The hooded Bat
Twirls softly by.

All but blind
In the burning day
The Barn-Owl blunders
On her way.

And blind as are
These three to me,
So blind to someone
I must be.

Summer Evening

The sandy cat by the Farmer's chair
Mews at his knee for dainty fare;
Old Rover in his moss-greened house
Mumbles a bone, and barks at a mouse
In the dewy fields the cattle lie
Chewing the cud 'neath a fading sky
Dobbin at manger pulls his hay:
Gone is another summer's day.

Day 9

1. Read these poems by Walter De La Mare.
2. What is the oak's "green crest"? (hint: What part of the oak tree is green?)
3. Where are the star's thrones set? (hint: Where are the stars?)

4. What words in the *Earth Folk* poem rhyme? (Answers)
5. In *Alone* what sounds does the woman hear now that she is old and there is no longer music and singing in her house? (Answers)

Earth Folk

The cat she walks on padded claws,
The wolf on the hills lays stealthy paws,
Feathered birds in the rain-sweet sky
At their ease in the air, flit low, flit high.

The oak's blind, tender roots pierce deep,
The oak's blind, tender roots pierce deep,
His green crest towers, dimmed in sleep,
Under the stars whose thrones are set
Where never prince hath journeyed yet.

Alone

A very old woman
Lives in yon house--
The squeak of the cricket,
The stir of the mouse,
Are all she knows
Of the earth and us.

Once she was young,
Would dance and play,
Like many another
Young popinjay;
And run to her mother
At dusk of day.

And colours bright
She delighted in;
The fiddle to hear,
And to lift her chin,
And sing as small
As a twittering wren.

But age apace
Comes at last to all;
And a lone house filled
With the cricket's call;
And the scampering mouse
In the hollow wall.

Day 10

1. Read these poems by Walter De La Mare.
2. In the horsemen, what color was the horse? (hint: last line)
3. Whose five eyes were "green and bright"? (hint: last line)

The Horseman

I heard a horseman
   Ride over the hill;
The moon shone clear,
The night was still;
His helm was silver,
   And pale was he;
And the horse he rode
   Was of ivory.

Five Eyes

In Hans' old Mill his three black cats
Watch the bins for the thieving rats.
Whisker and claw, they crouch in the night,
Their five eyes smouldering green and bright:
Squeaks from the flour sacks, squeaks from where
The cold wind stirs on the empty stair,
Squeaking and scampering, everywhere.

Then down they pounce, now in, now out,
At whisking tail, and sniffing snout;

While lean old Hans he snores away
Till peep of light at break of day;
Then up he climbs to his creaking mill,
Out come his cats all grey with meal--
Jekkel, and Jessup, and one-eyed Jill.

Day 11

1. You are going to read to a poem called, <u>When the Frost is on the Pumpkin</u>, by James Riley.
2. The line that is repeated in this poem is, "When the frost is on the punkin and the fodder's in the shock." Pumpkin is spelled that way on purpose. Say it the way it is written. The poem is written with a sort of accent. That's how the farmer sounds when he speaks. There are lots of words that end with n' such as cluckin' and struttin'. That means that there is a letter missing. Those words are clucking and strutting. Say them out loud both ways. Do you hear the difference? This poem is written the way the farmer would say it. Read this one out loud and just sound out the words to figure out what he's saying the best you can. You don't have to get every word. I'm not sure of every word. But you can get an idea of the time of year and what's going on and how he feels about it. If you are having a hard time, ask someone to read this poem to you.
3. Fodder is feed for animals. Below is a picture of grain in shocks. The grain has all been harvested, collected. It's ready to feed the animals.
4. What time of year is it when the harvest is all collected and there is frost on the pumpkin? (Answers)

5. How does the poet feel about the end of harvest? Is he happy that it's this time of year? (Answers)
6. What are some lines that show how he feels? I underlined some. What words show his feelings? I think the poem feels warm and homey. Is that a happy feeling? (Answers)

When the Frost is on the Punkin
BY JAMES WHITCOMB RILEY

When the frost is on the punkin and the fodder's in the shock,
   And you hear the kyouck and gobble of the struttin' turkey-cock,
   And the clackin' of the guineys, and the cluckin' of the hens,
   And the rooster's hallylooyer as he tiptoes on the fence;
   O, it's then's the times a feller is <u>a-feelin' at his best</u>,
   With the risin' sun to greet him from a night of peaceful rest,
   As he leaves the house, bareheaded, and goes out to feed the stock,
   When the frost is on the punkin and the fodder's in the shock.

They's something kindo' harty-like about the atmusfere
   When the heat of summer's over and the coolin' fall is here—
   Of course we miss the flowers, and the blossums on the trees,
   And the mumble of the hummin'-birds and buzzin' of the bees;
   But the air's so <u>appetizin'</u>; and the landscape through the haze
   Of a crisp and sunny morning of the airly autumn days
   Is a pictur' that no painter has the colorin' to mock—
   When the frost is on the punkin and the fodder's in the shock.

The husky, rusty russel of the tossels of the corn,
And the raspin' of the tangled leaves, as <u>golden as the morn</u>;
The stubble in the furries—kindo' lonesome-like, but still
A-preachin' sermuns to us of the barns they growed to fill;
The strawstack in the medder, and the reaper in the shed;
The hosses in theyr stalls below—the clover over-head!—
O, <u>it sets my hart a-clickin'</u> like the tickin' of a clock,
When the frost is on the punkin and the fodder's in the shock!

Then your apples all is gethered, and the ones a feller keeps
Is poured around the celler-floor in red and yeller heaps;
And your cider-makin' 's over, and your wimmern-folks is through
With their mince and apple-butter, and theyr souse and saussage, too! ...
I don't know how to tell it—but ef sich a thing could be
<u>As the Angels wantin' boardin'</u>, and they'd call around on *me*—
I'd want to 'commodate 'em—all the whole-indurin' flock—
When the frost is on the punkin and the fodder's in the shock!

Day 12

1. Read poems 01 through 04 by Christina Rossetti.
2. In the first two poems what is she describing? (Answers)
3. In poem 03, where are the two places she digs for flowers? (Answers)
4. Where will the flowers grow and where will flowers never grow? (Answers)
5. A linnet, in poem 04, is a bird.
6. What story does the bird tell? (Answers)

01

Bread and milk for breakfast,
And woolen frocks to wear,
And a crumb for robin redbreast
On the cold days of the year.

02

There's snow on the fields,
And cold in the cottage,

While I sit in the chimney nook
Supping hot pottage.

My clothes are soft and warm,
Fold upon fold,
But I'm so sorry for the poor
Out in the cold.

03

I dug and dug amongst the snow,
And thought the flowers would never grow;
I dug and dug amongst the sand,
And still no green thing came to hand.

Melt, O snow! the warm winds blow
To thaw the flowers and melt the snow;
But all the winds from every land
Will rear no blossom from the sand.

04

Hear what the mournful linnets say:
"We built our nest compact and warm,
But cruel boys came round our way
And took our summerhouse by storm.

"They crushed the eggs so neatly laid;
So now we sit with drooping wing,
And watch the ruin they have made,
Too late to build, too sad to sing."

Day 13

1. Read poems 08, 09 and 10.
2. Poem 08 talks about two linnets, two birds. One is outside in a tree and one is in a cage. The poet asks which is luckier. What is the poet's answer? (Answers)
3. Poem 09 is about rainbows. When it says "bow," it is talking about a rainbow. What does it say you need to have rainbows? (Answers)

4. Poem 10 mentions turf, meaning the ground or grass. The poet smells something sweet. The wind blows the smell her way. At the end of the poem she says that violets make the turf sweet. What does that mean? (Answers)

08

A linnet in a gilded cage,
A linnet on a bough,
In frosty winter one might doubt
Which bird is luckier now.

But let the trees burst out in leaf,
And nests be on the bough,
Which linnet is the luckier bird,
Oh who could doubt it now?

09

If all were rain and never sun,
No bow could span the hill;
If all were sun and never rain,
There'd be no rainbow still.

10

O wind, where have you been,
That you blow so sweet?
Among the violets
Which blossom at your feet.

The honeysuckle waits
For Summer and for heat.
But violets in the chilly Spring
Make the turf so sweet.

Day 14

1. Read poems 16, 17 and 18 by Christina Rossetti.
2. In poem 16 she describes how a flint rock just looks like a rock, but it really has a special purpose.
3. What happens when you strike flint rock? (Answers)
4. There are many things and people in this world that look ordinary but serve a special purpose.
5. In poem 17 it says that even the coldest May brings what? (Answers)
6. When it is summer in America, it is winter in Australia. America is in the north, what we call the northern hemisphere, and Australia is in the south or southern hemisphere. Also, you know that the sun rises and sets at different times everyday.
7. In the summer in America the days are long, the sun gets up early and goes down late so the nights are shorter. At the same time in Australia the opposite is happening. So when the days are long the nights are short and when the days are short the nights are long. Right?
8. The lark is known for singing in the morning, so when the sun is up early, the lark can sing for hours and hours.
9. The nightingale is known for singing at night. The poem says that even though the nights are long, they seem short because of the nightingale's singing. Does that mean she likes or doesn't like the nightingale's song? (Answers)

Vocabulary

1. **Admire** means to think well of someone or something, to have a good opinion of something, to respect someone.

16

Stroke a flint, and there is nothing to admire:
Strike a flint, and forthwith flash out sparks of fire.

17

There is but one May in the year,
And sometimes May is wet and cold;
There is but one May in the year
Before the year grows old.

Yet though it be the chilliest May,
With least of sun and most of showers,
Its wind and dew, its night and day,
Bring up the flowers.

18

The summer nights are short
Where northern days are long:
For hours and hours lark after lark
Trills out his song.

The summer days are short
Where southern nights are long:
Yet short the night when nightingales
Trill out their song.

Day 15

1. Read poems 20, 21 and 22 by Christina Rossetti.
2. What is poem 20 about? (Answers)
3. Draw a picture of the caterpillar in the poem.
4. What is the poet feeling in the first stanza of poem 21? (Answers)
   - A stanza is a section of a poem. There's a break between each stanza.
5. What is the poet feeling at the end of the second stanza? (Answers)
6. What words rhyme in poem 22? (Answers)

20

Brown and furry
Caterpillar in a hurry,
Take your walk
To the shady leaf, or stalk,
Or what not,
Which may be the chosen spot.
No toad spy you,
Hovering bird of prey pass by you;
Spin and die,
To live again a butterfly.

21

A pocket handkerchief to hem-
Oh dear, oh dear, oh dear!
How many stitches it will take
Before it's done, I fear.

Yet set a stitch and then a stitch,
And stitch and stitch away,
Till stitch by stitch the hem is done-
And after work is play!

22

If a pig wore a wig,
What could we say?
Treat him as a gentleman,
And say "Good day."

If his tail chanced to fail,
What could we do? -
Send him to the tailoress
To get one new.

Day 16

1. Read poems 24 and 25 by Christina Rossetti.
2. These poems teach. What is taught in poem 24? (Answers)
3. What do you think is being taught in poem 25? (hint: You would know if you lived in England.) (Answers)

Vocabulary

1. Use poem 25. Which is worth the most? the least? pound, shilling, pence? (Answers)
2. This is British money.

24

How many seconds in a minute?
Sixty, and no more in it.

How many minutes in an hour?
Sixty for sun and shower.

How many hours in a day?
Twenty-four for work and play.

How many days in a week?
Seven both to hear and speak.

How many weeks in a month?
Four, as the swift moon runn'th.

How many months in a year?
Twelve the almanack makes clear.

How many years in an age?
One hundred says the sage.

How many ages in time?
No one knows the rhyme.

25

What will you give me for my pound?
Full twenty shillings round.
What will you give me for my shilling?
Twelve pence to give I'm willing.
What will you give me for my penny?
Four farthings, just so many.

Day 17

1. Read poems 26, 27 and 28.
2. How many cherries did their family eat? (answer: 1 + 1 + 2 + 6 = 10)
3. Maybe you would like to make a picture or a calendar page based on poem 26 for whatever month it is right now. Example: It says that February is dripping wet, so you would write February at the top and draw rain drops and puddles.

26

January cold desolate;
February all dripping wet;
March wind ranges;
April changes;
Birds sing in tune
To flowers of May,
And sunny June
Brings longest day;
In scorched July
The storm-clouds fly
Lightning-torn;
August bears corn,
September fruit;
In rough October
Earth must disrobe her;
Stars fall and shoot
In keen November;
And night is long
And cold is strong
In bleak December.

27

What is pink? a rose is pink
By the fountain's brink.
What is red? a poppy's red
In its barley bed.
What is blue? the sky is blue
Where the clouds float thro'.
What is white? a swan is white
Sailing in the light.
What is yellow? pears are yellow,
Rich and ripe and mellow.
What is green? the grass is green,
With small flowers between.
What is violet? clouds are violet
In the summer twilight.
What is orange? why, an orange,
Just an orange!

28

Mother shake the cherry-tree,
Susan catch a cherry;
Oh how funny that will be,
Let's be merry!

One for brother, one for sister,
Two for mother more,
Six for father, hot and tired,
Knocking at the door.

Day 18

1. Read poems 29 and 34.
2. Both of these poems are about different uses of words. Like the peacock has eyes but can't see. Here is a picture of peacock feathers that look like eyes.

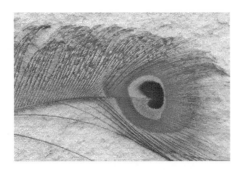

3. The poet is **observant**, pays attention to what's around her. I know you don't understand everything she points out, but find one in each poem and explain what it means to a parent or older sibling and then draw a picture of it. Example: The head of a pin is the top round part, but of course it doesn't have hair. You could draw a human head on the top of a pokey pin.

29

A pin has a head, but has no hair;
A clock has a face, but no mouth there;
Needles have eyes, but they cannot see;
A fly has a trunk without lock or key;
A timepiece may lose, but cannot win;
A corn-field dimples without a chin;
A hill has no leg, but has a foot;
A wine-glass a stem, but not a root;
A watch has hands, but no thumb or finger;
A boot has a tongue, but is no singer;
Rivers run, though they have no feet;
A saw has teeth, but it does not eat;
Ash-trees have keys, yet never a lock;
And baby crows, without being a cock.

34

The peacock has a score of eyes,
With which he cannot see;
The cod-fish has a silent sound,
However that may be;

No dandelions tell the time,
Although they turn to clocks;
Cat's-cradle does not hold the cat,
Nor foxglove fit the fox.

Day 19

1. Read poems 38, 39 and 40.
2. Poem 40: If you don't know what a ferry is, what clues are there in the poem to help you guess what it is? (hint: "across the water" and "boatman") What is a ferry? (Answers)
3. How much does a ferry ride cost in this poem? (Answers)
4. Poem 39: What does it mean that the milk is coming when the cows come home? (Answers)
5. A drake is a duck. Brake and rushes are plants.
6. Poem 38: What is happening in this poem? First, what is a swallow? (look for clues in the poem like "fly away") (Answers)
7. When does the swallow leave and fly away? (Answers)
8. When does the swallow come home? (Answers)
9. What is happening in this poem? (Answers)

38

Fly away, fly away over the sea,
Sun-loving swallow, for summer is done;
Come again, come again, come back to me,
Bringing the summer and bringing the sun.

39

When the cows come home the milk is coming,
Honey's made while the bees are humming;
Duck and drake on the rushy lake,
And the deer live safe in the breezy brake;
And timid, funny, brisk little bunny,
Winks his nose and sits all sunny.

40

"Ferry me across the water,
Do, boatman, do."
"If you've a penny in your purse
I'll ferry you."

"I have a penny in my purse,
And my eyes are blue;
So ferry me across the water,
Do, boatman, do."

"Step into my ferry-boat,
Be they black or blue,
And for the penny in your purse
I'll ferry you."

Day 20

1. Read poems 45, 46 and 47.
2. What does the poet compare to a boat sailing? (Answers)
3. What does the poet compare to a bridge? (If you don't know, use the clues. What bow looks like a bridge from the earth to the sky?) (Answers)
4. What is the message of poem 46? (Answers)
5. What is the message of poem 47? (Answers)

45

Boats sail on the rivers,
And ships sail on the seas;
But clouds that sail across the sky
Are prettier far than these.

There are bridges on the rivers,
As pretty as you please;
But the bow that bridges heaven,
And overtops the trees,
And builds a road from earth to sky,
Is prettier far than these.

46

The lily has a smooth stalk,
Will never hurt your hand;
But the rose upon her briar
Is lady of the land.

There's sweetness in an apple tree,
And profit in the corn;
But lady of all beauty
Is a rose upon a thorn.

When with moss and honey
She tips her bending briar,
And half unfolds her glowing heart,
She sets the world on fire.

47

Hurt no living thing:
Ladybird, nor butterfly,
Nor moth with dusty wing,
Nor cricket chirping cheerily,
Nor grasshopper so light of leap,
Nor dancing gnat, nor beetle fat,
Nor harmless worms that creep.

Day 21

1. Read the first half of <u>The City Zoo</u> by George Comninos.
2. What problem did the zoo have? (Answers)
3. What kind of person was the zookeeper? (hint: look at the beginning of the story)
   (Answers)

Vocabulary

1. These are words from the story in the order that they appear. Try to spot them
   as you read.
   1. **tirelessly** – with endless energy, working without getting tired

2. **disrepair** – poor condition of a building because no one is caring for it
3. **contented** – happy and at ease

2. Write each word and draw a picture that shows what it means.

<u>The City Zoo</u> (first half)

The kind old keeper was popular at City Zoo. He never locked the animals up and they roamed the zoo visiting each other for a chat, or spent their days playing with one another. All the animals were fed and protected by their faithful zookeeper, who worked tirelessly to take care of their needs and keep the zoo running smoothly. Not many people visited the zoo as it was old and in disrepair but all the animals lived contented and extremely lazy lives.

One day Billy Big Ears the bat was hanging around the zookeeper's office snoozing. Bats like to slumber during the day. Nothing much happened at this zoo, so Billy was surprised to be woken with a start by the telephone ringing. "Hello, City Zoo," said the keeper, smiling. The keeper's smile left his face as he listened to the person on the other end of the line. "What will become of the animals? They will have to be separated and sent off to other zoos. I hadn't realized the zoo was that badly in debt. I could never raise so much money myself!"

The keeper listened intently and then, sighing sadly, he said, "Well, I guess the zoo will have to close, then." The kind old zookeeper, not knowing Billy was in the office, put his head on the office desk and muttered to himself, "How will I ever be able to tell the animals this sad news?" Billy Big Ears silently soared through the open window of the office and rushed off to tell the other animals this shocking news.

Hearing Billy's story, the animals held a meeting with the Wise Old Owl as the chairman. "I now call this meeting to order," said Wise Old Owl. "The topic for the meeting will be how to save the City Zoo." He hooted with much authority, "Does anyone have any suggestions?" The animals all fell silent as they concentrated on this problem, until many moments later, the bat Billy Big Ears piped up, "I know, we can find some money for the kind Old keeper and give it to him." The other animals all smiled and nodded in agreement, until Horrace Hippo, with a puzzled look on his face, asked, "What's money and where can money be found?"

By now the Wise Old Owl had heard enough; he knew the animals were not knowledgeable of the outside world but could not help feeling impatient at the time it was taking them to arrive at an answer. Puffing up his feathers as he always did when feeling exasperated at the other animals' ignorance he hooted, "You don't find money! Money is something you earn by getting a job!" The animals all looked at one another, appearing none the wiser, and finally Percy Pelican rather timidly asked, "What is a job?" "A job is doing something useful to help others. Sometimes it's done voluntarily and other times special colored paper, called money, is paid to the worker," Hooted Owl, adding, "Money is what the zoo keeper uses to buy us the things we need."

The animals seemed quite satisfied with Owl's explanation. The answer to their problem was now obvious: they would all go outside City Zoo and get jobs. As the animals were of many different sizes and shapes, the meeting lasted late into the night as they discussed with the Owl the sorts of work that would best suit their individual attributes. At the close of the meeting the animals went to their cages to sleep and prepare for the big day that lay ahead.

Day 22

1. Read the second half of <u>The City Zoo</u> by George Comninos.
2. It mentions the sport rugby which is sort of similar to American football. The story mentions a **scrum**. It's not really important, but a scrum is a sort of huddle where both teams crunch into a circle to try to get the ball. Also in the story is a mention of an **accountant**, or someone who keeps track of the money for a business.
3. How did they solve the problem? Tell a parent or older sibling.

Vocabulary

1. Here are some more words to look for.
    1. **gleam** – shine brightly
    2. **wallow** – lie relaxed in mud or water
    3. **bulge** – swelling or protruding
2. Write each word and draw a picture to show what the word means.
3. Look for these while you read. You might see "gleaming" and "wallowing" for example, but you should know what those words mean by the definitions above.

The City Zoo (second half)

The next day the animals rose early to start their first day at work. The keeper couldn't work out the reason for the animals' departure, they had never desired to leave the confines of the zoo before. He waved goodbye as they paraded out of the main gate, a puzzled look on his face. "Be sure to be home in time for dinner!" he yelled after them.

The Giraffes Gerry and Jenny went straight to the local telephone company. Their long necks and legs made them ideal for work on the tallest of telephone poles. Gerry and Jenny loved their new job, even if it did mean being tangled up in telephone cable occasionally.

The two cheeky chimps and Big Bertha the Elephant set up a car wash in a nearby car park. The nimble Chimps scampered about scrubbing the dirty cars clean, making a game of the work at hand. Big Bertha, loading her trunk with water from a bucket, rinsed the soap suds off the now gleaming cars. The chimps and Bertha the Elephant made a great car washing team.

Horrace the Hippo spent his days working as a lifeguard at the local council swimming pool. The children at the pool were delighted at Horrace's antics in the pool. Horrace loved his new job, as he was doing what Hippos love best: wallowing in the water and sun baking.

Sylvia Snake spent her days helping a local plumber. Sylvia slithered down plug holes, helping the plumber clear blocked drains. This was hard work for Sylvia, but work a slithering snake could do well. The plumber was delighted with Sylvia's work and paid her well.

Percy Pelican worked for the Postal Service delivering air mail. Percy flew far and wide, his large bill bulging with mail. Percy loved flying low over the city, enjoying the view and meeting the people he had mail for. This was a fine job for a pelican, indeed.

Russell Rhino, heavy and strong with his big rhino horn, applied for work at a building firm. Russell was well suited to his new career, charging headlong through brick walls demolishing old buildings. Rhinos love to charge at things and to be paid to do this was a dream come true for Russell.

The Zoo's gorillas tried out for the local professional rugby league team. The coach was delighted with the two of them, and they found themselves playing as front row forwards. Needless to say, their team never lost a scrum and the other players admired the playing skill of the gorillas, often trying to emulate it.

At the end of each day, the animals made their way home to the zoo, tired but happy that they were secretly helping the keeper save the zoo from closing. All the animals gave their money to the wise old owl, who was their accountant, and he worked late into the night counting their hard-earned money.

Finally the big day arrived, and the animals gathered around the kind old keeper and presented him with the money needed to save the City Zoo. Needless to say the keeper was overcome with joy and thanked the animals, adding, "Now I know what you all were getting up to when you left the zoo."

The animals raised so much money that enough was left over to renovate the zoo. The animals were no longer lazy; they liked to work and set about transforming the zoo. The keeper looked on in amazement as the animals made City Zoo beautiful. People of the city soon heard news of this and visited in great numbers, assuring the Zoo of its future. The kind keeper and all the animals lived happily ever after.

THE END

Day 23

1. Read the first part of The City Zoo.
2. Find the first part of the story on Day 21.

Vocabulary

1. Here are some more words to look for.
   - **slumber** – sleep
   - **intently** – with great focus, with eager attention
   - **exasperated** – frustrated, very irritated
2. Write each word and draw a picture to show what the word means.
3. Look for these words while you read.

Day 24

1. Read the second part of The City Zoo.

2. Find the second part of the story on Day 22.

Vocabulary

1. Here are some more words to look for.
    1. **demolish** – tear down, destroy
    2. **emulate** – imitate someone to try to achieve what they have
2. Write each word and draw a picture to show what the word means.
3. Look for these words as you read.

Day 25

Vocabulary

1. Do you know what all of the words mean now? Can you match the words to their definitions? You can write the matching numbers and letters on a piece of paper. (Answers)

1.	happy	A.	contented
2.	sleep	B.	wallow
3.	hardworking	C.	exasperated
4.	to be full of	D.	bulge
5.	poor condition	E.	disrepair
6.	shine brightly	F.	demolish
7.	extremely annoyed	G.	intently
8.	with concentration	H.	slumber
9.	knock down a building	I.	gleam
10.	lie relaxed in mud or water	J.	emulate
11.	copy someone to try and be as good as them	K.	tirelessly

Day 26

1. We're going to start a new book, *The Adventures of Old Mr. Toad.*
2. Read chapter 1.
3. What happened in chapter 1? Tell someone. Tell them who the chapter was about and what that person did.

Chapter I   Jimmy Skunk Is Puzzled

Old Mother West Wind had just come down from the Purple Hills and turned loose her children, the Merry Little Breezes, from the big bag in which she had been carrying them. They were very lively and very merry as they danced and raced across the Green Meadows in all directions, for it was good to be back there once more. Old Mother West Wind almost sighed as she watched them for a few minutes. She felt that she would like to join them. Always the springtime made her feel this way, young, mad, carefree, and happy. But she had work to do. She had to turn the windmill to pump water for Farmer Brown's cows, and this was only one of many mills standing idle as they waited for her. So she puffed her cheeks out and started about her business.

Jimmy Skunk sat at the top of the hill that overlooks the Green Meadows and watched her out of sight. Then he started to amble down the Lone Little Path to look for some beetles. He was ambling along in his lazy way, for you know he never hurries, when he heard some one puffing and blowing behind him. Of course he turned to see who it was, and he was greatly surprised when he discovered Old Mr. Toad. Yes, Sir, it was Old Mr. Toad, and he seemed in a great hurry. He was quite short of breath, but he was hopping along in the most determined way as if he were in a great hurry to get somewhere.

Now it is a very unusual thing for Mr. Toad to hurry, very unusual indeed. As a rule he hops a few steps and then sits down to think it over. Jimmy had never before seen him hop more than a few steps unless he was trying to get away from danger, from Mr. Blacksnake for instance. Of course the first thing Jimmy thought of was Mr. Blacksnake, and he looked for him. But there was no sign of Mr. Blacksnake nor of any other danger. Then he looked very hard at Old Mr. Toad, and he saw right away that Old Mr. Toad didn't seem to be frightened at all, only very determined, and as if he had something important on his mind.

"Well, well," exclaimed Jimmy Skunk, "whatever has got into those long hind legs of yours to make them work so fast?"

Old Mr. Toad didn't say a word, but simply tried to get past Jimmy and keep on his way. Jimmy put out one hand and turned Old Mr. Toad right over on his back, where he kicked and struggled in an effort to get on his feet again, and looked very ridiculous.

"Don't you know that it isn't polite not to speak when you are spoken to?" demanded Jimmy severely, though his eyes twinkled.

"I- I beg your pardon. I didn't have any breath to spare," panted Old Mr. Toad. "You see I'm in a great hurry."

"Yes, I see," replied Jimmy. "But don't you know that it isn't good for the health to hurry so? Now, pray, what are you in such a hurry for? I don't see anything to run away from."

"I'm not running away," retorted Old Mr. Toad indignantly. "I've business to attend to at the Smiling Pool, and I'm late as it is."

"Business!" exclaimed Jimmy as if he could hardly believe his ears. "What business have you at the Smiling Pool?"

"That is my own affair," retorted Old Mr. Toad, "but if you really want to know, I'll tell you. I have a very important part in the spring chorus, and I'm going down there to sing. I have a very beautiful voice."

That was too much for Jimmy Skunk. He just lay down and rolled over and over with laughter. The idea of any one so homely, almost ugly-looking, as Mr. Toad thinking that he had a beautiful voice! "Ha, ha, ha! Ho, ho, ho!" roared Jimmy.

When at last he stopped because he couldn't laugh any more, he discovered that Old Mr. Toad was on his way again. Hop, hop, hipperty-hop, hop, hop, hipperty-hop went Mr. Toad. Jimmy watched him, and he confessed that he was puzzled.

Day 27

1. Read chapter 2.
2. What is Jimmy trying to figure out? (Answers)
3. What is Jimmy going to do to try to find out the answer? (Answers)
4. Review your "City Zoo" vocabulary by going to Day 25 or looking for it under Level 2 on the Review Games page of the Easy Peasy All-in-One Homeschool site.

Chapter II Jimmy Skunk Consults His Friends

Jimmy Skunk scratched his head thoughtfully as he watched Old Mr. Toad go down the Lone Little Path, hop, hop, hipperty-hop, towards the Smiling Pool. He certainly was puzzled, was Jimmy Skunk. If Old Mr. Toad had told him that he could fly, Jimmy would not have been more surprised, or found it harder to believe than that Old Mr. Toad had a beautiful voice. The truth is, Jimmy didn't believe it. He thought that Old Mr. Toad was trying to fool him.

Presently Peter Rabbit came along. He found Jimmy Skunk sitting in a brown study. He had quite forgotten to look for fat beetles, and when he forgets to do that you may make up your mind that Jimmy is doing some hard thinking.

"Hello, old Striped-coat, what have you got on your mind this fine morning?" cried Peter Rabbit.

"Him," said Jimmy simply, pointing down the Lone Little Path.

Peter looked. "Do you mean Old Mr. Toad!" he asked.

Jimmy nodded. "Do you see anything queer about him?" he asked in his turn.

Peter stared down the Lone Little Path. "No," he replied, "except that he seems in a great hurry."

"That's just it," Jimmy returned promptly. "Did you ever see him hurry unless he was frightened?"

Peter confessed that he never had.

"Well, he isn't frightened now, yet just look at him go," retorted Jimmy. "Says he has got a beautiful voice, and that he has to take part in the spring chorus at the Smiling Pool and that he is late."

Peter looked very hard at Jimmy to see if he was fooling or telling the truth. Then he began to laugh. "Old Mr. Toad sing! The very idea!" he cried. "He can sing about as much as I can, and that is not at all."

Jimmy grinned. "I think he's crazy, if you ask me," said he. "And yet he was just as earnest about it as if it were really so. I think he must have eaten something that has gone to his head. There's Unc' Billy Possum over there. Let's ask him what he thinks."

So Jimmy and Peter joined Unc' Billy, and Jimmy told the story about Old Mr. Toad all over again. Unc' Billy chuckled and laughed just as they had at the idea of Old Mr. Toad's saying he had a beautiful voice. But Unc' Billy has a shrewd little head on his shoulders. After a few minutes he stopped laughing.

"Ah done learn a right smart long time ago that Ah don' know all there is to know about *mah* neighbors," said he. "We-*uns* done think of Brer Toad as ugly-lookin' fo' so long that we-*uns* may have overlooked something. Ah don' reckon Brer Toad can sing, but Ah 'lows that perhaps he thinks he can. What do you-alls say to we-*uns* going down to the Smiling Pool and finding out what he really is up to?"

"The very thing!" cried Peter, kicking up his heels. You know Peter is always ready to go anywhere or do anything that will satisfy his curiosity.

Jimmy Skunk thought it over for a few minutes, and then he decided that as he hadn't anything in particular to do, and as he might find some fat beetles on the way, he would go too. So off they started after Old Mr. Toad, Peter Rabbit in the lead as usual, Unc' Billy Possum next, grinning as only he can grin, and in the rear Jimmy Skunk, taking his time and keeping a sharp eye out for fat beetles.

Day 28

1. Read chapter 3.
2. When they got to Smiling Pool, where was Mr. Toad? (Answers)

Chapter III The Hunt for Old Mr. Toad

Now, though Old Mr. Toad was hurrying as fast as ever he could and was quite out of breath, he wasn't getting along very fast compared with the way Peter Rabbit or Jimmy Skunk or Unc' Billy Possum could cover the ground. You see he cannot make long jumps like his cousin, Grandfather Frog, but only little short hops.

So Peter and Jimmy and Unc' Billy took their time about following him. They stopped to hunt for fat beetles for Jimmy Skunk, and at every little patch of sweet clover for Peter Rabbit to help himself. Once they wasted a lot of time while Unc' Billy Possum hunted for a nest of Carol the Meadow Lark, on the chance that he would find some fresh eggs there. He didn't find the nest for the very good reason that Carol hadn't built one yet. Peter was secretly glad. You know he doesn't eat eggs, and he is always sorry for his feathered friends when their eggs are stolen.

Half way across the Green Meadows they stopped to play with the Merry Little Breezes, and because it was very pleasant there, they played longer than they realized. When at last they started on again, Old Mr. Toad was out of sight. You see all the time he had kept right on going, hop, hop, hipperty-hop.

"Never mind," said Peter, "we can catch up with him easy enough, he's such a slow-poke."

But even a slow-poke who keeps right on doing a thing without wasting any time always gets somewhere sooner or later, very often sooner than those who are naturally quicker, but who waste their time. So it was with Old Mr. Toad. He kept right on, hop, hop, hipperty-hop, while the others were playing, and so it happened that when at last Peter and Jimmy and Unc' Billy reached the Smiling Pool, they hadn't caught another glimpse of Old Mr. Toad.

"Do you suppose he hid somewhere, and we passed him?" asked Peter.

Unc' Billy shook his head. "Ah don' reckon so," said he. "We-*uns* done been foolin' away our time, an' Brer Toad done stole a march on us. Ah reckons we-*uns* will find him sittin' on the bank here somewhere."

So right away the three separated to look for Old Mr. Toad. All along the bank of the Smiling Pool they looked. They peeped under old leaves and sticks. They looked in every place where Old Mr. Toad might have hidden, but not a trace of him did they find.

"*Tra-la-la*-lee! Oka-chee! Oka-chee! Happy am I as I can be!" sang Mr. Redwing, as he swayed to and fro among the bulrushes.

"Say, Mr. Redwing, have you seen Old Mr. Toad?" called Peter Rabbit.

"No," replied Mr. Redwing. "Is that whom you fellows are looking for? I wondered if you had lost something. What do you want with Old Mr. Toad?"

Peter explained how they had followed Old Mr. Toad just to see what he really was up to. "Of course we know that he hasn't any more voice than I have," declared Peter, "but we are curious to know if he really thinks he has, and why he should be in such a hurry to reach the Smiling Pool. It looks to us as if the spring has made Old Mr. Toad crazy."

"Oh, that's it, is it?" replied Mr. Redwing, his bright eyes twinkling. "Some people don't know as much as they might. I've been wondering where Old Mr. Toad was, and I'm ever so glad to learn that he hasn't forgotten that he has a very important part in our beautiful spring chorus." Then once more Mr. Redwing began to sing.

Day 29

1. Read chapter 4.
2. What does Peter wish he could do? (Answers)

Vocabulary

1. **Envy** means to be jealous of.

Chapter IV   Peter Rabbit Finds Old Mr. Toad

It isn't often that Peter Rabbit is truly envious, but sometimes in the joyousness of spring he is. He envies the birds because they can pour out in beautiful song the joy that is in them. The only way he can express his feelings is by kicking his long heels, jumping about, and such foolish things. While that gives Peter a great deal of satisfaction, it doesn't add to the joy of other people as do the songs of the birds, and you know to give joy to others is to add to your own joy. So there are times when Peter wishes he could sing.

He was wishing this very thing now, as he sat on the bank of the Smiling Pool, listening to the great spring chorus.

"*Tra-la-la*-lee! Oka-chee! Oka-chee! There's joy in the spring for you and for me." sang Redwing the Blackbird from the bulrushes.

From over in the Green Meadows rose the clear lilt of Carol the Meadow Lark, and among the alders just where the Laughing Brook ran into the Smiling Pool a flood of happiness was pouring from the throat of Little Friend the Song Sparrow. Winsome Bluebird's sweet, almost plaintive, whistle seemed to fairly float in the air, so that it was hard to say just where it did come from, and in the top of the Big Hickory-tree, Welcome Robin was singing as if his heart were bursting with joy. Even Sammy Jay was adding a beautiful, bell-like note instead of his usual harsh scream. As for the Smiling Pool, it seemed as if the very water itself sang, for a mighty chorus of clear piping voices from unseen singers rose from all around its banks. Peter knew who those singers were, although look as he would he could see none of them. They were hylas, the tiny cousins of Stickytoes the Tree Toad.

Listening to all these joyous voices, Peter forgot for a time what had brought him to the Smiling Pool. But Jimmy Skunk and Unc' Billy Possum didn't forget. They were still hunting for Old Mr. Toad.

"Well, old Mr. Dreamer, have you found him yet?" asked Jimmy Skunk, stealing up behind Peter and poking him in the back.

Peter came to himself with a start. "No," said he. "I was just listening and wishing that I could sing, too. Don't you ever wish you could sing, Jimmy?"

"No," replied Jimmy. "I never waste time wishing I could do things it was never meant I should do. It's funny where Old Mr. Toad is. He said that he was coming down here to sing, and Redwing the Blackbird seemed to be expecting him. I've looked everywhere I can think of without finding him, but I don't believe in giving up without another try. Stop your dreaming and come help us hunt."

So Peter stopped his dreaming and joined in the search. Now there was one place where neither Peter nor Jimmy nor Unc' Billy had thought of looking. That was in the Smiling Pool itself. They just took it for granted that Old Mr. Toad was somewhere on the bank. Presently Peter came to a place where the bank was very low and the water was shallow for quite a little distance out in the Smiling Pool. From out of that shallow water came the piping voice of a hyla, and Peter stopped to stare, trying to see the tiny singer.

Suddenly he jumped right up in the air with surprise. There was a familiar-looking head sticking out of the water. Peter had found Old Mr. Toad!

Day 30

1. Read chapter 5.
2. The chapter numbers are in Roman numerals. What letter is the Roman numeral for 5? (Check out the chapter heading to find out.)
3. How does Mr. Toad make his song? (Answers)
4. Tell someone what happened in this chapter.

Chapter V   Old Mr. Toad's Music Bag

Never think that you have learned
   All there is to know.
 That's the surest way of all
   Ignorance to show.

"I've found Old Mr. Toad!" cried Peter Rabbit, hurrying after Jimmy Skunk.

"Where?" demanded Jimmy.

"In the water," declared Peter. "He's sitting right over there where the water is shallow, and he didn't notice me at all. Let's get Unc' Billy, and then creep over to the edge of the Smiling Pool and watch to see if Old Mr. Toad really does try to sing."

So they hunted up Unc' Billy Possum, and the three stole very softly over to the edge of the Smiling Pool, where the bank was low and the water shallow. Sure enough, there sat Old Mr. Toad with just his head out of water. And while they were watching him, something very strange happened.

"What what's the matter with him?" whispered Peter, his big eyes looking as if they might pop out of his head.

"If he don't watch out, he'll blow up and bust!" exclaimed Jimmy.

"Listen!" whispered Unc' Billy Possum. "*Do mah* ol' ears hear right? 'Pears to me that that song is coming right from where Brer Toad is sitting."

It certainly did appear so, and of all the songs that glad spring day there was none sweeter. Indeed there were few as sweet. The only trouble was the song was so very short. It lasted only for two or three seconds. And when it ended, Old Mr. Toad looked quite his natural self again; just as commonplace, almost ugly, as ever. Peter looked at Jimmy Skunk, Jimmy looked at Unc' Billy Possum, and Unc' Billy looked at Peter. And no one had a word to say. Then all three looked back at Old Mr. Toad.

And even as they looked, his throat began to swell and swell and swell, until it was no wonder that Jimmy Skunk had thought that he was in danger of blowing up. And then, when it stopped swelling, there came again those beautiful little notes, so sweet and tremulous that Peter actually held his breath to listen. There was no doubt that Old Mr. Toad was singing just as he had said he was going to, and it was just as true that his song was one of the sweetest if not *the* sweetest of all the chorus from and around the Smiling Pool. It was very hard to believe, but Peter and Jimmy and Unc' Billy both saw and heard, and that was enough. Their respect for Old Mr. Toad grew tremendously as they listened.

"How does he do it?" whispered Peter.

"With that bag under his chin, of course," replied Jimmy Skunk. "Don't you see it's only when that is swelled out that he sings? It's a regular music bag. And I didn't know he had any such bag there at all."

"I wish," said Peter Rabbit, feeling of his throat, "that I had a music bag like that in my throat."

And then he joined in the laugh of Jimmy and Unc' Billy, but still with something of a look of wistfulness in his eyes.

Day 31

1. Read chapter 6.
2. Tell someone what happened in this chapter.
3. Review your "City Zoo" vocabulary by going to Day 25 or looking for it under

Level 2 on the Review Games page of the Easy Peasy website.

Chapter VI   Peter Discovers Something More

There are stranger things in the world to-day
   Than ever you dreamed could be.
 There's beauty in some of the commonest things
   If only you've eyes to see.

Ever since Peter Rabbit was a little chap and had first ran away from home, he had known Old Mr. Toad, and never once had Peter suspected that he could sing. Also he had thought Old Mr. Toad almost ugly-looking, and he knew that most of his neighbors thought the same way. They were fond of Old Mr. Toad, for he was always good-natured and attended strictly to his own affairs; but they liked to poke fun at him, and as for there being anything beautiful about him, such a thing never entered their heads.

Now that they had discovered that he really has a very beautiful voice, they began to look on him with a great deal more respect. This was especially so with Peter. He got in the habit of going over to the Smiling Pool every day, when the way was clear, just to sit on the bank and listen to Old Mr. Toad.

"Why didn't you ever tell us before that you could sing?" he asked one day, as Old Mr. Toad looked up at him from the Smiling Pool.

"What was the use of wasting my breath?" demanded Old Mr. Toad. "You wouldn't have believed me if I had. You didn't believe me when I did tell you."

Peter knew that this was true, and he couldn't find any answer ready. At last he ventured another question. "Why haven't I ever heard you sing before?"

"You have," replied Old Mr. Toad tartly. "I sang right in this very place last spring, and the spring before, and the spring before that. You've sat on that very bank lots of times while I was singing. The trouble with you, Peter, is that you don't use your eyes or your ears."

Peter looked more foolish than ever. But he ventured another question. It wouldn't be Peter to let a chance for questions go by. "Have I ever heard you singing up on the meadows or in the Old Orchard?"

"No," replied Old Mr. Toad, "I only sing in the springtime. That's the time for singing. I just *have* to sing then. In the summer it is too hot, and in the winter I sleep. I always return to my old home to sing. You know I was born here. All my family gathers here in the spring to sing, so of course I come too."

Old Mr. Toad filled out his queer music bag under his chin and began to sing again. Peter watched him. Now it just happened that Old Mr. Toad was facing him, and so Peter looked down straight into his eyes. He never had looked into Mr. Toad's eyes before, and now he just stared and stared, for it came over him that those eyes were very beautiful, very beautiful indeed.

"Oh!" he exclaimed, "what beautiful eyes you have, Mr. Toad!"

"So I've been told before," replied Old Mr. Toad. "My family always has had beautiful eyes. There is an old saying that every Toad has jewels in his head, but of course he hasn't, not real jewels. It is just the beautiful eyes. Excuse me, Peter, but I'm needed in that chorus." Old Mr. Toad once more swelled out his throat and began to sing.

Peter watched him a while longer, then hopped away to the dear Old Briarpatch, and he was very thoughtful.

"Never again will I call anybody homely and ugly until I know all about him," said Peter, which was a very wise decision. Don't you think so?

Day 32

1. Read chapter 7.
2. Who wanted to eat Mr. Toad? (Answers)

Chapter VII   A Shadow Passes Over the Smiling Pool

Here's what Mr. Toad says;
  Heed it well, my dear:
 "Time to watch for clouds is
  When the sky is clear."

He says that that is the reason that he lives to a good old age, does Old Mr. Toad. I suppose he means that when the sky is cloudy, everybody is looking for rain and is prepared for it, but when the sun is shining, most people forget that there is such a thing as a storm, so when it comes suddenly very few are prepared for it. It is the same way with danger and trouble. So Old Mr. Toad very wisely watches out when there seems to be the least need of it, and he finds it always pays.

It was a beautiful spring evening. Over back of the Purple Hills to which Old Mother West Wind had taken her children, the Merry Little Breezes, and behind which jolly, round, red Mr. Sun had gone to bed, there was still a faint, clear light. But over the Green Meadows and the Smiling Pool the shadows had drawn a curtain of soft dusk which in the Green Forest became black. The little stars looked down from the sky and twinkled just to see their reflections twinkle back at them from the Smiling Pool. And there and all around it was perfect peace. Jerry Muskrat swam back and forth, making little silver lines on the surface of the Smiling Pool and squeaking contentedly, for it was the hour which he loves best. Little Friend the Song Sparrow had tucked his head under his wing and gone to sleep among the alders along the Laughing Brook and Redwing the Blackbird had done the same thing among the bulrushes. All the feathered songsters who had made joyous the bright day had gone to bed.

But this did not mean that the glad spring chorus was silent. Oh, my, no! No indeed! The Green Meadows were silent, and the Green Forest was silent, but as if to make up for this, the sweet singers of the Smiling Pool, the hylas and the frogs and Old Mr. Toad, were pouring out their gladness as if they had not been singing most of the departed day. You see it was the hour they love best of all, the hour which seems to them just made for singing, and they were doing their best to tell Old Mother Nature how they love her, and how glad they were that she had brought back sweet Mistress Spring to waken them from their long sleep.

It was so peaceful and beautiful there that it didn't seem possible that danger of any kind could be lurking near. But Old Mr. Toad, swelling out that queer music bag in his throat and singing with all his might, never once forgot that wise saying of his, and so he was the first to see what looked like nothing so much as a little detached bit of the blackness of the Green Forest floating out towards the Smiling Pool. Instantly he stopped singing. Now that was a signal. When he stopped singing, his nearest neighbor stopped singing, then the next one and the next, and in a minute there wasn't a sound from the Smiling Pool save the squeak of Jerry Muskrat hidden among the bulrushes. That great chorus stopped as abruptly as the electric lights go out when you press a button.

Back and forth over the Smiling Pool, this way and that way, floated the shadow, but there was no sign of any living thing in the Smiling Pool. After awhile the shadow floated away over the Green Meadows without a sound.

"Hooty the Owl didn't get one of us that time," said Old Mr. Toad to his nearest neighbor with a chuckle of satisfaction. Then he swelled out his music bag and began to sing again. And at once, as abruptly as it had stopped, the great chorus began again as joyous as before, for nothing had happened to bring sadness as might have but for the watchfulness of Old Mr. Toad.

Day 33

1. Read chapter 8.
2. Peter thought Mr. Toad's babies looked like whose? (Answers)

Chapter VIII   Old Mr. Toad's Babies

The Smiling Pool's a nursery
   Where all the sunny day
 A thousand funny babies
   Are taught while at their play.

Really the Smiling Pool is a sort of kindergarten, one of the most interesting kindergartens in the world. Little Joe Otter's children learn to swim there. So do Jerry Muskrat's babies and those of Billy Mink, the Trout and Minnow babies, and a lot more. And there you will find the children and grandchildren of Grandfather Frog and Old Mr. Toad.

Peter Rabbit had known for a long time about the Frog babies, but though he knew that Old Mr. Toad was own cousin to Grandfather Frog, he hadn't known anything about Toad babies, except that at a certain time in the year he was forever running across tiny Toads, especially on rainy days, and each little Toad was just like Old Mr. Toad, except for his size. Peter had heard it said that Toads rain down from the sky, and sometimes it seems as if this must be so. Of course he knew it couldn't be, but it puzzled him a great deal. There wouldn't be a Toad in sight. Then it would begin to rain, and right away there would be so many tiny Toads that it was hard work to jump without stepping on some.

He remembered this as he went to pay his daily call on Old Mr. Toad in the Smiling Pool and listen to his sweet song. He hadn't seen any little Toads this year, but he remembered his experiences with them in other years, and he meant to ask about them.

Old Mr. Toad was sitting in his usual place, but he wasn't singing. He was staring at something in the water. When Peter said "Good morning," Old Mr. Toad didn't seem to hear him. He was too much interested in what he was watching. Peter stared down into the water to see what was interesting Old Mr. Toad so much, but he saw nothing but a lot of wriggling tadpoles.

"What are you staring at so, Mr. Sobersides?" asked Peter, speaking a little louder than before.

Old Mr. Toad turned and looked at Peter, and there was a look of great pride in his face. "I'm just watching my babies. Aren't they lovely?" said he.

Peter stared harder than ever, but he couldn't see anything that looked like a baby Toad.

"Where are they?" asked he. "I don't see any babies but those of Grandfather Frog, and if you ask me, I always did think tadpoles about the homeliest things in th' world."

Old Mr. Toad grew indignant. "Those are not Grandfather Frog's children; they're mine!" he sputtered. "And I'll have you know that they are the most beautiful babies in th' world!"

Peter drew a hand across his mouth to hide a smile. "I beg your pardon, Mr. Toad," said he. "I- I thought all tadpoles were Frog babies. They all look alike to me."

"Well, they're not," declared Old Mr. Toad. "How any one can mistake my babies for their cousins I cannot understand. Now mine are beautiful, while "

"Chug-arum!" interrupted the great deep voice of Grandfather Frog. "What are you talking about? Why, your babies are no more to be compared with my babies for real beauty than nothing at all! I'll leave it to Peter if they are."

But Peter wisely held his tongue. To tell the truth, he couldn't see beauty in any of them. To him they were all just wriggling pollywogs. They were more interesting now, because he had found out that some of them were Toads and some were Frogs, and he hadn't known before that baby Toads begin life as tadpoles, but he had no intention of being drawn into the dispute now waxing furious between Grandfather Frog and Old Mr. Toad.

Day 34

1. Read chapter 9.
2. What did the pollywog do that surprised Peter? (Answers)

Chapter IX   The Smiling Pool Kindergarten

Play a little, learn a little, grow a little too;
　That's what every pollywoggy tries his best to do.

Of course. That's what a kindergarten is for. And you may be sure that the babies of Grandfather Frog and Old Mr. Toad and Stickytoes the Tree Toad did all of these things in the kindergarten of the Smiling Pool. They looked considerably alike, did these little cousins, for they were all pollywogs to begin with. Peter Rabbit came over every day to watch them. Always he had thought pollywogs just homely, wriggling things, not the least bit interesting, but since he had discovered how proud of them were Grandfather Frog and Old Mr. Toad, he had begun to wonder about them and then to watch them.

"There's one thing about them, and that is they are not in danger the way any babies are," said Peter, talking to himself as is his way when there is no one else to talk to. Just then a funny little black pollywog wriggled into sight, and while Peter was watching him, a stout-jawed water-beetle suddenly rushed from among the water grass, seized the pollywog by his tail, and dragged him down. Peter stared. Could it be that that ugly-looking bug was as dangerous an enemy to the baby Toad as Reddy Fox is to a baby Rabbit? He began to suspect so, and a little later he knew so, for there was that same little pollywog trying hard to swim and making bad work of it, because he had lost half of his long tail.

That set Peter to watching sharper than ever, and presently he discovered that pollywogs have to keep their eyes open quite as much as do baby Rabbits, if they would live to grow up. There were several kinds of queer, ugly-looking bugs forever darting out at the wriggling pollywogs. Hungry-looking fish lay in wait for them, and Longlegs the Blue Heron seemed to have a special liking for them. But the pollywogs were spry, and seemed to have learned to watch out. They seemed to Peter to spend all their time swimming and eating and growing. They grew so fast that it seemed to him that he could almost *see* them grow. And just imagine how surprised Peter was to discover one day that that very pollywog which he had seen lose his tail had grown a *new* one. That puzzled Peter more than anything he had seen in a long time.

"Why, I couldn't do that!" he exclaimed right out loud.

"Do what?" demanded Jerry Muskrat, who happened along just then.

"Why, grow a new tail like that pollywog," replied Peter, and told Jerry all that he had seen. Jerry laughed.

"You'll see queerer things than that if you watch those pollywogs long enough," said he. "They are a queer lot of babies, and very interesting to watch if you've got the time for it. I haven't. This Smiling Pool is a great kindergarten, and there's something happening here every minute. There's no place like it."

"Are those great big fat pollywogs Grandfather Frog's children, or Old Mr. Toad's?" asked Peter.

"Grandfather Frog's last year's children," replied Jerry. "They'll grow into real Frogs this summer, if nothing happens to them."

"Where are Old Mr. Toad's last year's children?" asked Peter.

"Don't ask me," replied Jerry. "They hopped away last summer. Never saw anything like the way those Toad youngsters grow. Those Toad pollywogs you see now will turn into real Toads, and be leaving the Smiling Pool in a few weeks. People think Old Mr. Toad is slow, but there is nothing slow about his children. Look at that little fellow over there; he's begun to grow legs already."

Peter looked, and sure enough there was a pollywog with a pair of legs sprouting out. They were his fore legs, and they certainly did make him look funny. And only a few days before there hadn't been a sign of legs.

"My gracious!" exclaimed Peter. "What a funny sight! I thought my babies grew fast, but these beat them."

Day 35

1. Read chapter 10.
2. Tell someone what happened in this chapter.

Chapter X   The Little Toads Start Out to See the World

The world is a wonderful great big place
  And in it the young must roam
To learn what their elders have long since learned
  There's never a place like home.

It had been some time since Peter Rabbit had visited the Smiling Pool to watch the pollywogs. But one cloudy morning he happened to think of them, and decided that he would run over there and see how they were getting along. So off he started, lipperty-lipperty-lip. He wondered if those pollywog children of Old Mr. Toad would be much changed. The last time he saw them some of them had just begun to grow legs, although they still had long tails.

He had almost reached the Smiling Pool when great big drops of rain began to splash down. And with those first raindrops something funny happened. Anyway, it seemed funny to Peter. Right away he was surrounded by tiny little Toads. Everywhere he looked he saw Toads, tiny little Toads just like Old Mr. Toad, only so tiny that one could have sat comfortably on a ten-cent piece and still had plenty of room.

Peter's big eyes grew round with surprise as he stared. Where had they all come from so suddenly? A minute before he hadn't seen a single one, and now he could hardly move without stepping on one. It seemed, it really seemed, as if each raindrop turned into a tiny Toad the instant it struck the ground. Of course Peter knew that that couldn't be, but it was very puzzling. And all those little Toads were bravely hopping along as if they were bound for some particular place.

Peter watched them for a few minutes, then he once more started for the Smiling Pool. On the very bank whom should he meet but Old Mr. Toad. He looked rather thin, and his back was to the Smiling Pool. Yes, Sir, he was hopping away from the Smiling Pool where he had been all the spring, singing in the great chorus. Peter was almost as surprised to see him as he had been to see the little Toads, but just then he was most interested in those little Toads.

"Good morning, Old Mr. Toad," said Peter in his most polite manner. "Can you tell me where all these little Toads came from?"

"Certainly," replied Old Mr. Toad. "They came from the Smiling Pool, of course. Where did you suppose they came from?"

"I- I didn't know. There wasn't one to be seen, and then it began to rain, and right away they were everywhere. It it almost seemed as if they had rained down out of the sky."

Old Mr. Toad chuckled. "They've got good sense, if I must say it about my own children," said he. "They know that wet weather is the only weather for Toads to travel in. They left the Smiling Pool in the night while it was damp and comfortable, and then, when the sun came up, they hid, like sensible children, under anything they could find, sticks, stones, pieces of bark, grass. The minute this shower came up, they knew it was good traveling weather and out they popped."

"But what did they leave the Smiling Pool for?" Peter asked.

"To see the Great World," replied Old Mr. Toad. "Foolish, very foolish of them, but they would do it. I did the same thing myself when I was their age. Couldn't stop me any more than I could stop them. They don't know when they're well off, but young folks never do. Fine weather, isn't it?"

Day 36

1. Read chapter 11.
2. Tell someone what happened in this chapter.

Vocabulary

1. Do you remember what **envy** means? (Answers)

Chapter XI   Old Mr. Toad's Queer Tongue

Old Mother Nature doth provide
  For all her children, large or small.
 Her wisdom foresees all their needs
  And makes provision for them all.

If you don't believe it, just you go ask Old Mr. Toad, as Peter Rabbit did, how such a slow-moving fellow as he is can catch enough bugs and insects to keep him alive. Perhaps you'll learn something just as Peter did. Peter and Old Mr. Toad sat in the rain watching the tiny Toads, who, you know, were Mr. Toad's children, leaving their kindergarten in the Smiling Pool and starting out to see the Great World. When the last little Toad had passed them, Old Mr. Toad suddenly remembered that he was hungry, very hungry indeed.

"Didn't have time to eat much while I was in the Smiling Pool," he explained. "Couldn't eat and sing too, and while I was down there, I was supposed to sing. Now that it is time to quit singing, I begin to realize that I've got a stomach to look out for as well as a voice. See that bug over there on that leaf? Watch him."

Peter looked, and sure enough there was a fat bug crawling along on an old leaf. He was about two inches from Old Mr. Toad, and he was crawling very fast. And right while Peter was looking at him he disappeared. Peter turned to look at Old Mr. Toad. He hadn't budged. He was sitting exactly where he had been sitting all the time, but he was smacking his lips, and there was a twinkle of satisfaction in his eyes. Peter opened his eyes very wide.

"Wha what " he began.

"Nice bug," interrupted Old Mr. Toad. "Nicest bug I've eaten for a longtime."

"But I didn't see you catch him!" protested Peter, looking at Old Mr. Toad as if he suspected him of joking.

"Anything wrong with your eyes?" inquired Old Mr. Toad.

"No," replied Peter just a wee bit crossly. "My eyes are just as good as ever."

"Then watch me catch that fly over yonder," said Old Mr. Toad. He hopped towards a fly which had lighted on a blade of grass just ahead. About two inches from it he stopped, and so far as Peter could see, he sat perfectly still. But the fly disappeared, and it wasn't because it flew away, either. Peter was sure of that. As he told Mrs. Peter about it afterwards, "It was there, and then it wasn't, and that was all there was to it."

Old Mr. Toad chuckled. "Didn't you see that one go, Peter?" he asked.

Peter shook his head. "I wish you Would stop fooling me," said Peter. "The joke is on me, but now you've had your laugh at my expense, I wish you would tell me how you do it. Please, Mr. Toad."

Now when Peter said please that way, of course Old Mr. Toad couldn't resist him. Nobody could.

"Here comes an ant this way. Now you watch my mouth instead of the ant and see what happens," said Old Mr. Toad.

Peter looked and saw a big black ant coming. Then he kept his eyes on Old Mr. Toad's mouth. Suddenly there was a little flash of red from it, so tiny and so quick that Peter couldn't be absolutely sure that he saw it. But when he looked for the ant, it was nowhere to be seen. Peter looked at Old Mr. Toad very hard.

"Do you mean to tell me, Mr. Toad, that you've got a tongue long enough to reach way over to where that ant was?" he asked.

Old Mr. Toad chuckled again. With every insect swallowed he felt better natured. "You've guessed it, Peter," said he. "Handy tongue, isn't it?"

"I think it's a very queer tongue," retorted Peter, "and I don't understand it at all. If it's so long as all that, where do you keep it when it isn't in use? I should think you'd have to swallow it to get it out of the way, or else leave it hanging out of your mouth."

"Ha, ha, ha, ha, ha!" laughed Old Mr. Toad. "My tongue never is in the way, and it's the handiest tongue in the world. I'll show it to you."

Day 37

1. Read chapter 12.
2. What makes Mr. Toad's tongue so wonderful? (Answers)
3. Why does Peter think Mr. Toad's tongue is attached in the wrong place?   (Answers)

Chapter XII   Old Mr. Toad Shows His Tongue

To show one's tongue, as you well know,
  Is not considered nice to do;
 But if it were like Mr. Toad's
  I'd want to show it wouldn't you?

I'm quite sure you would. You see, if it were like Old Mr. Toad's, it would be such a wonderful tongue that I suspect you would want everybody to see it. Old Mr. Toad thinks his tongue the most satisfactory tongue in the world. In fact, he is quite sure that without it he couldn't get along at all, and I don't know as he could. And yet very few of his neighbors know anything about that tongue and how different it is from most other tongues. Peter Rabbit didn't until Old Mr. Toad showed him after Peter had puzzled and puzzled over the mysterious way in which bugs and flies disappeared whenever they happened to come within two inches or less of Old Mr. Toad.

What Peter couldn't understand was what Old Mr. Toad did with a tongue that would reach two inches beyond his mouth. He said as much.

"I'll show you my tongue, and then you'll wish you had one just like it," said Old Mr. Toad, with a twinkle in his eyes.

He opened his big mouth and slowly ran his tongue out its full length. "Why! Why-ee!" exclaimed Peter. "It's fastened at the wrong end!"

"No such thing!" replied Old Mr. Toad indignantly. "If it was fastened at the other end, how could I run it out so far?"

"But mine and all other tongues that I ever have seen are fastened way down in the throat," protested Peter. "Yours is fastened at the other end, way in the very front of your mouth. I never heard of such a thing."

"There are a great many things you have never heard of, Peter Rabbit," replied Old Mr. Toad drily. "Mine is the right way to have a tongue. Because it is fastened way up in the front of my mouth that way, I can use the whole of it. You see it goes out its full length. Then, when I draw it in with a bug on the end of it, I just turn it over so that the end that was out goes way back in my throat and takes the bug with it to just the right place to swallow."

Peter thought this over for a few minutes before he ventured another question. "I begin to understand," said he, "but how do you hold on to the bug with your tongue?"

"My tongue is sticky, of course, Mr. Stupid," replied Old Mr. Toad, looking very much disgusted. "Just let me touch a bug with it, and he's mine every time."

Peter thought this over. Then he felt of his own tongue. "Mine isn't sticky," said he very innocently.

Old Mr. Toad laughed right out. "Perhaps if it was, you couldn't ask so many questions," said he. "Now watch me catch that fly." His funny little tongue darted out, and the fly was gone.

"It certainly is very handy," said Peter politely. "I think we are going to have more rain, and I'd better be getting back to the dear Old Briarpatch. Very much obliged to you, Mr. Toad. I think you are very wonderful."

"Not at all," replied Old Mr. Toad. "I've simply got the things I need in order to live, just as you have the things you need. I couldn't get along with your kind of a tongue, but no more could you get along with mine. If you live long enough, you will learn that Old Mother Nature makes no mistakes. She gives each of us what we need, and each one has different needs."

Day 38

1. Read chapter 13. Are you paying attention to the Roman numerals? How do you make 13?
2. Tell someone what happened in this chapter.

Chapter XIII   Peter Rabbit Is Impolite

Peter Rabbit couldn't get Old Mr. Toad off his mind. He had discovered so many interesting things about Old Mr. Toad that he was almost on the point of believing him to be the most interesting of all his neighbors. And his respect for Old Mr. Toad had become very great indeed. Of course. Who wouldn't respect any one with such beautiful eyes and such a sweet voice and such a wonderful tongue? Yet at the same time Peter felt very foolish whenever he remembered that all his life he had been acquainted with Old Mr. Toad without really knowing him at all. There was one comforting thought, and that was that most of his neighbors were just as ignorant regarding Old Mr. Toad as Peter had been.

"Funny," mused Peter, "how we can live right beside people all our lives and not really know them at all. I suppose that is why we should never judge people hastily. I believe I will go hunt up Old Mr. Toad and see if I can find out anything more."

Off started Peter, lipperty-lipperty-lip. He didn't know just where to go, now that Old Mr. Toad had left the Smiling Pool, but he had an idea that he would not be far from their meeting place of the day before, when Old Mr. Toad had explained about his wonderful tongue. But when he got there, Peter found no trace of Old Mr. Toad. You see, it had rained the day before, and that is just the kind of weather that a Toad likes best for traveling. Peter ought to have thought of that, but he didn't. He hunted for awhile and finally gave it up and started up the Crooked Little Path with the idea of running over for a call on Johnny Chuck in the Old Orchard.

Jolly, round, bright Mr. Sun was shining his brightest, and Peter soon forgot all about Old Mr. Toad. He scampered along up the Crooked Little Path, thinking of nothing in particular but how good it was to be alive, and occasionally kicking up his heels for pure joy. He had just done this when his ears caught the sound of a queer noise a little to one side of the Crooked Little Path. Instantly Peter stopped and sat up to listen. There it was again, and it seemed to come from under an old piece of board. It was just a little, rustling sound, hardly to be heard.

"There's some one under that old board," thought Peter, and peeped under. All he could see was that there was something moving. Instantly Peter was all curiosity. Whoever was there was not very big. He was sure of that. Of course that meant that he had nothing to fear. So what do you think Peter did? Why, he just pulled that old board over. And when he did that, he saw, whom do you think? Why, Old Mr. Toad, to be sure.

But such a sight as Old Mr. Toad was! Peter just stared. For a full minute he couldn't find his voice. Old Mr. Toad was changing his clothes! Yes, Sir, that is just what Old Mr. Toad was doing. He was taking off his old suit, and under it was a brand new one. But such a time as he was having! He was opening and shutting his big mouth, and drawing his hind legs under him, and rubbing them against his body. Then Peter saw a strange thing. He saw that Old Mr. Toad's old suit had split in several places, and he was getting it off by sucking it into his mouth!

In a few minutes his hind legs were free of the old suit, and little by little it began to be pulled free from his body. All the time Old Mr. Toad was working very hard to suck it at the corners of his big mouth. He glared angrily at Peter, but he couldn't say anything because his mouth was too full. He looked so funny that Peter just threw himself on the ground and rolled over and over with laughter. This made Old Mr. Toad glare more angrily than ever, but he couldn't say anything, not a word.

When he had got his hands free by pulling the sleeves of his old coat off inside out, he used his hands to pull the last of it over his head. Then he gulped very hard two or three times to swallow his old suit, and when the last of it had disappeared, he found his voice.

"Don't you know that it is the most impolite thing in the world to look at people when they are changing their clothes?" he sputtered.

Day 39

1. Read chapter 14.
2. Look for the word **indignant** in the beginning of today's reading.
3. Look for the word **hastily** at the end of today's reading.
4. **Indignant** means feeling angered or annoyed.
5. **Hastily** means doing something in a hurry.
6. It's time to act. Say this line **indignantly**, "I can't believe you did that!" Say it like you are really annoyed!
7. Now say it with **envy**, like you are really jealous that they got to do that great thing. "I can't believe you did that!"
8. Now say it **hastily**, really fast! If that's too hard, you can do something hastily. Picking up things from the floor would be a great thing to do hastily. :)

Chapter XIV   Old Mr. Toad Disappears

Admit your fault when you've done wrong,
 And don't postpone it over long.

Peter Rabbit didn't blame Old Mr. Toad a bit for being indignant because Peter had watched him change his suit. It wasn't a nice thing to do. Old Mr. Toad had looked very funny while he was struggling out of his old suit, and Peter just couldn't help laughing at him. But he realized that he had been very impolite, and he very meekly told Old Mr. Toad so.

"You see, it was this way," explained Peter. "I heard something under that old board, and I just naturally turned it over to find out what was there."

"Hump!" grunted Old Mr. Toad.

"I didn't have the least idea that you were there," continued Peter. "When I found who it was, and what you were doing, I couldn't help watching because it was so interesting, and I couldn't help laughing because you really did look so funny. But I'm sorry, Mr. Toad. Truly I am. I didn't mean to be so impolite. I promise never to do it again. I don't suppose, Mr. Toad, that it seems at all wonderful to you that you can change your suit that way, but it does to me. I had heard that you swallowed your old suits, but I never half believed it. Now I know it is so and just how you do it, and I feel as if I had learned something worth knowing. Do you know, I think you are one of the most interesting and wonderful of all my neighbors, and I'll never laugh at or tease you again, Mr. Toad."

"Hump!" grunted Old Mr. Toad again, but it was very clear that he was a little flattered by Peter's interest in him and was rapidly recovering his good nature.

"There is one thing I don't understand yet," said Peter, "and that is where you go to to sleep all winter. Do you go down into the mud at the bottom of the Smiling Pool the way Grandfather Frog does?"

"Certainly not!" retorted Old Mr. Toad. "Use your common sense, Peter Rabbit. If I had spent the winter in the Smiling Pool, do you suppose I would have left it to come way up here and then have turned right around and gone back there to sing? I'm not so fond of long journeys as all that."

"That's so." Peter looked foolish. "I didn't think of that when I spoke."

"The trouble with you, and with a lot of other people, is that you speak first and do your thinking afterward, when you do any thinking at all," grunted Old Mr. Toad. "Now if I wanted to, I could disappear right here."

"You mean that you would hide under that old board just as you did before," said Peter, with a very wise look.

"Nothing of the sort!" snapped Old Mr. Toad. "I could disappear and not go near that old board, not a step nearer than I am now."

Peter looked in all directions carefully, but not a thing could he see under which Old Mr. Toad could possibly hide except the old board, and he had said he wouldn't hide under that. "I don't like to doubt your word, Mr. Toad," said he, "but you'll have to show me before I can believe that."

Old Mr. Toad's eyes twinkled. Here was a chance to get even with Peter for watching him change his suit. "If you'll turn your back to me and look straight down the Crooked Little Path for five minutes, I'll disappear," said he. "More than that, I give you my word of honor that I will not hop three feet from where I am sitting."

"All right," replied Peter promptly, turning his back to Old Mr. Toad. "I'll look down the Crooked Little Path for five minutes and promise not to peek."

So Peter sat and gazed straight down the Crooked Little Path. It was a great temptation to roll his eyes back and peep behind him, but he had given his word that he wouldn't, and he didn't. When he thought the five minutes were up, he turned around. Old Mr. Toad was nowhere to be seen. Peter looked hastily this way and that way, but there was not a sign of Old Mr. Toad. He had disappeared as completely as if he never had been there.

Day 40

1. Read chapter 15.
2. Where does Peter look for Mr. Toad? (Answers)
3. Where does Mr. Toad hide? (Answers)

Chapter XV   Old Mr. Toad Gives Peter a Scare

> If you play pranks on other folks
>   You may be sure that they
> Will take the first chance that they get
>   A joke on you to play.

Old Mr. Toad was getting even with Peter for laughing at him. While Peter's back had been turned, Old Mr. Toad had disappeared.

It was too much for Peter. Look as he would, he couldn't see so much as a chip under which Old Mr. Toad might have hidden, excepting the old board, and Old Mr. Toad had given his word of honor that he wouldn't hide under that. Nevertheless, Peter hopped over to it and turned it over again, because he couldn't think of any other place to look. Of course, Old Mr. Toad wasn't there. Of course not. He had given his word that he wouldn't hide there, and he always lives up to his word. Peter should have known better than to have looked there.

Old Mr. Toad had also said that he would not go three feet from the spot where he was sitting at the time, so Peter should have known better than to have raced up the Crooked Little Path as he did. But if Old Mr. Toad had nothing to hide under, of course he must have hopped away, reasoned Peter. He couldn't hop far in five minutes, that was sure, and so Peter ran this way and that way a great deal farther than it would have been possible for Old Mr. Toad to have gone. But it was a wholly useless search, and presently Peter returned and sat down on the very spot where he had last seen Old Mr. Toad. Peter never had felt more foolish in all his life. He began to think that Old Mr. Toad must be bewitched and had some strange power of making himself invisible.

For a long time Peter sat perfectly still, trying to puzzle out how Old Mr. Toad had disappeared, but the more he puzzled over it, the more impossible it seemed. And yet Old Mr. Toad had disappeared. Suddenly Peter gave a frightened scream and jumped higher than he ever had jumped before in all his life. A voice, the voice of Old Mr. Toad himself, had said, "Well, now are you satisfied?" *And that voice had come from right under Peter!* Do you wonder that he was frightened? When he turned to look, there sat Old Mr. Toad right where he himself had been sitting a moment before. Peter rubbed his eyes and stared very foolishly.

"Wh-wh-where did you come from?" he stammered at last.

Old Mr. Toad grinned. "I'll show you," said he. And right while Peter was looking at him, he began to sink down into the ground until only the top of his head could be seen. Then that disappeared. Old Mr. Toad had gone down, and the sand had fallen right back over him. Peter just had to rub his eyes again. He had to! Then, to make sure, he began to dig away the sand where Old Mr. Toad had been sitting. In a minute he felt Old Mr. Toad, who at once came out again.

Old Mr. Toad's beautiful eyes twinkled more than ever. "I guess we are even now, Peter," said he.

Peter nodded. "More than that, Mr. Toad. I think you have a little the best of it," he replied. "Now won't you tell me how you did it?"

Old Mr. Toad held up one of his stout hind feet, and on it was a kind of spur. "There's another just like that on the other foot," said he, "and I use them to dig with. You go into a hole headfirst, but I go in the other way. I make my hole in soft earth and back into it at the same time, this way." He began to work his stout hind feet, and as he kicked the earth out, he backed in at the same time. When he was deep enough, the earth just fell back over him, for you see it was very loose and not packed down at all. When he once more reappeared, Peter thanked him. Then he asked one more question.

"Is that the way you go into winter quarters?"

Old Mr. Toad nodded. "And it's the way I escape from my enemies."

Day 41

1. Read chapter 16.
2. Why do you think Old Mr. Toad turns pale and leaves at the end of the chapter? (hint: It has to do with who Jimmy saw that day.) (Answers)

Vocabulary

1. To **amble** means to walk slowly.
2. If you are **smug**, it means you have too much pride in yourself.
3. **Anxious** means worried.
4. Always be on the lookout in your reading for words I give you.

Chapter XVI   Jimmy Skunk Is Surprised

Jimmy Skunk ambled along the Crooked Little Path down the hill. He didn't hurry because Jimmy doesn't believe in hurrying. The only time he ever hurries is when he sees a fat beetle trying to get out of sight. Then Jimmy *does* hurry. But just now he didn't see any fat beetles, although he was looking for them. So he just ambled along as if he had all the time in the world, as indeed he had. He was feeling very good-natured, was Jimmy Skunk. And why shouldn't he? There was everything to make him feel good-natured. Summer had arrived to stay. On every side he heard glad voices. Bumble the Bee was humming a song. Best of all, Jimmy had found three beetles that very morning, and he knew that there were more if he could find them. So why shouldn't he feel good?

Jimmy had laughed at Peter Rabbit for being so anxious for Summer to arrive, but he was just as glad as Peter that she had come, although he wouldn't have said so for the world. His sharp little eyes twinkled as he ambled along, and there wasn't much that they missed. As he walked he talked, quite to himself of course, because there was nobody near to hear, and this is what he was saying:

"Beetle, beetle, smooth and smug,
You are nothing but a bug.
Bugs were made for Skunks to eat,
So come out from your retreat.

"Hello! There's a nice big piece of bark over there that looks as if it ought to have a dozen fat beetles under it. It's great fun to pull over pieces of bark and see fat beetles run all ways at once. I'll just have to see what is under that piece."

Jimmy tiptoed softly over to the big piece of bark, and then as he made ready to turn it over, he began again that foolish little verse.

"Beetle, beetle, smooth and smug,
You are nothing but a bug."

As he said the last word, he suddenly pulled the piece of bark over.

"Who's a bug?" asked a funny voice, and it sounded rather cross. Jimmy Skunk nearly tumbled over backward in surprise, and for a minute he couldn't find his tongue. There, instead of the fat beetles he had been so sure of, sat Old Mr. Toad, and he didn't look at all pleased.

"Who's a bug?" he repeated.

Instead of answering, Jimmy Skunk began to laugh. "Who's a bug?" demanded Old Mr. Toad, more crossly than before.

"There isn't any bug, Mr. Toad, and I beg your pardon," replied Jimmy, remembering his politeness. "I just thought there was. You see, I didn't know you were under that piece of bark. I hope you will excuse me, Mr. Toad. Have you seen any fat beetles this morning?"

"No," said Old Mr. Toad grumpily, and yawned and rubbed his eyes.

"Why," exclaimed Jimmy Skunk, "I believe you have just waked up!"

"What if I have?" demanded Old Mr. Toad.

"Oh, nothing, nothing at all, Mr. Toad," replied Jimmy Skunk, "only you are the second one I've met this morning who had just waked up."

"Who was the other?" asked Old Mr. Toad.

"Mr. Blacksnake," replied Jimmy. "He inquired for you."

Old Mr. Toad turned quite pale. "I I think I'll be moving along," said he.

Day 42

1. Read chapter 17.
2. Who did Mr. Toad see on the path? (Answers)

Chapter XVII   Old Mr. Toad's Mistake

If is a very little word to look at, but the biggest word you have ever seen doesn't begin to have so much meaning as little "if." *If* Jimmy Skunk hadn't ambled down the Crooked Little Path just when he did; *if* he hadn't been looking for fat beetles; *if* he hadn't seen that big piece of bark at one side and decided to pull it over; *if* it hadn't been for all these "*ifs*," why Old Mr. Toad wouldn't have made the mistake he did, and you wouldn't have had this story.   But Jimmy Skunk *did* amble down the Crooked Little Path, he *did* look for beetles, and he *did* pull over that big piece of bark.   And when he had pulled it over, he found Old Mr. Toad there.

Old Mr. Toad had crept under that piece of bark because he wanted to take a nap.   But when Jimmy Skunk told him that he had seen Mr. Blacksnake that very morning, and that Mr. Blacksnake had asked after Old Mr. Toad, the very last bit of sleepiness left Old Mr. Toad.   Yes, Sir, he was wide awake right away.   You see, he knew right away why Mr. Blacksnake had asked after him.   He knew that Mr. Blacksnake has a fondness for Toads.   He turned quite pale when he heard that Mr. Blacksnake had asked after him, and right then he made his mistake.   He was in such a hurry to get away from that neighborhood that he forgot to ask Jimmy Skunk just where he had seen Mr. Blacksnake.   He hardly waited long enough to say good-by to Jimmy Skunk, but started off as fast as he could go.

Now it just happened that Old Mr. Toad started up the Crooked Little Path, and it just happened that Mr. Blacksnake was coming down the Crooked Little Path.   Now when people are very much afraid, they almost always seem to think that danger is behind instead of in front of them.   It was so with Old Mr. Toad.   Instead of watching out in front as he hopped along, he kept watching over his shoulder, and that was his second mistake.   He was so sure that Mr. Blacksnake was somewhere behind him that he didn't look to see where he was going, and you know that people who don't look to see where they are going are almost sure to go headfirst right into trouble.

Old Mr. Toad went hopping up the Crooked Little Path as fast as he could, which wasn't very fast, because he never can hop very fast.   And all the time he kept looking behind for Mr. Blacksnake.   Presently he came to a turn in the Crooked Little Path, and as he hurried around it, he almost ran into Mr. Blacksnake himself.   It was a question which was more surprised.   For just a wee second they stared at each other.   Then Mr. Blacksnake's eyes began to sparkle.

"Good morning, Mr. Toad. Isn't this a beautiful morning? I was just thinking about you," said he.

But poor Old Mr. Toad didn't say good morning. He didn't say anything. He couldn't, because he was too scared. He just gave a frightened little squeal, turned around, and started down the Crooked Little Path twice as fast as he had come up. Mr. Blacksnake grinned and started after him, not very fast because he knew that he wouldn't have to run very fast to catch Old Mr. Toad, and he thought the exercise would do him good.

And this is how it happened that summer morning that jolly, bright Mr. Sun, looking down from the blue, blue sky and smiling to see how happy everybody seemed, suddenly discovered that there was one of the little meadow people who wasn't happy, but instead was terribly, terribly unhappy. It was Old Mr. Toad hopping down the Crooked Little Path for his life, while after him, and getting nearer and nearer, glided Mr. Blacksnake.

Day 43

1. Read chapter 18.
2. Who saved Mr. Toad? (Answers)

Chapter XVIII   Jimmy Skunk Is Just in Time

Jimmy Skunk ambled slowly along, chuckling as he thought of what a hurry Mr. Toad had been in, when he had heard that Mr. Blacksnake had asked after him. It had been funny, very funny indeed, to see Mr. Toad try to hurry.

Suddenly Jimmy stopped chuckling. Then he stopped ambling along the Crooked Little Path. He turned around and looked back, and as he did so he scratched his head thoughtfully. He had just happened to think that Old Mr. Toad had gone up the Crooked Little Path, and it was *up* the Crooked Little Path that Mr. Blacksnake had shown himself that morning.

"If he's still up there," thought Jimmy, "Old Mr. Toad is hopping right straight into the very worst kind of trouble. How stupid of him not to have asked me where Mr. Blacksnake was! Well, it's none of my business. I guess I'll go on."

But he had gone on down the Crooked Little Path only a few steps when he stopped again. You see, Jimmy is really a very kind-hearted little fellow, and somehow he didn't like to think of what might happen to Old Mr. Toad.

"I hate to go way back there," he grumbled, for you know he is naturally rather lazy. "Still, the Green Meadows wouldn't be quite the same without Old Mr. Toad. I should miss him if anything happened to him. I suppose it would be partly my fault, too, for if I hadn't pulled over that piece of bark, he probably would have stayed there the rest of the day and been safe."

"Maybe he won't meet Mr. Blacksnake," said a little voice inside of Jimmy.

"And maybe he will," said Jimmy right out loud. And with that, he started back up the Crooked Little Path, and strange to say Jimmy hurried.

He had just reached a turn in the Crooked Little Path when who should run right plump into him but poor Old Mr. Toad. He gave a frightened squeal and fell right over on his

69

back, and kicked foolishly as he tried to get on his feet again. But he was all out of breath, and so frightened and tired that all he could do was to kick and kick. He hadn't seen Jimmy at all, for he had been looking behind him, and he didn't even know who it was he had run into.

Right behind him came Mr. Blacksnake. Of course he saw Jimmy, and he stopped short and hissed angrily.

"What were you going to do to Mr. Toad?" demanded Jimmy.

"None of your business!" hissed Mr. Blacksnake. "Get out of my way, or you'll be sorry."

Jimmy Skunk just laughed and stepped in front of poor Old Mr. Toad. Mr. Blacksnake coiled himself up in the path and darted his tongue out at Jimmy in the most impudent way. Then he tried to make himself look very fierce. Then he jumped straight at Jimmy Skunk with his mouth wide open, but he took great care not to jump quite far enough to reach Jimmy. You see, he was just trying to scare Jimmy. But Jimmy didn't scare. He knows all about Mr. Blacksnake and that really he is a coward. So he suddenly gritted his teeth in a way not at all pleasant to hear and started for Mr. Blacksnake. Mr. Blacksnake didn't wait. No, Sir, he didn't wait. He suddenly turned and glided back up the Crooked Little Path, hissing angrily. Jimmy followed him a little way, and then he went back to Old Mr. Toad.

"Oh," panted Mr. Toad, "you came just in time! I couldn't have hopped another hop."

"I guess I did," replied Jimmy. "Now you get your breath and come along with me." And Old Mr. Toad did.

Day 44

1. Read chapter 19.

Vocabulary

1. **Scorn** means thinking that someone or something is worthless or despicable.
2. **Feeble** means not having physical strength.

3. Who was feeble in this chapter? (hint: He was feeble because he was so scared.) (Answers)

Chapter XIX   Old Mr. Toad Gets His Stomach Full

Pray do not tip your nose in scorn
    At things which others eat,
For things to you not good at all
    To others are most sweet.

There are ants, for instance. You wouldn't want to eat them even if you were dreadfully hungry. But Old Mr. Toad and Buster Bear think there is nothing much nicer. Now Buster Bear had found Old Mr. Toad catching ants, one at a time, as he kept watch beside their home, and it had pleased Buster to find some one else who liked ants. Right away he invited Old Mr. Toad to dine with him. But poor Old Mr. Toad was frightened almost to death when he heard the deep, grumbly-rumbly voice of Buster Bear, for he had been so busy watching the ants that he hadn't seen Buster coming.

He fell right over on his back, which wasn't at all dignified, and made Buster Bear laugh. That frightened Mr. Toad more than ever. You see he didn't have the least doubt in the world that Buster Bear meant to eat him, and when Buster invited him to dinner, he was sure that that was just a joke on Buster's part.

But there was no way to escape, and after a little Old Mr. Toad thought it best to be polite, because, you know, it always pays to be polite. So he said in a very faint voice that he would be pleased to dine with Buster. Then he waved his feet feebly, trying to get on his feet again. Buster Bear laughed harder than ever. It was a low, deep, grumbly-rumbly laugh, and sent cold shivers all over poor Old Mr. Toad. But when Buster reached out a great paw with great cruel-looking claws Mr. Toad quite gave up. He didn't have strength enough left to even kick. He just closed his eyes and waited for the end.

What do you think happened? Why, he was rolled over on to his feet so gently that he just gasped with surprise. It didn't seem possible that such a great paw could be so gentle.

"Now," said Buster Bear in a voice which he tried to make sound pleasant, but which was grumbly-rumbly just the same, "I know where there is a fine dinner waiting for us just a little way from here. You follow me, and we'll have it in no time."

So Buster Bear led the way, and Old Mr. Toad followed as fast as he could, because he didn't dare not to. Presently Buster stopped beside a big decayed old log. "If you are ready, Mr. Toad, we will dine now," said he.

Old Mr. Toad didn't see anything to eat. His heart sank again, and he shook all over. "I I'm not hungry," said he in a very faint voice.

Buster Bear didn't seem to hear. He hooked his great claws into the old log and gave a mighty pull. Over rolled the log, and there were ants and ants and ants, hurrying this way and scurrying that way, more ants than Mr. Toad had seen in all his life before!

"Help yourself," said Buster Bear politely.

Old Mr. Toad didn't wait to be told twice. He forgot all about his fright. He forgot all about Buster Bear. He forgot that he wasn't hungry. He forgot his manners. He jumped right in among those ants, and for a little while he was the busiest Toad ever seen. Buster Bear was busy too. He swept his long tongue this way, and he swept it that way, and each time he drew it back into his mouth, it was covered with ants. At last Old Mr. Toad couldn't hold another ant. Then he remembered Buster Bear and looked up a little fearfully. Buster was smacking his lips, and there was a twinkle in each eye.

"Good, aren't they?" said he.

"The best I ever ate," declared Old Mr. Toad with a sigh of satisfaction.

"Come dine with me again," said Buster Bear, and somehow this time Old Mr. Toad didn't mind because his voice sounded grumbly-rumbly.

Day 45

1. Read chapter 20.
2. Tell someone what happens in this chapter.

Chapter XX   Old Mr. Toad Is Puffed Up

Old Mr. Toad hopped slowly down the Lone Little Path. He usually does hop slowly, but this time he hopped slower than ever. You see, he was so puffed up that he couldn't have hopped fast if he had wanted to, and he didn't want to. In the first place his stomach was so full of ants that there wasn't room for another one. No, Sir, Old Mr. Toad couldn't have swallowed another ant if he had tried. Of course they made his stomach stick out, but it wasn't the ants that puffed him out all over. Oh, my, no! It was pride. That's what it was pride. You know nothing can puff any one up quite like foolish pride.

Old Mr. Toad was old enough to have known better. It is bad enough to see young and foolish creatures puffed up with pride, but it is worse to see any one as old as Old Mr. Toad that way. He held his head so high that he couldn't see his own feet, and more than once he stubbed his toes. Presently he met his old friend, Danny Meadow Mouse. He tipped his head a little higher, puffed himself out a little more, and pretended not to see Danny.

"Hello, Mr. Toad," said Danny.

Mr. Toad pretended not to hear. Danny looked puzzled. Then he spoke again, and this time he shouted: "Hello, Mr. Toad! I haven't seen you for some time."

It wouldn't do to pretend not to hear this time. "Oh, how do you do, Danny?" said Old Mr. Toad with a very grand air, and pretending to be much surprised. "Sorry I can't stop, but I've been dining with, my friend, Buster Bear, and now I must get home." When he mentioned the name of Buster Bear, he puffed himself out a little more.

Danny grinned as he watched him hop on down the Lone Little Path. "Can't talk with common folks any more," he muttered. "I've heard that pride is very apt to turn people's heads, but I never expected to see Old Mr. Toad proud."

Mr. Toad kept on his way, and presently he met Peter Rabbit. Peter stopped to gossip, as is his way. But Old Mr. Toad took no notice of him at all. He kept right on with his head high, and all puffed out. Peter might have been a stick or a stone for all the notice Old Mr. Toad took of him. Peter looked puzzled. Then he hurried down to tell Danny Meadow Mouse about it.

"Oh," said Danny, "he's been to dine with Buster Bear, and now he has no use for his old friends."

Pretty soon along came Johnny Chuck, and he was very much put out because he had been treated by Old Mr. Toad just as Peter Rabbit had. Striped Chipmunk told the same story. So did Unc' Billy Possum. It was the same with all of Old Mr. Toad's old friends and neighbors, excepting Bobby Coon, who, you know, is Buster Bear's little cousin. To him Old Mr. Toad was very polite and talked a great deal about Buster Bear, and thought that Bobby must be very proud to be related to Buster.

At first everybody thought it a great joke to see Old Mr. Toad so puffed up with, pride, but after a little they grew tired of being snubbed by their old friend and neighbor, and began to say unpleasant things about him. Then they decided that what Old Mr. Toad needed was a lesson, so they put their heads together and planned how they would teach Old Mr. Toad how foolish it is for any one to be puffed up with pride.

Day 46

1. Read chapter 21.
2. Tell someone what happens in this chapter.

Vocabulary

1. Play charades. Go through the list below and act out your vocabulary words. Have someone watch you and guess which word you are acting out. You could take turns acting and guessing. Keep going until you've done all the words.
2. Choose your word to act out from this list and then give the book to the guesser.
   - Scorn – thinking something or someone is worthless or despicable
   - Amble – walking in a slow, relaxed way
   - Indignant – angered or annoyed
   - Hastily – doing something in a hurry
   - Envy – jealous
   - Feeble – lacking physical strength
   - Anxious – worried
   - Smug – having too much pride in yourself

Chapter XXI   Old Mr. Toad Receives Another Invitation

The friends and neighbors of Old Mr. Toad decided that he needed to be taught a lesson. At first, you know, every one had laughed at him, because he had grown too proud to speak to them, but after a little they grew tired of being treated so, and some of them put their heads together to think of some plan to teach Old Mr. Toad a lesson and what a very, very foolish thing false pride is. The very next day Jimmy Skunk went into the Green Forest to look for Buster Bear. You know Jimmy isn't afraid of Buster. He didn't have to look long, and when he had found him, the very first thing he did was to ask Buster if he had seen any fat beetles that morning. You know Jimmy is very fond of fat beetles, and the first thing he asks any one he may happen to meet is if they have seen any.

Buster Bear grinned and said he thought he knew where there might be a few, and he would be pleased to have Jimmy go with him to see. Sure enough, under an old log he found five fat beetles, and these Jimmy gobbled up without even asking Buster if he would have one. Jimmy is usually very polite, but this time he quite forgot politeness. I am afraid he is rather apt to when fat beetles are concerned. But Buster didn't seem to mind. When the last beetle had disappeared Jimmy smacked his lips, and then he told Buster Bear what he had come for. Of course, at first Buster had thought it was for the fat beetles. But it wasn't. No, Sir, it wasn't for the fat beetles at all. It was to get Buster Bear's help in a plan to teach Old Mr. Toad a lesson.

First Jimmy told Buster all about how puffed up Old Mr. Toad was because he had dined with Buster, and how ever since then he had refused even to speak to his old friends and neighbors. It tickled Buster Bear so to think that little homely Old Mr. Toad could be proud of anything that he laughed and laughed, and his laugh was deep and grumbly-rumbly. Then Jimmy told him the plan to teach Old Mr. Toad a lesson and asked Buster if he would help. Buster's eyes twinkled as he promised to do what Jimmy asked.

Then Jimmy went straight to where Old Mr. Toad was sitting all puffed up, taking a sun-bath.

"Buster Bear has just sent word by me to ask if you will honor him by dining with him to-morrow at the rotted chestnut stump near the edge of the Green Forest," said Jimmy in his politest manner.

Now if Old Mr. Toad was puffed up before, just think how he swelled out when he heard that. Jimmy Skunk was actually afraid that he would burst.

"You may tell my friend, Buster Bear, that I shall be very happy to honor him by dining with him," replied Old Mr. Toad with a very grand air.

Jimmy went off to deliver his reply, and Old Mr. Toad sat and puffed himself out until he could hardly breathe. "Honor him by dining with him," said he over and over to himself. "I never was so flattered in my life."

Day 47

1. Read chapter 22.
2. What lesson does Old Mr. Toad learn? (Answers)

Chapter XXII   Old Mr. Toad Learns a Lesson

Pride is like a great big bubble;
    You'll find there's nothing in it.
  Prick it and for all your trouble
    It has vanished in a minute.

Old Mr. Toad was so puffed out with pride as he started for the Green Forest to dine with Buster Bear that those who saw him wondered if he wouldn't burst before he got there. Everybody knew where he was going, and this made Old Mr. Toad feel more important and proud than ever. He might not have felt quite so puffed up if he had known just how it had come about that he received this second invitation to dine with Buster Bear. When Jimmy Skunk brought it to him, Jimmy didn't tell him that Buster had been asked to send the invitation, and that it was all part of a plan on the part of some of Old Mr. Toad's old friends and neighbors to teach him a lesson. No, indeed, Jimmy didn't say anything at all about that!

So Old Mr. Toad went hopping along and stumbling over his own feet, because his head was held so high and he was so puffed out that he couldn't see where he was going. He could think of nothing but how important Buster Bear must consider him to invite him to dinner a second time, and of the delicious ants he was sure he would have to eat.

"What very good taste Buster Bear has," thought he, "and how very fortunate it is that he found out that I also am fond of ants."

He was so busy with these pleasant thoughts and of the good dinner that he expected to have that he took no notice of what was going on about him. He didn't see his old friends and neighbors peeping out at him and laughing because he looked so foolish and silly. He was dressed in his very best, which was nothing at all to be proud of, for you know Old Mr. Toad has no fine clothes. And being puffed up so, he was homelier than ever, which is saying a great deal, for at best Mr. Toad is anything but handsome.

He was beginning to get pretty tired by the time he reached the Green Forest and came in sight of the rotted old chestnut stump where he was to meet Buster Bear.

Buster was waiting for him. "How do you do this fine day? You look a little tired and rather warm, Mr. Toad," said he.

"I am a little warm," replied Mr. Toad in his most polite manner, although he couldn't help panting for breath as he said it. "I hope you are feeling as well as you are looking, Mr. Bear."

Buster Bear laughed a great, grumbly-rumbly laugh. "I always feel fine when there is a dinner of fat ants ready for me," said he. "It is fine of you to honor me by coming to dine."

Here Mr. Toad put one hand on his stomach and tried to make a very grand bow. Peter Rabbit, hiding behind a near-by tree, almost giggled aloud, he looked so funny.

"I have ventured to invite another to enjoy the dinner with us," continued Buster Bear. Mr. Toad's face fell. You see he was selfish. He wanted to be the only one to have the honor of dining with Buster Bear. "He's a little late," went on Buster, "but I think he will be here soon, and I hope you will be glad to meet him. Ah, there he comes now!"

Old Mr. Toad looked in the direction in which Buster Bear was looking. He gave a little gasp and turned quite pale. All his puffiness disappeared. He didn't look like the same Toad at all. The newcomer was Mr. Blacksnake. "Oh!" cried Old Mr. Toad, and then, without even asking to be excused, he turned his back on Buster Bear and started back the way he had come, with long, frightened hops.

"Ha, ha, ha!" shouted Peter Rabbit, jumping out from behind a tree.

"Ho, ho, ho!" shouted Jimmy Skunk from behind another.

"Hee, hee, hee!" shouted Johnny Chuck from behind a third.

Then Old Mr. Toad knew that his old friends and neighbors had planned this to teach him a lesson.

Day 48

1. Read chapter 23. This is the last chapter.
2. Tell someone what happens at the end of the story.

Chapter XXIII   Old Mr. Toad is Very Humble

When Old Mr. Toad saw Mr. Blacksnake and turned his back on Buster Bear and the fine dinner to which Buster had invited him, he had but just one idea in his head, and that was to get out of sight of Mr. Blacksnake as soon as possible. He forgot to ask Buster Bear to excuse him. He forgot that he was tired and hot. He forgot all the pride with which he had been so puffed up. He forgot everything but the need of getting out of sight of Mr. Blacksnake as soon as ever he could. So away went Old Mr. Toad, hop, hop, hipperty-hop, hop, hop, hipperty-hop! He heard Peter Rabbit and Jimmy Skunk and Johnny Chuck and others of his old friends and neighbors shouting with laughter. Yes, and he heard the deep, grumbly-rumbly laugh of Buster Bear. But he didn't mind it. Not then, anyway. He hadn't room for any feeling except fear of Mr. Blacksnake.

But Old Mr. Toad had to stop after a while. You see, his legs were so tired they just wouldn't go any longer. And he was so out of breath that he wheezed. He crawled under a big piece of bark, and there he lay flat on the ground and panted and panted for breath. He would stay there until jolly, round, bright Mr. Sun went to bed behind the Purple Hills. Then Mr. Blacksnake would go to bed too, and it would be safe for him to go home. Now, lying there in the dark, for it was dark under that big piece of bark, Old Mr. Toad had time to think. Little by little he began to understand that his invitation to dine with Buster Bear had been part of a plan by his old friends and neighbors whom he had so snubbed and looked down on when he had been puffed up with pride, to teach him a lesson. At first he was angry, very angry indeed. Then he began to see how foolish and silly he had been, and shame took the place of anger. As he remembered the deep, grumbly-rumbly laughter of Buster Bear, the feeling of shame grew.

"I deserve it," thought Old Mr. Toad. "Yes, Sir, I deserve every bit of it. The only thing that I have to be proud of is that I'm honest and work for my living. Yes, Sir, that's all."

When darkness came at last, and he crawled out to go home, he was feeling very humble. Peter Rabbit happened along just then. Old Mr. Toad opened his mouth to speak, but Peter suddenly threw his head up very high and strutted past as if he didn't see Old Mr. Toad at all. Mr. Toad gulped and went on. Pretty soon he met Jimmy Skunk. Jimmy went right on about his business and actually stepped right over Old Mr. Toad as if he had been a stick or a stone. Old Mr. Toad gulped again and went on. The next day he went down to see Danny Meadow Mouse. He meant to tell Danny how ashamed he was for the way he had treated Danny and his other friends. But Danny brushed right past without even a glance at him. Old Mr. Toad gulped and started up to see Johnny Chuck. The same thing happened again. So it did when he met Striped Chipmunk.

At last Old Mr. Toad gave up and went home, where he sat under a big mullein leaf the rest of the day, feeling very miserable and lonely. He didn't have appetite enough to snap at a single fly. Late that afternoon he heard a little noise and looked up to find all his old friends and neighbors forming a circle around him. Suddenly they began to dance and shout:

"Old Mr. Toad is a jolly good fellow!
His temper is sweet, disposition is mellow!
And now that his bubble of pride is quite busted
We know that he knows that his friends can be trusted."

Then Old Mr. Toad knew that all was well once more, and presently he began to dance too, the funniest dance that ever was seen.

This is all for now about homely Old Mr. Toad, because I have just got to tell you about another homely fellow, Prickly Porky the Porcupine, who carries a thousand little spears. The next book will tell you all about *his* adventures.

Day 49

1. Write a book report about *The Adventures of Old Mr. Toad.*
    1. Write the author's name.

2. Write the name of the book.

3. Write about who the book was about and where the story took place.

4. Write what was your favorite part.

5. Add a picture if you like.

2. You could save this for your portfolio.

Day 50

Vocabulary

1. Either read this story to someone and ask someone else to act it out as you read or ask someone to read the story and you act it out. Or, both take turns acting it out. I used boys but you could read it Jacqueline and Johanna and use feminine pronouns if you like.

2. You will just act out the story without talking. You can play all the characters.
   - Jack **ambled** down the street, humming a song, smiling in the sun. He was on his way to his friend's house for a birthday party. Suddenly he stopped. He had forgotten a present! Now he started feeling very **anxious**. What was he going to do? He decided he better go get a present. He **hastily** returned home and searched for a present. He didn't know what else to do, so he grabbed his stack of baseball cards and put them in a paper bag. He ran out of the house and down the street. He was huffing and puffing and had to sit because he was so **feeble** from running so fast so far. Joe was already at the party.

   - (The actor has to be Joe now.) Joe took one look at Jack's bag and felt very **smug**. "That's your present?" he said **scornfully**. "What? Did you bring him your lunch?"

   - (Now the actor can be Jack again.) Jack was **indignant**. He knew it wasn't the best looking present, but he still thought it was a good present.

   - (Now the actor can be Joe.) Soon their friend started opening presents. He opened Joe's first. It turned out that their friend already had one. Joe was upset that he wasn't more excited about it. He opened Jack's bag last. His eyes grew wide. He jumped up and started saying how great it was. He couldn't believe Jack had given him so many. Jack was really happy he had brought them, but Joe was **envious** that Jack had brought the best present.

Day 51

1. Read the first half of *The Emperor's New Clothes.* This is by Hans Christian Anderson.

Many years ago, there was an Emperor, who was so excessively fond of new clothes, that he spent all his money in dress. He did not trouble himself in the least about his soldiers; nor did he care to go either to the theatre or the chase, except for the opportunities then afforded him for displaying his new clothes. He had a different suit for each hour of the day; and as of any other king or emperor, one is accustomed to say, "he is sitting in council," it was always said of him, "The Emperor is sitting in his wardrobe."

Time passed merrily in the large town which was his capital; strangers arrived every day at the court. One day, two rogues, calling themselves weavers, made their appearance. They gave out that they knew how to weave stuffs of the most beautiful colors and elaborate patterns, the clothes manufactured from which should have the wonderful property of remaining invisible to everyone who was unfit for the office he held, or who was extraordinarily simple in character.

"These must, indeed, be splendid clothes!" thought the Emperor. "Had I such a suit, I might at once find out what men in my realms are unfit for their office, and also be able to distinguish the wise from the foolish! This stuff must be woven for me immediately." And he caused large sums of money to be given to both the weavers in order that they might begin their work directly.

So the two pretended weavers set up two looms, and affected to work very busily, though in reality they did nothing at all. They asked for the most delicate silk and the purest gold thread; put both into their own knapsacks; and then continued their pretended work at the empty looms until late at night.

"I should like to know how the weavers are getting on with my cloth," said the Emperor to himself, after some little time had elapsed; he was, however, rather embarrassed, when he remembered that a simpleton, or one unfit for his office, would be unable to see the manufacture. To be sure, he thought he had nothing to risk in his own person; but yet, he would prefer sending somebody else, to bring him intelligence about the weavers, and their work, before he troubled himself in the affair. All the people throughout the city had heard of the wonderful property the cloth was to possess; and all were anxious to learn how wise, or how ignorant, their neighbors might prove to be.

"I will send my faithful old minister to the weavers," said the Emperor at last, after some deliberation, "he will be best able to see how the cloth looks; for he is a man of sense, and no one can be more suitable for his office than be is."

So the faithful old minister went into the hall, where the knaves were working with all their might, at their empty looms. "What can be the meaning of this?" thought the old man, opening his eyes very wide. "I cannot discover the least bit of thread on the looms." However, he did not express his thoughts aloud.

The impostors requested him very courteously to be so good as to come nearer their looms; and then asked him whether the design pleased him, and whether the colors were not very beautiful; at the same time pointing to the empty frames. The poor old minister looked and looked, he could not discover anything on the looms, for a very good reason: there was nothing there. "What!" thought he again. "Is it possible that I am a simpleton? I have never thought so myself; and no one must know it now if I am so. Can it be, that I am unfit for my office? No, that must not be said either. I will never confess that I could not see the stuff."

"Well, Sir Minister!" said one of the knaves, still pretending to work. "You do not say whether the stuff pleases you."

"Oh, it is excellent!" replied the old minister, looking at the loom through his spectacles. "This pattern, and the colors, yes, I will tell the Emperor without delay, how very beautiful I think them."

"We shall be much obliged to you," said the impostors, and then they named the different colors and described the pattern of the pretended stuff. The old minister listened attentively to their words, in order that he might repeat them to the Emperor; and then the knaves asked for more silk and gold, saying that it was necessary to complete what they had begun. However, they put all that was given them into their knapsacks; and continued to work with as much apparent diligence as before at their empty looms.

The Emperor now sent another officer of his court to see how the men were getting on, and to ascertain whether the cloth would soon be ready. It was just the same with this gentleman as with the minister; he surveyed the looms on all sides, but could see nothing at all but the empty frames.

"Does not the stuff appear as beautiful to you, as it did to my lord the minister?" asked the impostors of the Emperor's second ambassador; at the same time making the same gestures as before, and talking of the design and colors which were not there.

"I certainly am not stupid!" thought the messenger. "It must be, that I am not fit for my good, profitable office! That is very odd; however, no one shall know anything about it." And accordingly he praised the stuff he could not see, and declared that he was delighted with both colors and patterns. "Indeed, please your Imperial Majesty," said he to his sovereign when he returned, "the cloth which the weavers are preparing is extraordinarily magnificent."

Day 52

1.   Read the second half of *The Emperor's New Clothes.*

The whole city was talking of the splendid cloth which the Emperor had ordered to be woven at his own expense.

And now the Emperor himself wished to see the costly manufacture, while it was still in the loom. Accompanied by a select number of officers of the court, among whom were the two honest men who had already admired the cloth, he went to the crafty impostors, who, as soon as they were aware of the Emperor's approach, went on working more diligently than ever; although they still did not pass a single thread through the looms.

"Is not the work absolutely magnificent?" said the two officers of the crown, already mentioned. "If your Majesty will only be pleased to look at it! What a splendid design! What glorious colors!" and at the same time they pointed to the empty frames; for they imagined that everyone else could see this exquisite piece of workmanship.

"How is this?" said the Emperor to himself. "I can see nothing! This is indeed a terrible affair! Am I a simpleton, or am I unfit to be an Emperor? That would be the worst thing that could happen–Oh! the cloth is charming," said he, aloud. "It has my complete approbation." And he smiled most graciously, and looked closely at the empty looms; for on no account would he say that he could not see what two of the officers of his court had praised so much. All his retinue now strained their eyes, hoping to discover something on the looms, but they could see no more than the others; nevertheless, they all exclaimed, "Oh, how beautiful!" and advised his majesty to have some new clothes made from this splendid material, for the approaching procession. "Magnificent! Charming! Excellent!" resounded on all sides; and everyone was uncommonly gay. The Emperor shared in the general satisfaction; and presented the impostors with the riband of an order of knighthood, to be worn in their button-holes, and the title of "Gentlemen Weavers."

The rogues sat up the whole of the night before the day on which the procession was to take place, and had sixteen lights burning, so that everyone might see how anxious they were to finish the Emperor's new suit. They pretended to roll the cloth off the looms; cut the air with their scissors; and sewed with needles without any thread in them. "See!" cried they, at last. "The Emperor's new clothes are ready!"

And now the Emperor, with all the grandees of his court, came to the weavers; and the rogues raised their arms, as if in the act of holding something up, saying, "Here are your Majesty's trousers! Here is the scarf! Here is the mantle! The whole suit is as light as a cobweb; one might fancy one has nothing at all on, when dressed in it; that, however, is the great virtue of this delicate cloth."

"Yes indeed!" said all the courtiers, although not one of them could see anything of this exquisite manufacture.

"If your Imperial Majesty will be graciously pleased to take off your clothes, we will fit on the new suit, in front of the looking glass."

The Emperor was accordingly undressed, and the rogues pretended to array him in his new suit; the Emperor turning round, from side to side, before the looking glass.

"How splendid his Majesty looks in his new clothes, and how well they fit!" everyone cried out. "What a design! What colors! These are indeed royal robes!"

"The canopy which is to be borne over your Majesty, in the procession, is waiting," announced the chief master of the ceremonies.

"I am quite ready," answered the Emperor. "Do my new clothes fit well?" asked he, turning himself round again before the looking glass, in order that he might appear to be examining his handsome suit.

The lords of the bedchamber, who were to carry his Majesty's train felt about on the ground, as if they were lifting up the ends of the mantle; and pretended to be carrying something; for they would by no means betray anything like simplicity, or unfitness for their office.

So now the Emperor walked under his high canopy in the midst of the procession, through the streets of his capital; and all the people standing by, and those at the windows, cried out, "Oh! How beautiful are our Emperor's new clothes! What a magnificent train there is to the mantle; and how gracefully the scarf hangs!" in short, no one would allow that he could not see these much-admired clothes; because, in doing so, he would have declared himself either a simpleton or unfit for his office. Certainly, none of the Emperor's various suits, had ever made so great an impression, as these invisible ones.

"But the Emperor has nothing at all on!" said a little child.

"Listen to the voice of innocence!" exclaimed his father; and what the child had said was whispered from one to another.

"But he has nothing at all on!" at last cried out all the people. The Emperor was vexed, for he knew that the people were right; but he thought the procession must go on now! And the lords of the bedchamber took greater pains than ever, to appear holding up a train, although, in reality, there was no train to hold.

Day 53

1. Read the first part of *How the Leopard Got His Spots* by Kipling.
2. "'sclusively" is the word exclusively. Read it out loud when you need to.
3. If this one is trouble for you, you can ask someone to read it aloud to you or listen to it online at lightupyourbrain.com.

In the days when everybody started fair, Best Beloved, the Leopard lived in a place called the High Veldt. 'Member it wasn't the Low Veldt, or the Bush Veldt, or the Sour Veldt, but the 'sclusively bare, hot, shiny High Veldt, where there was sand and sandy-coloured rock and 'sclusively tufts of sandy- yellowish grass. The Giraffe and the Zebra and the Eland and the Koodoo and the Hartebeest lived there; and they were 'sclusively sandy-yellow-brownish all over; but the Leopard, he was the 'sclusivest sandiest-yellowishbrownest of them all–a greyish-yellowish catty-shaped kind of beast, and he matched the 'sclusively yellowish-greyish-brownish colour of the High Veldt to one hair. This was very bad for the Giraffe and the Zebra and the rest of them; for he would lie down by a 'sclusively yellowish-greyish-brownish stone or clump of grass, and when the Giraffe or the Zebra or the Eland or the Koodoo or the Bush-Buck or the Bonte-Buck came by he would surprise them out of their jumpsome lives. He would indeed! And, also, there was an Ethiopian with bows and arrows (a 'sclusively greyish-brownish-yellowish man he was then), who lived on the High Veldt with the Leopard; and the two used to hunt together– the Ethiopian with his bows and arrows, and the Leopard 'sclusively with his teeth and claws–till the Giraffe and the Eland and the Koodoo and the Quagga and all the rest of them didn't know which way to jump, Best Beloved. They didn't indeed!

After a long time–things lived for ever so long in those days–they learned to avoid anything that looked like a Leopard or an Ethiopian; and bit by bit–the Giraffe began it, because his legs were the longest–they went away from the High Veldt. They scuttled for days and days and days till they came to a great forest, 'sclusively full of trees and bushes and stripy, speckly, patchy-blatchy shadows, and there they hid: and after another long time, what with standing half in the shade and half out of it, and what with the slippery-slidy shadows of the trees falling on them, the Giraffe grew blotchy, and the Zebra grew stripy, and the Eland and the Koodoo grew darker, with little wavy grey lines on their backs like bark on a tree trunk; and so, though you could hear them and smell them, you could very seldom see them, and then only when you knew precisely where to look. They had a beautiful time in the 'sclusively speckly-spickly shadows of the forest, while the Leopard and the Ethiopian ran about over the 'sclusively greyish-yellowish-reddish High Veldt outside, wondering where all their breakfasts and their dinners and their teas had gone. At last they were so hungry that they ate rats and beetles and rock-rabbits, the Leopard and the Ethiopian, and then they had the Big Tummy-ache, both together; and then they met Baviaan–the dog-headed, barking Baboon, who is Quite the Wisest Animal in All South Africa.

Said Leopard to Baviaan (and it was a very hot day), "Where has all the game gone?"

And Baviaan winked. He knew.

Said the Ethiopian to Baviaan, "Can you tell me the present habitat of the aboriginal Fauna?" (That meant just the same thing, but the Ethiopian always used long words. He was a grown-up.)

And Baviaan winked. He knew.

Day 54

1. Read the second part of *How the Leopard Got His Spots* by Kipling.
2. I'll start you with a little reminder of where you are in the story.

Said the Ethiopian to Baviaan, "Can you tell me the present habitat of the aboriginal Fauna?" (That meant just the same thing, but the Ethiopian always used long words. He was a grown-up.)

And Baviaan winked. He knew.

Then said Baviaan, "The game has gone into other spots; and my advice to you, Leopard, is to go into other spots as soon as you can."

And the Ethiopian said, "That is all very fine, but I wish to know whither the aboriginal Fauna has migrated."

Then said Baviaan, "The aboriginal Fauna has joined the aboriginal Flora because it was high time for a change; and my advice to you, Ethiopian, is to change as soon as you can."

That puzzled the Leopard and the Ethiopian, but they set off to look for the aboriginal Flora, and presently, after ever so many days, they saw a great, high, tall forest full of tree trunks all 'sclusively speckled and sprottled and spotted, dotted and splashed and slashed and hatched and cross-hatched with shadows. (Say that quickly aloud, and you will see how very shadowy the forest must have been.)

"What is this," said the Leopard, "that is so 'sclusively dark, and yet so full of little pieces of light?"

"I don't know," said the Ethiopian, "but it ought to be the aboriginal Flora. I can smell Giraffe, and I can hear Giraffe, but I can't see Giraffe."

"That's curious," said the Leopard. "I suppose it is because we have just come in out of the sunshine. I can smell Zebra, and I can hear Zebra, but I can't see Zebra."

"Wait a bit," said the Ethiopian. "It's a long time since we've hunted 'em. Perhaps we've forgotten what they were like."

"Fiddle!" said the Leopard. "I remember them perfectly on the High Veldt, especially their marrow-bones. Giraffe is about seventeen feet high, of a 'sclusively fulvous golden-yellow from head to heel; and Zebra is about four and a half feet high, of a 'sclusively grey-fawn colour from head to heel."

"Umm," said the Ethiopian, looking into the speckly-spickly shadows of the aboriginal Flora-forest. "Then they ought to show up in this dark place like ripe bananas in a smokehouse."

But they didn't. The Leopard and the Ethiopian hunted all day; and though they could smell them and hear them, they never saw one of them.

"For goodness' sake," said the Leopard at tea-time, "let us wait till it gets dark. This daylight hunting is a perfect scandal."

So they waited till dark, and then the Leopard heard something breathing sniffily in the starlight that fell all stripy through the branches, and he jumped at the noise, and it smelt like Zebra, and it felt like Zebra, and when he knocked it down it kicked like Zebra, but he couldn't see it. So he said, "Be quiet, O you person without any form. I am going to sit on your head till morning, because there is something about you that I don't understand."

Presently he heard a grunt and a crash and a scramble, and the Ethiopian called out, "I've caught a thing that I can't see. It smells like Giraffe, and it kicks like Giraffe, but it hasn't any form."

"Don't you trust it," said the Leopard. "Sit on its head till the morning–same as me. They haven't any form–any of 'em."

So they sat down on them hard till bright morning-time, and then Leopard said, "What have you at your end of the table, Brother?"

The Ethiopian scratched his head and said, "It ought to be 'sclusively a rich fulvous orange-tawny from head to heel, and it ought to be Giraffe; but it is covered all over with chestnut blotches. What have you at your end of the table, Brother?"

And the Leopard scratched his head and said, "It ought to be 'sclusively a delicate greyish-fawn, and it ought to be Zebra; but it is covered all over with black and purple stripes. What in the world have you been doing to yourself, Zebra? Don't you know that if you were on the High Veldt I could see you ten miles off? You haven't any form."

"Yes," said the Zebra, "but this isn't the High Veldt. Can't you see?"

"I can now," said the Leopard. "But I couldn't all yesterday. How is it done?"

"Let us up," said the Zebra, "and we will show you."

Day 55

1. Read the last part of *How the Leopard Got His Spots* by Kipling.
2. How did the leopard get its spots?

They let the Zebra and the Giraffe get up; and Zebra moved away to some little thorn-bushes where the sunlight fell all stripy, and Giraffe moved off to some tallish trees where the shadows fell all blotchy.

"Now watch," said the Zebra and the Giraffe. "This is the way it's done. One–two–three! And where's your breakfast?"

Leopard stared, and Ethiopian stared, but all they could see were stripy shadows and blotched shadows in the forest, but never a sign of Zebra and Giraffe. They had just walked off and hidden themselves in the shadowy forest.

"Hi! Hi!" said the Ethiopian. "That's a trick worth learning. Take a lesson by it, Leopard. You show up in this dark place like a bar of soap in a coal-scuttle."

"Ho! Ho!" said the Leopard. "Would it surprise you very much to know that you show up in this dark place like a mustard-plaster on a sack of coals?"

"Well, calling names won't catch dinner," said the Ethiopian. "The long and the little of it is that we don't match our backgrounds. I'm going to take Baviaan's advice. He told me I ought to change; and as I've nothing to change except my skin I'm going to change that."

"What to?" said the Leopard, tremendously excited.

"To a nice working blackish-brownish colour, with a little purple in it, and touches of slaty-blue. It will be the very thing for hiding in hollows and behind trees."

So he changed his skin then and there, and the Leopard was more excited than ever; he had never seen a man change his skin before.

"But what about me?" he said, when the Ethiopian had worked his last little finger into his fine new black skin.

"You take Baviaan's advice too. He told you to go into spots."

"So I did," said the Leopard. "I went into other spots as fast as I could. I went into this spot with you, and a lot of good it has done me."

"Oh," said the Ethiopian, "Baviaan didn't mean spots in South Africa. He meant spots on your skin."

"What's the use of that?" said the Leopard.

"Think of Giraffe," said the Ethiopian. "Or if you prefer stripes, think of Zebra. They find their spots and stripes give them per-feet satisfaction."

"Umm," said the Leopard. "I wouldn't look like Zebra–not for ever so."

"Well, make up your mind," said the Ethiopian, "because I'd hate to go hunting without you, but I must if you insist on looking like a sun-flower against a tarred fence."

"I'll take spots, then," said the Leopard; "but don't make 'em too vulgar-big. I wouldn't look like Giraffe–not for ever so."

"I'll make 'em with the tips of my fingers," said the Ethiopian. "There's plenty of black left on my skin still. Stand over!"

Then the Ethiopian put his five fingers close together (there was plenty of black left on his new skin still) and pressed them all over the Leopard, and wherever the five fingers touched they left five little black marks, all close together. You can see them on any Leopard's skin you like, Best Beloved. Sometimes the fingers slipped and the marks got a little blurred; but if you look closely at any Leopard now you will see that there are always five spots–off five fat black finger-tips.

"Now you are a beauty!" said the Ethiopian. "You can lie out on the bare ground and look like a heap of pebbles. You can lie out on the naked rocks and look like a piece of pudding-stone. You can lie out on a leafy branch and look like sunshine sifting through the leaves; and you can lie right across the centre of a path and look like nothing in particular. Think of that and purr!"

"But if I'm all this," said the Leopard, "why didn't you go spotty too?"

"Oh, plain black's best for a black man," said the Ethiopian. "Now come along and we'll see if we can't get even with Mr. One-Two- Three-Where's-your-Breakfast!"

So they went away and lived happily ever afterward, Best Beloved. That is all.

Oh, now and then you will hear grown-ups say, "Can the Ethiopian change his skin or the Leopard his spots?" I don't think even grown-ups would keep on saying such a silly thing if the Leopard and the Ethiopian hadn't done it once–do you? But they will never do it again, Best Beloved. They are quite contented as they are.

Day 56

1. Read *The Three Little Pigs* by Hans Christian Anderson.

Once upon a time there was an old Sow with three little Pigs, and since she did not have enough to give them to eat, she sent them out on their own to seek their fortune.

The first little pig that went off met a Man with a bundle of straw, and said to him, "Please, sir, give me that straw so I can build myself a house"; which the Man did, and the little Pig built a house with it.

Then along came a Wolf, who knocked at the door, and said, "Little Pig, little Pig, let me come in."

To which the Pig answered, "Not by the hair of my chinny chin chin!"

"Then I'll huff and I'll puff, and I'll blow your house in!" said the Wolf. So he huffed and he puffed, and he blew his house in, and the Wolf ate up the first little Pig.

Now the second little Pig met a Man with a bundle of shrubs, and said, "Please, sir…give me those shrubs so I can build myself a house"; which the Man did, and the Pig built his house.

Then along came that same Wolf and he said, "Little Pig, little Pig, let me come in."

"Not by the hair of my chinny chin chin!"

"Then I'll puff and I'll huff, and I'll blow your house in!" So he huffed and he puffed, and he puffed and he huffed, and at last he blew the house down, and ate up the second little Pig.

Now the third little Pig met a Man with a load of bricks, and said, "Please, sir, give me those bricks to build a house with"; so the Man gave him the bricks, and he built his house with them.

So the Wolf came, as he did to the other little Pigs, and said, "Little Pig, little Pig, let me come in."

"Not by the hair of my chinny chin chin!"

"Then I'll huff and I'll puff, and I'll blow your house in."

Well, he huffed and he puffed, and he huffed and he puffed, and he puffed and he huffed; but he could not get the house to fall down. When he found that he could not, with all his huffing and puffing, blow the house down, he said, "Little Pig, I know where there is a nice field of turnips."

"Where?" said the little Pig.

"Oh, in Mr. Smith's home-field; and if you'll be ready tomorrow morning, I will call for you, and we will go together and get some for dinner."

"Very well," said the little Pig, "I will be ready. What time do you mean to go?"

"Oh, at six o'clock."

Well, the little Pig got up at five, and went and found the field, got the turnips and was home again before six. When the Wolf came he said, "Little Pig, are you ready?"

"Ready!" said the little Pig, "I have already been to the field and come back again, and I got myself a nice pot-full of turnips for dinner."

When he heard this, the Wolf felt very angry…but he thought he could outsmart the little Pig somehow or other; so he said, "Little Pig, I know where there is a nice apple-tree."

"Where?" said the Pig.

"Down at Merry-garden," replied the Wolf; "and if you will not deceive me I will come for you, at five o'clock tomorrow, and we will go together and get some apples."

Well, the little Pig woke at four the next morning, and got up in hurry, and went off for the apples, hoping to get back before the Wolf came. But he had farther to go, and he had to climb the tree…so that, just as he was coming down from it, he saw the Wolf coming (which, as you may suppose, frightened him very much). When the Wolf came up he said, "Little Pig! What…are you here before me once again? Are they nice apples?"

"Oh yes, very!" said the little Pig; "I will throw you down one." And he threw it so far that, while the Wolf was gone to pick it up, the little Pig jumped down and ran home.

Well, the next day the Wolf came once again, and said to the little Pig, "Little Pig, there is a Fair in the Town this afternoon: would you like you go?"

"Oh, yes," said the Pig, "I will go; what time should I be ready?"

"At three," said the Wolf.

So, as he had done before, the little Pig went off before the time they had discussed. He got to the Fair, bought a butter churn, and was on his way home with it when he saw the Wolf coming. He did not know what to do. So he got into the churn to hide, and in doing so it got turned around, and then… it began to roll, and it rolled down the hill with the Pig inside it, which frightened the Wolf so much that he ran home without going to the Fair.

After awhile, the Wolf went to the little Pig's house, and told him all about how frightened he had been by a great round thing which came down the hill past him.

Then the little Pig said, "Haha! I frightened you, did I? I had been to the Fair and bought a butter churn, and when I saw you I got into it, and rolled down the hill."

Then the Wolf was very angry indeed, and he declared that he would eat up the little Pig, and that, in fact…right now…he was going to come down the chimney after him!

When the little Pig understood the Wolf's plans, he hung up a pot full of water, made a blazing fire in the fireplace, and, just as the Wolf was coming down the chimney, he took the cover off the pot, and in fell the Wolf. And the little Pig put the cover back on again in an instant, boiled him up, ate him for supper, and lived happy ever after.

Day 57

1. Read the first half of *The Tale of Benjamin Bunny.*

One morning a little rabbit sat on a bank. He pricked his ears and listened to the trit-trot, trit-trot of a pony. A gig was coming along the road; it was driven by Mr. McGregor, and beside him sat Mrs. McGregor in her best bonnet. As soon as they had passed, little Benjamin Bunny slid down into the road, and set off–with a hop, skip, and a jump–to call upon his relations, who lived in the wood at the back of Mr. McGregor's garden.

That wood was full of rabbit holes; and in the neatest, sandiest hole of all lived Benjamin's aunt and his cousins–Flopsy, Mopsy, Cotton-tail, and Peter. Old Mrs. Rabbit was a widow; she earned her living by knitting rabbit-wool mittens and muffatees (I once bought a pair at a bazaar). She also sold herbs, and rosemary tea, and rabbit-tobacco (which is what we call lavender). Little Benjamin did not very much want to see his Aunt. He came round the back of the fir-tree, and nearly tumbled upon the top of his Cousin Peter.

Peter was sitting by himself. He looked poorly, and was dressed in a red cotton pocket-handkerchief. "Peter," said little Benjamin, in a whisper, "who has got your clothes?" Peter replied, "The scarecrow in Mr. McGregor's garden," and described how he had been chased about the garden, and had dropped his shoes and coat. Little Benjamin sat down beside his cousin and assured him that Mr. McGregor had gone out in a gig, and Mrs. McGregor also; and certainly for the day, because she was wearing her best bonnet.

Peter said he hoped that it would rain. At this point old Mrs. Rabbit's voice was heard inside the rabbit hole, calling: "Cotton-tail! Cotton-tail! fetch some more camomile!" Peter said he thought he might feel better if he went for a walk. They went away hand in hand, and got upon the flat top of the wall at the bottom of the wood. From here they looked down into Mr. McGregor's garden. Peter's coat and shoes were plainly to be seen upon the scarecrow, topped with an old tam-o'-shanter of Mr. McGregor's.

Little Benjamin said: "It spoils people's clothes to squeeze under a gate; the proper way to get in is to climb down a pear-tree." Peter fell down head first; but it was of no consequence, as the bed below was newly raked and quite soft. It had been sown with lettuces. They left a great many odd little footmarks all over the bed, especially little Benjamin, who was wearing clogs.

Little Benjamin said that the first thing to be done was to get back Peter's clothes, in order that they might be able to use the pocket-handkerchief. They took them off the scarecrow. There had been rain during the night; there was water in the shoes, and the coat was somewhat shrunk. Benjamin tried on the tam-o'-shanter, but it was too big for him. Then he suggested that they should fill the pocket-handkerchief with onions, as a little present for his Aunt. Peter did not seem to be enjoying himself; he kept hearing noises.

Benjamin, on the contrary, was perfectly at home, and ate a lettuce leaf. He said that he was in the habit of coming to the garden with his father to get lettuces for their Sunday dinner. (The name of little Benjamin's papa was old Mr. Benjamin Bunny.) The lettuces certainly were very fine. Peter did not eat anything; he said he should like to go home. Presently he dropped half the onions.

Day 58

1. Read the second half of *The Tale of Benjamin Bunny.*

Little Benjamin said that it was not possible to get back up the pear-tree with a load of vegetables. He led the way boldly towards the other end of the garden. They went along a little walk on planks, under a sunny, red brick wall. The mice sat on their doorsteps cracking cherry-stones; they winked at Peter Rabbit and little Benjamin Bunny. Presently Peter let the pocket-handkerchief go again.

They got amongst flower-pots, and frames, and tubs. Peter heard noises worse than ever; his eyes were as big as lolly-pops! He was a step or two in front of his cousin when he suddenly stopped. This is what those little rabbits saw round that corner! Little Benjamin took one look, and then, in half a minute less than no time, he hid himself and Peter and the onions underneath a large basket....

The cat got up and stretched herself, and came and sniffed at the basket. Perhaps she liked the smell of onions! Anyway, she sat down upon the top of the basket. She sat there for five hours. I cannot draw you a picture of Peter and Benjamin underneath the basket, because it was quite dark, and because the smell of onions was fearful; it made Peter Rabbit and little Benjamin cry. The sun got round behind the wood, and it was quite late in the afternoon; but still the cat sat upon the basket.

At length there was a pitter-patter, pitter-patter, and some bits of mortar fell from the wall above. The cat looked up and saw old Mr. Benjamin Bunny prancing along the top of the wall of the upper terrace. He was smoking a pipe of rabbit-tobacco, and had a little switch in his hand. He was looking for his son. Old Mr. Bunny had no opinion whatever of cats. He took a tremendous jump off the top of the wall on to the top of the cat, and cuffed it off the basket, and kicked it into the greenhouse, scratching off a handful of fur. The cat was too much surprised to scratch back.

When old Mr. Bunny had driven the cat into the greenhouse, he locked the door. Then he came back to the basket and took out his son Benjamin by the ears, and whipped him with the little switch. Then he took out his nephew Peter. Then he took out the handkerchief of onions, and marched out of the garden.

When Mr. McGregor returned about half an hour later he observed several things which perplexed him. It looked as though some person had been walking all over the garden in a pair of clogs–only the footmarks were too ridiculously little! Also he could not understand how the cat could have managed to shut herself up inside the greenhouse, locking the door upon the outside.

When Peter got home his mother forgave him, because she was so glad to see that he had found his shoes and coat. Cotton-tail and Peter folded up the pocket-handkerchief, and old Mrs. Rabbit strung up the onions and hung them from the kitchen ceiling, with the bunches of herbs and the rabbit-tobacco.

Day 59

1. Read the first half of *The Tale of Flopsy Bunnies.*
2. Tell someone about what's happening in the story.

It is said that the effect of eating too much lettuce is "soporific." I have never felt sleepy after eating lettuces; but then I am not a rabbit. They certainly had a very soporific effect upon the Flopsy Bunnies! When Benjamin Bunny grew up, he married his Cousin Flopsy. They had a large family, and they were very improvident and cheerful. I do not remember the separate names of their children; they were generally called the "Flopsy Bunnies."

As there was not always quite enough to eat, Benjamin used to borrow cabbages from Flopsy's brother, Peter Rabbit, who kept a nursery garden. Sometimes Peter Rabbit had no cabbages to spare.

When this happened, the Flopsy Bunnies went across the field to a rubbish heap, in the ditch outside Mr. McGregor's garden. Mr. McGregor's rubbish heap was a mixture. There were jam pots and paper bags, and mountains of chopped grass from the mowing machine (which always tasted oily), and some rotten vegetable marrows and an old boot or two. One day…oh joy!…there were a quantity of overgrown lettuces, which had "shot" into flower.

The Flopsy Bunnies simply stuffed lettuces. By degrees, one after another, they were overcome with slumber, and lay down in the mown grass. Benjamin was not so much overcome as his children. Before going to sleep he was sufficiently wide awake to put a paper bag over his head to keep off the flies. The little Flopsy Bunnies slept delightfully in the warm sun. From the lawn beyond the garden came the distant clacketty sound of the mowing machine. The bluebottles buzzed about the wall, and a little old mouse picked over the rubbish among the jam pots. (I can tell you her name, she was called Thomasina

Tittlemouse, a woodmouse with a long tail.)

She rustled across the paper bag, and awakened Benjamin Bunny. The mouse apologized profusely, and said that she knew Peter Rabbit. While she and Benjamin were talking, close under the wall, they heard a heavy tread above their heads; and suddenly Mr. McGregor emptied out a sackful of lawn mowings right upon the top of the sleeping Flopsy Bunnies! Benjamin shrank down under his paper bag. The mouse hid in a jam pot.

The little rabbits smiled sweetly in their sleep under the shower of grass; they did not awake because the lettuces had been so soporific. They dreamt that their mother Flopsy was tucking them up in a hay bed. Mr. McGregor looked down after emptying his sack. He saw some funny little brown tips of ears sticking up through the lawn mowings. He stared at them for some time. Presently a fly settled on one of them and it moved. Mr. McGregor climbed down on to the rubbish heap. "One, two, three, four! five! six leetle rabbits!" said he as he dropped them into his sack. The Flopsy Bunnies dreamt that their mother was turning them over in bed. They stirred a little in their sleep, but still they did not wake up.

Mr. McGregor tied up the sack and left it on the wall. He went to put away the mowing machine. While he was gone, Mrs. Flopsy Bunny (who had remained at home) came across the field. She looked suspiciously at the sack and wondered where everybody was?

Day 60

1. Read the second half of *The Tale of Flopsy Bunnies.*
2. I'll start with a reminder of what's happening.

Mr. McGregor tied up the sack and left it on the wall. He went to put away the mowing machine. While he was gone, Mrs. Flopsy Bunny (who had remained at home) came across the field. She looked suspiciously at the sack and wondered where everybody was?

Then the mouse came out of her jam pot, and Benjamin took the paper bag off his head, and they told the doleful tale. Benjamin and Flopsy were in despair, they could not undo the string. But Mrs. Tittlemouse was a resourceful person. She nibbled a hole in the bottom corner of the sack.

The little rabbits were pulled out and pinched to wake them. Their parents stuffed the empty sack with three rotten vegetable marrows, an old blacking-brush and two decayed turnips.

Then they all hid under a bush and watched for Mr. McGregor.

Mr. McGregor came back and picked up the sack, and carried it off. He carried it hanging down, as if it were rather heavy. The Flopsy Bunnies followed at a safe distance.

The watched him go into his house. And then they crept up to the window to listen.

Mr. McGregor threw down the sack on the stone floor in a way that would have been extremely painful to the Flopsy Bunnies, if they had happened to have been inside it. They could hear him drag his chair on the flags, and chuckle "One, two, three, four, five, six leetle rabbits!" said Mr. McGregor.

"Eh? What's that? What have they been spoiling now?" enquired Mrs. McGregor. "One, two, three, four, five, six leetle fat rabbits!" repeated Mr. McGregor, counting on his fingers "one, two, three" "Don't you be silly; what do you mean, you silly old man?" "In the sack! one, two, three, four, five, six!" replied Mr. McGregor. (The youngest Flopsy Bunny got upon the window sill.) Mrs. McGregor took hold of the sack and felt it. She said she could feel six, but they must be old rabbits, because they were so hard and all different shapes. "Not fit to eat; but the skins will do fine to line my old cloak." "Line your old cloak?" shouted Mr. McGregor "I shall sell them and buy myself baccy!" "Rabbit tobacco! I shall skin them and cut off their heads."

Mrs. McGregor untied the sack and put her hand inside. When she felt the vegetables she became very very angry. She said that Mr. McGregor had "done it a purpose."

And Mr. McGregor was very angry too. One of the rotten marrows came flying through the kitchen window, and hit the youngest Flopsy Bunny. It was rather hurt.

Then Benjamin and Flopsy thought that it was time to go home.

So Mr. McGregor did not get his tobacco, and Mrs. McGregor did not get her rabbit skins.

But next Christmas Thomasina Tittlemouse got a present of enough rabbit-wool to make herself a cloak and a hood, and a handsome muff and a pair of warm mittens.

Day 61

1. You are starting a new book today, *The Adventures of Jimmy Skunk*, by Thornton Burgess. I think this will be the last book you will read by this author for school,

but he wrote 170 books, so if you like to read them, your parents can help you search for more.

2. Read chapter 1 of *The Adventures of Jimmy Skunk.*

3. Who were all of the characters in this chapter? (Answers)

Chapter I   Peter Rabbit Plans a Joke

The Imp of Mischief, woe is me,
  Is always busy as a bee.

That is why so many people are forever getting into trouble. He won't keep still. No, Sir, he won't keep still unless he is made to. Once let him get started there is no knowing where he will stop. Peter Rabbit had just seen Jimmy Skunk disappear inside an old barrel, lying on its side at the top of the hill, and at once the Imp of Mischief began to whisper to Peter. Of course Peter shouldn't have listened. Certainly not. But he did. You know Peter dearly loves a joke when it is on some one else. He sat right where he was and watched to see if Jimmy would come out of the barrel. Jimmy didn't come out, and after a little Peter stole over to the barrel and peeped inside. There was Jimmy Skunk curled up for a nap.

Peter tiptoed away very softly. All the time the Imp of Mischief was whispering to him that this was a splendid chance to play a joke on Jimmy. You know it is very easy to play a joke on any one who is asleep. Peter doesn't often have a chance to play a joke on Jimmy Skunk. It isn't a very safe thing to do, not if Jimmy is awake. No one knows that better than Peter. He sat down some distance from the barrel but where he could keep an eye on it. Then he went into a brown study, which is one way of saying that he thought very hard. He wanted to play a joke on Jimmy, but like most jokers he didn't want the joke to come back on himself. In fact, he felt that it would be a great deal better for him if Jimmy shouldn't know that he had anything to do with the joke.

As he sat there in a brown study, he happened to glance over on the Green Meadows and there he saw something red. He looked very hard, and in a minute he saw that it was Reddy Fox. Right away, Peter's nimble wits began to plan how he could use Reddy Fox to play a joke on Jimmy. All in a flash an idea came to him, an idea that made him laugh right out. You see, the Imp of Mischief was very, very busy whispering to Peter.

"If Reddy were only up here, I believe I could do it, and it would be a joke on Reddy as well as on Jimmy," thought Peter, and laughed right out again.

"What are you laughing at?" asked a voice. It was the voice of Sammy Jay.

Right away a plan for getting Reddy up there flashed into Peter's head. He would get Sammy angry, and that would make Sammy scream. Reddy would be sure to come up there to see what Sammy Jay was making such a fuss about. Sammy, you know, is very quick-tempered. No one knows this better than Peter. So instead of replying politely to Sammy, as he should have done, Peter spoke crossly:

"Fly away, Sammy, fly away! It is no business of yours what I am laughing at," said he.

Right away Sammy's quick temper flared up. He began to call Peter names, and Peter answered back. This angered Sammy still more, and as he always screams when he is angry, he was soon making such a racket that Reddy Fox down on the Green Meadows couldn't help but hear it. Peter saw him lift his head to listen. In a few minutes he began to trot that way. He was coming to find out what that fuss was about. Peter knew that Reddy wouldn't come straight up there. That isn't Reddy's way. He would steal around back of the old stone wall on the edge of the Old Orchard, which was back of Peter, and would try to see what was going on without being seen himself.

"As soon as he sees me he will think that at last he has a chance to catch me," thought Peter. "I shall have to run my very fastest, but if everything goes right, he will soon forget all about me. I do hope that the noise Sammy Jay is making will not waken Jimmy Skunk and bring him out to see what is going on."

So with one eye on the barrel where Jimmy Skunk was taking a nap, and the other eye on the old stone wall behind which he expected Reddy Fox to come stealing up, Peter waited and didn't mind in the least the names that Sammy Jay was calling him.

Day 62

1. Read chapter 2 of *The Adventures of Jimmy Skunk.*
2. Do you remember who is sleeping in the barrel?
3. What is the "problem with **thoughtlessness**?" (hint: The answer is in the very last sentence of the first paragraph—or section—of the chapter.) (Answers)

4. So, what is the opposite? What does **thoughtfulness** do? (hint: It's the opposite of thoughtlessness.) (Answers)
5. Talk with your parents about how you can be thoughtful of them.

Chapter II   Peter Makes a Flying Jump

To risk your life unless there's need
 Is downright foolishness indeed.

Never forget that. Never do such a crazy thing as Peter Rabbit was doing. What was he doing? Why, he was running the risk of being caught by Reddy Fox all for the sake of a joke. Did you ever hear of anything more foolish? Yet Peter was no different from a lot of people who every day risk their lives in the most careless and heedless ways just to save a few minutes of time or for some other equally foolish reason. The fact is, Peter didn't stop to think what dreadful thing might happen if his plans didn't work out as he intended. He didn't once think of little Mrs. Peter over in the dear Old Briar-patch and how she would feel if he never came home again.   That's the trouble with thoughtlessness; it never remembers other people.

All the time that Reddy Fox was creeping along behind the old stone wall on the edge of the Old Orchard, Peter knew just where he was, though Reddy didn't know that. If he had known it, he would have suspected one of Peter's tricks.

"He'll peep over that wall, and just as soon as he sees me, he will feel sure that this time he will catch me," thought Peter. "He will steal along to that place where the wall is lowest and will jump over it right there. I must be ready to jump the very second he does."

It all happened just as Peter had expected. While seeming to be paying no attention to anything but to Sammy Jay, he kept his eyes on that low place in the old wall, and presently he saw Reddy's sharp nose, as Reddy peeped over to make sure that he was still there. The instant that sharp nose dropped out of sight, Peter made ready to run for his life. A second later, Reddy leaped over the wall, and Peter was off as hard as he could go, with Reddy almost at his heels. Sammy Jay, who had been so busy calling Peter names that he hadn't seen Reddy at all, forgot all about his quarrel with Peter.

"Go it, Peter! Go it!" he screamed excitedly. That was just like Sammy.

Peter did go it. He had to. He ran with all his might. Reddy grinned as he saw Peter start towards the Green Meadows. It was a long way to the dear Old Briar-patch, and Reddy didn't have any doubt at all that he would catch Peter before he got there. He watched sharply for Peter to dodge and try to get back to the old stone wall. He didn't mean to let Peter do that. But Peter didn't even try. He ran straight for the edge of the hill above the Green Meadows. Then, for the first time, Reddy noticed an old barrel there lying on its side.

"I wonder if he thinks he can hide in that," thought Reddy, and grinned again, for he remembered that he had passed that old barrel a few days before, and that one end was open while the other end was closed. "If he tries that, I will get him without the trouble of much of a chase," thought Reddy, and chuckled.

Lipperty-lipperty-lip ran Peter, lipperty-lipperty-lip, Reddy right at his heels! To Sammy Jay it looked as if in a few more jumps Reddy certainly would catch Peter. "Go it, Peter! Oh, go it! Go it!" screamed Sammy, for in spite of his quarrels with Peter, he didn't want to see him come to any real harm.

Just as he reached the old barrel, Reddy was so close to him that Peter was almost sure that he could feel Reddy's breath. Then Peter made a splendid flying jump right over the old barrel and kept on down the hill, lipperty-lipperty-lip, as fast as ever he could, straight for an old house of Johnny Chuck's of which he knew. When he reached it, he turned to see what was happening behind him, for he knew by the screaming of Sammy Jay and by other sounds that a great deal was happening. In fact, he suspected that the joke which he had planned was working out just as he had hoped it would.

Day 63

1. Read chapter 3 of *The Adventures of Jimmy Skunk.*
2. Why did Peter Rabbit become afraid? (Answers)

Chapter III   What Happened at the Old Barrel

Peter Rabbit's jump over the old barrel on the edge of the hill was unexpected to Reddy Fox. In fact, Reddy was so close on Peter's heels that he had no thought of anything but catching Peter. He was running so fast that when Peter made his flying jump over the barrel, Reddy did not have time to jump too, and he ran right smack bang against that old barrel. Now you remember that that barrel was right on the edge of the hill. When Reddy ran against it, he hit it so hard that he rolled it over, and of course that started it down the hill. You know a barrel is a very rolly sort of thing, and once it has started down a hill, nothing can stop it.

It was just so this time. Reddy Fox had no more than picked himself up when the barrel was half way down the hill and going faster and faster. It bounced along over the ground, and every time it hit a little hummock it seemed to jump right up in the air. And all the time it was making the strangest noises. Reddy quite forgot the smarting sore places where he had bumped into the barrel. He simply stood and stared at the runaway.

"As I live," he exclaimed, "I believe there was some one in that old barrel!" There was. You remember that Jimmy Skunk had curled up in there for a nap. Now Jimmy was awake, very much awake. You see, for once in his life he was moving fast, very much faster than ever he had moved before since he was born. And it wasn't at all comfortable. No, Sir, it wasn't at all a comfortable way in which to travel. He went over and over so fast that it made him dizzy. First he was right side up and then wrong side up, so fast that he couldn't tell which side up he was. And every time that old barrel jumped when it went over a hummock, Jimmy was tossed up so that he hit whatever part of the barrel happened to be above him. Of course, he couldn't get out, because he was rolled over and over so fast that he didn't have a chance to try.

Now Reddy didn't know who was in the barrel. He just knew by the sounds that some one was. So he started down the hill after the barrel to see what would happen when it stopped. All the time Peter Rabbit was dancing about in the greatest excitement, but taking the greatest care to keep close to that old house of Johnny Chuck's so as to pop into it in case of danger. He saw that Reddy Fox had quite forgotten all about him in his curiosity as to who was in the barrel, and he chuckled as he thought of what might happen when the barrel stopped rolling and Reddy found out. Sammy Jay was flying overhead, screaming enough to split his throat. Altogether, it was quite the most exciting thing Peter had ever seen.

Now it just happened that Old Man Coyote had started to cross the Green Meadows right at the foot of the hill just as the barrel started down. Of course, he heard the noise and looked up to see what it meant. When he saw that barrel rushing right down at him, it frightened him so that he just gave one yelp and started for the Old Pasture like a gray streak. He gave Peter a chance to see just how fast he can run, and Peter made up his mind right then that he never would run a race with Old Man Coyote.

Down at the bottom of the hill was a big stone, and when the barrel hit this, the hoops broke, and the barrel fell all apart. Peter decided that it was high time for him to get out of sight. So he dodged into the old house of Johnny Chuck and lay low in the doorway, where he could watch. He saw Jimmy Skunk lay perfectly still, and a great fear crept into his heart. Had Jimmy been killed? He hadn't once thought of what might happen to Jimmy when he planned that joke. But presently Jimmy began to wave first one leg and then another, as if to make sure that he had some legs left. Then slowly he rolled over and got on to his feet. Peter breathed a sigh of relief.

Day 64

1. Read chapter 4 of *The Adventures of Jimmy Skunk.*
2. Who did Jimmy blame for rolling the barrel? (Answers)
3. What did Jimmy Skunk do to him? (Answers)
4. Jimmy Skunk walked away "with a great deal of **dignity**." Dignity means he had honor and respect. He was sure he had done the right thing.
5. Try walking "with a great deal of **dignity**."

Chapter IV   Jimmy Skunk Is Very Mad Indeed

When Jimmy Skunk is angry
  Then every one watch out!
  It's better far at such a time
  To be nowhere about.

Jimmy Skunk was angry this time and no mistake. He was just plain *mad,* and when Jimmy Skunk feels that way, no one wants to be very near him. You know he is one of the very best-natured little fellows in the world ordinarily. He minds his own business, and if no one interferes with him, he interferes with no one. But once he is aroused and feels that he hasn't been treated fairly, look out for him!

And this time Jimmy was mad clear through, as he got to his feet and shook himself to see that he was all there. I don't know that any one could blame him. To be wakened from a comfortable nap by being rolled over and over and shaken nearly to death as Jimmy had been by that wild ride down the hill in the old barrel was enough to make any one mad. So he really is not to be blamed for feeling as he did.

Now Jimmy can never be accused of being stupid. He knew that an old barrel which has been lying in one place for a long time doesn't move of its own accord. He knew that that barrel couldn't possibly have started off down the hill unless some one had made it start, and he didn't have a doubt in the world that whoever had done it, had known that he was inside and had done it to make him uncomfortable. So just as soon as he had made sure that he was really alive and quite whole, he looked about to see who could have played such a trick on him.

The first person he saw was Reddy Fox. In fact, Reddy was right close at hand. You see, he had raced down the hill after the barrel to see who was in it when he heard the strange noises coming from it as it rolled and bounded down. If Reddy had known that it was Jimmy Skunk, he would have been quite content to remain at the top of the hill. But he didn't know, and if the truth be known, he had hopes that it might prove to be some one who would furnish him with a good breakfast. So, quite out of breath with running, Reddy arrived at the place where the old barrel had broken to pieces just as Jimmy got to his feet.

Now when Jimmy Skunk is angry, he doesn't bite and he doesn't scratch. You know Old Mother Nature has provided him with a little bag of perfume which Jimmy doesn't object to in the least, but which makes most people want to hold their noses and run. He never uses it, excepting when he is angry or in danger, but when he does use it, his enemies always turn tail and run. That is why he is afraid of no one, and why every one respects Jimmy and his rights.

He used it now, and he didn't waste any time about it. He threw some of that perfume right in the face of Reddy Fox before Reddy had a chance to turn or to say a word.

"Take that!" snapped Jimmy Skunk. "Perhaps it will teach you not to play tricks on your honest neighbors!"

Poor Reddy! Some of that perfume got in his eyes and made them smart dreadfully. In fact, for a little while he couldn't see at all. And then the smell of it was so strong that it made him quite sick. He rolled over and over on the ground, choking and gasping and rubbing his eyes. Jimmy Skunk just stood and looked on, and there wasn't a bit of pity in his eyes.

"How do you like that?" said he. "You thought yourself very smart, rolling me down hill in a barrel, didn't you? You might have broken my neck."

"I didn't know you were in that barrel, and I didn't mean to roll it down the hill anyway," whined Reddy, when he could get his voice.

"Huh!" snorted Jimmy Skunk, who didn't believe a word of it.

"I didn't. Honestly I didn't," protested Reddy. "I ran against the barrel by accident, chasing Peter Rabbit. I didn't have any idea that any one was in it."

"Huh!" said Jimmy Skunk again. "If you were chasing Peter Rabbit, where is he now?"

Reddy had to confess he didn't know. He was nowhere in sight, and he certainly hadn't had time to reach the dear Old Briar-patch. Jimmy looked this way and that way, but there was no sign of Peter Rabbit.

"Huh!" said he again, turning his back on Reddy Fox and walking away with a great deal of dignity.

Day 65

1. Read chapter 5 of *The Adventures of Jimmy Skunk*.
2. Copy this sentence: *He stopped and into his yellow eyes crept a look of suspicion.*
3. **Suspicion** means a feeling or belief that someone is guilty or that a certain thought is true.
4. Finish this sentence: I have a **suspicion** that… (You don't have to write it. Just say it.) Here's an example: I have a suspicion that Andrew's gotten into the cookie jar.

Chapter V   Reddy Fox Sneaks Away

To sneak away is to steal away trying to keep out of sight of everybody, and is usually done only by those who for some reason or other are ashamed to be seen. Just as soon as Reddy Fox could see after Jimmy Skunk had thrown that terrible perfume in Reddy's face he started for the Green Forest. He wanted to get away by himself. But he didn't trot with his head up and his big plumey tail carried proudly as is usual with him. No indeed. Instead he hung his head, and his handsome tail was dropped between his legs;

he was the very picture of shame. You see that terrible perfume which Jimmy Skunk had thrown at him clung to his red coat and he knew that he couldn't get rid of it, not for a long time anyway. And he knew, too, that wherever he went his neighbors would hold their noses and make fun of him, and that no one would have anything to do with him. So he sneaked away across the Green Meadows towards the Green Forest and he felt too sick and mean and unhappy to even be angry with Sammy Jay, who was making fun of him and saying that he had got no more than he deserved.

Poor Reddy! He didn't know what to do or where to go. He couldn't go home, for old Granny Fox would drive him out of the house. She had warned him time and again never to provoke Jimmy Skunk, and he knew that she never would forgive him if he should bring that terrible perfume near their home. He knew, too, that it would not be long before all the little people of the Green Forest and the Green Meadows would know what had happened to him. Sammy Jay would see to that. He knew just how they would point at him and make fun of him. He would never hear the last of it. He felt as if he never, never would be able to hold his head and his tail up again. Every few minutes he stopped to roll over and over on the ground trying to get rid of that dreadful perfume.

When he reached the Green Forest he hurried over to the Laughing Brook to wash out his eyes. It was just his luck to have Billy Mink come along while he was doing this. Billy didn't need to be told what had happened. "Phew!" he exclaimed, holding on to his nose. Then he turned and hurried beyond the reach of that perfume. There he stopped and made fun of Reddy Fox and said all the provoking things he could think of. Reddy took no notice at all. He felt too miserable to quarrel.

After he had washed his face he felt better. Water wouldn't take away the awful smell, but it did take away the smart from his eyes. Then he tried to plan what to do next.

"The only thing I can do is to get as far away from everybody as I can," thought he. "I guess I'll have to go up to the Old Pasture to live for a while."

So he started for the Old Pasture, keeping as much out of sight as possible. On the way he remembered that Old Man Coyote lived there. Of course it would never do to go near Old Man Coyote's home for if he smelled that awful perfume and discovered that he, Reddy, was the cause of it he would certainly drive him out of the Old Pasture and then where could he go? So Reddy went to the loneliest part of the Old Pasture and crept into an old house that he and Granny had dug there long ago when they had been forced to live in the Old Pasture in the days when Farmer Brown's boy and Bowser the

Hound had hunted them for stealing chickens. There he stretched himself out and was perfectly miserable.

"It wouldn't be so bad if I had really been to blame, but I wasn't. I didn't know Jimmy Skunk was in that barrel and I didn't mean to start it rolling down the hill anyway," he muttered. "It was all an accident and " He stopped and into his yellow eyes crept a look of suspicion. "I wonder," said he slowly, "if Peter Rabbit knew that Jimmy Skunk was there and planned to get me into all this trouble. I wonder."

Day 66

1. Read chapter 6 of *The Adventures of Jimmy Skunk*.
2. What do you think it means that he "smarted all over"? Use the story to help you figure it out. Here is the sentence it is from: *He ached and smarted all over.* This is at the end of the chapter. What had just happened? (Answers)

Chapter VI   Peter Rabbit Doesn't Enjoy His Joke

All the time that Jimmy Skunk was punishing Reddy Fox for rolling him down hill in a barrel, and while Reddy was sneaking away to the Green Forest to get out of sight, Peter Rabbit was lying low in the old house of Johnny Chuck, right near the place where Jimmy Skunk's wild ride had come to an end. It had been a great relief to Peter when he had seen Jimmy Skunk get to his feet, and he knew that Jimmy hadn't been hurt in that wild ride. Lying flat in the doorway of Johnny Chuck's old house, Peter could see all that went on without being seen himself, and he could hear all that was said.

He chuckled as he saw Reddy Fox come up and his eyes were popping right out with excitement as he waited for what would happen next. He felt sure that Reddy Fox was in for something unpleasant, and he was glad. Of course, that wasn't a bit nice of Peter. Right down in his heart Peter knew it, but he had been chased so often by Reddy and given so many dreadful frights, that he felt now that he was getting even. So he chuckled as he waited for what was to happen. Suddenly that chuckle broke right off in the middle, and Peter cried "Ouch!" He had felt a pain as if a hot needle had been thrust into him. It made him almost jump out of the doorway. But he remembered in time that it would never, never do for him to show himself outside, for right away Reddy

Fox and Jimmy Skunk would suspect that he had had something to do with that wild ride of Jimmy's in the barrel. So it would not do to show himself now. No, indeed!

All he could do was to kick and squirm and twist his head around to see what was happening. It didn't take long to find out. Even as he looked, he felt another sharp pain which brought another "Ouch!" from him and made him kick harder than ever. Two very angry little insects were just getting ready to sting him again, and more were coming. They were Yellow Jackets, which you know belong to the wasp family and carry very sharp little lances in their tails. The fact is, this old house of Johnny Chuck's had been deserted so long the Yellow Jackets had decided that as no one else was using it, they would, and they had begun to build their home just inside the hall.

Poor Peter! What could he do? He didn't dare go out, and he simply couldn't stay where he was. Whatever he did must be done quickly, for it looked to him as if a regular army of Yellow Jackets was coming, and those little lances they carried were about the most painful things he knew of. By this time he had lost all interest in what was going on outside. There was quite enough going on inside; too much, in fact. He remembered that Johnny Chuck digs his house deep down in the ground. He looked down the long hall. It was dark down there. Perhaps if he went down there, these angry little warriors wouldn't follow him. It was worth trying, anyway.

So Peter scrambled to his feet and scurried down the long hall, and as he ran, he cried "Ouch! Ouch! Oh! Ohoo!" Those sharp little lances were very busy, and there was no way of fighting back. At the end of the long hall was a snug little room, very dark but cool and comfortable. It was just as he had hoped; the Yellow Jackets did not follow him down there. They had driven him away from their home, which was right near the entrance, and they were satisfied.

But what a fix he was in! What a dreadful fix! He ached and smarted all over. My goodness, how he did smart! And to get out he would have to go right past the Yellow Jacket home again.

"Oh, dear, I wish I had never thought of such a joke," moaned Peter, trying in vain to find a comfortable position. "I guess I am served just right."

I rather think he was, don't you?

Day 67

1. Read chapter 7 of *The Adventures of Jimmy Skunk*.
2. What is Sammy Jay's **suspicion**? (Answers)

Chapter VII   Sammy Jay Does Some Guessing

Sammy Jay is a queer fellow. Although he is a scamp and dearly loves to make trouble for his neighbors, he is always ready to take their part when others make trouble for them. Many are the times he has given them warning of danger. This is one reason they are quite willing to overlook his own shortcomings. So, though in many ways he is no better than Reddy Fox, he dearly loves to upset Reddy's plans and is very apt to rejoice when Reddy gets into trouble. Of course, being right there, he saw all that happened when Reddy ran against the old barrel at the top of the hill and sent it rolling. He had been quite as much surprised as Reddy to find that there was some one inside, and he had followed Reddy to see who it was. So, of course, he had seen what happened to Reddy.

Now, instead of being sorry for Reddy, he had openly rejoiced. It seems to be just that way with a great many people. They like to see others who are considered very smart get into trouble. So Sammy had laughed and made fun of poor Reddy. In the first place it was very exciting, and Sammy dearly loves excitement. And then it would make such a splendid story to tell, and no one likes to carry tales more than does Sammy Jay. He watched Reddy sneak away to the Green Forest, and Jimmy Skunk slowly walk away in a very dignified manner. Then Sammy flew back to the Old Orchard to spread the news among the little people there. It wasn't until he reached the Old Orchard that he remembered Peter Rabbit. Instead of flying about telling every one what had happened to Jimmy Skunk and Reddy Fox, he found a comfortable perch in an old apple-tree and was strangely silent. The fact is, Sammy Jay was doing some hard thinking. He had suddenly begun to wonder. It had popped into that shrewd little head of his that it was very strange how suddenly Peter Rabbit had disappeared.

"Of course," thought Sammy, "Jimmy Skunk is sure that Reddy rolled that barrel down hill purposely, and I don't wonder that he does think so. But I saw it all, and I know that it was all an accident so far as Reddy was concerned. I didn't know that Jimmy was in that barrel, and Reddy couldn't have known it, because he didn't come up here until after I did. But Peter Rabbit may have known. Why did Peter run so that he would have to jump over that barrel when he could have run right past it?

"Of course, he may have thought that if he could make Reddy run right slam bang against that barrel it would stop Reddy long enough to give him a chance to get away. That would have been pretty smart of Peter and quite like him. But somehow I have a feeling that he knew all the time that Jimmy Skunk was taking a nap inside and that something was bound to happen if he was disturbed. The more I think of it, the more I believe that Peter did know and that he planned the whole thing. If he did, it was one of the smartest tricks I ever heard of. I didn't think Peter had it in him. It was rather hard on Jimmy Skunk, but it got rid of Reddy Fox for a while. He won't dare show his face around here for a long time. That means that Peter will have one less worry on his mind. Hello! Here comes Jimmy Skunk. I'll ask him a few questions."

Jimmy came ambling along in his usual lazy manner. He had quite recovered his good nature. He felt that he was more than even with Reddy Fox, and as he was none the worse for his wild ride in the barrel, he had quite forgotten that he had lost his temper.

"Hello, Jimmy. Have you seen Peter Rabbit this morning?" cried Sammy Jay.

Jimmy looked up and grinned. "Yes," said he. "I saw him up here early this morning. Why?"

"Did he see you go into that old barrel?" persisted Sammy.

"I don't know," confessed Jimmy. "He may have. What have you got on your mind, Sammy Jay?"

"Nothing much, only Reddy Fox was chasing him when he ran against that barrel and sent you rolling down the hill," replied Sammy.

Jimmy pricked up his ears. "Then Reddy didn't do it purposely!" he exclaimed.

"No," replied Sammy. "He didn't do it purposely. I am quite sure that he didn't know you were in it. But how about Peter Rabbit? I am wondering. And I'm doing a little guessing, too."

Day 68

1. Read chapter 8 of *The Adventures of Jimmy Skunk.*

2. Tell someone about the chapter.

Vocabulary

1. In this chapter it says that Jimmy Skunk is **shrewd**. It means that he's clever and crafty.
2. Jimmy thinks maybe he did Reddy an **injustice**. That means he thinks maybe he wasn't fair to Reddy when he sprayed him.

Chapter VIII   Jimmy Skunk Looks for Peter

Jimmy Skunk looked very hard at Sammy Jay. Sammy Jay looked very hard at Jimmy Skunk. Then Sammy slowly shut one eye and as slowly opened it again. It was a wink.

"You mean," said Jimmy Skunk, "that you guess that Peter Rabbit knew that I was in that barrel, and that he jumped over it so as to make Reddy Fox run against it. Is that it?"

Sammy Jay said nothing, but winked again. Jimmy grinned. Then he looked thoughtful. "I wonder," said he slowly, "if Peter did it so as to gain time to get away from Reddy Fox."

"I wonder," said Sammy Jay.

"And I wonder if he did it just to get Reddy into trouble," continued Jimmy.

"I wonder," repeated Sammy Jay.

"And I wonder if he did it for a joke, a double joke on Reddy and myself," Jimmy went on, scratching his head thoughtfully.

"I wonder," said Sammy Jay once more, and burst out laughing.

Now Jimmy Skunk has a very shrewd little head on his shoulders. "So that is your guess, is it? Well, I wouldn't be a bit surprised if you are right," said he, nodding his head. "I think I will go look for Peter. I think he needs a lesson. Jokes that put other people in danger or make them uncomfortable can have no excuse. My neck might have been broken in that wild ride down the hill, and certainly I was made most uncomfortable. I felt as if everything inside me was shaken out of place and all mixed up. Even now my stomach feels a bit queer, as if it might not be just where it ought to be. By the way, what became of Peter after he jumped over the barrel?"

Sammy shook his head. "I don't know," he confessed. "You see, it was very exciting when that barrel started rolling, and we knew by the sounds that there was some one inside it. I guess Reddy Fox forgot all about Peter. I know I did. And when the barrel broke to pieces against that stone down there, and you and Reddy faced each other, it was still more exciting. After it was over, I looked for Peter, but he was nowhere in sight. He hadn't had time to reach the Old Briar-patch. I really would like to know myself what became of him."

Jimmy Skunk turned and looked down the hill. Then in his usual slow way he started back towards the broken barrel.

"Where are you going?" asked Sammy.

"To look for Peter Rabbit," replied Jimmy. "I want to ask him a few questions."

Jimmy Skunk ambled along down the hill. At first he was very angry as he thought of what Peter had done, and he made up his mind that Peter should be taught a lesson he would never forget. But as he ambled along, the funny side of the whole affair struck him, for Jimmy Skunk has a great sense of humor, and before he reached the bottom of the hill his anger had all gone and he was chuckling.

"I'm sorry if I did Reddy Fox an injustice," thought he, "but he makes so much trouble for other people that I guess no one else will be sorry. He isn't likely to bother any one for some time. Peter really ought to be punished, but somehow I don't feel so much like punishing him as I did. I'll just give him a little scare and let the scamp off with that. Now, I wonder where he can be. I have an idea he isn't very far away. Let me see. Seems to me I remember an old house of Johnny Chuck's not very far from here. I'll have a look in that."

Day 69

1. Read chapter 9 of *The Adventures of Jimmy Skunk.*
2. Tell someone about the chapter.

Vocabulary

1. *Jimmy Skunk was smiling as he ambled towards the old house of Johnny Chuck.*
2. How was Jimmy Skunk walking towards Johnny Chuck's old house? Demonstrate.

Chapter IX Jimmy Visit's Johnny Chuck's Old House

Jimmy Skunk was smiling as he ambled towards the old house of Johnny Chuck near the foot of the hill. There was no one near to see him, and this made him smile still more. You see, the odor of that perfume which he had thrown at Reddy Fox just a little while before was very, very strong there, and Jimmy knew that until that had disappeared no one would come near the place because it was so unpleasant for every one. To Jimmy himself it wasn't unpleasant at all, and he couldn't understand why other people disliked it so. He had puzzled over that a great deal. He was glad that it was so, because on account of it every one treated him with respect and took special pains not to quarrel with him.

"I guess it's a good thing that Old Mother Nature didn't make us all alike," said he to himself. "I think there must be something the matter with their noses, and I suppose they think there is something the matter with mine. But there isn't. Not a thing. Hello! There is Johnny Chuck's old house just ahead of me. Now we will see what we shall see."

He walked softly as he drew near to the old house. If Peter was way down inside, it wouldn't matter how he approached. But if Peter should happen to be only just inside the doorway, he might take it into his head to run if he should hear footsteps, particularly if those footsteps were not heavy enough to be those of Reddy or Granny Fox or Old Man Coyote. Jimmy didn't intend to give Peter a chance to do any such thing. If Peter once got outside that old house, his long legs would soon put him beyond Jimmy's reach, and Jimmy knew it. If he was to give Peter the fright that he had made up his mind to give him, he would first have to get him where he couldn't run away. So Jimmy walked as softly as he knew how and approached the old house in such a way as to keep out of sight of Peter, should he happen to be lying so as to look out of the doorway.

At last he reached a position where with one jump he could land right on the doorstep. He waited a few minutes and cocked his head on one side to listen. There wasn't a sound to tell him whether Peter was there or not. Then lightly he jumped over to the doorstep and looked in at the doorway. There was no Peter to be seen.

"If he is here, he is way down inside," thought Jimmy. "I wonder if he really is here. I think I'll look about a bit before I go in."

Now the doorstep was of sand, as Johnny Chuck's doorsteps always are. Almost at once Jimmy chuckled. There were Peter's tracks, and they pointed straight towards the inside of Johnny Chuck's old house. Jimmy looked carefully, but not a single track pointing the other way could he find. Then he chuckled again. "The scamp is here all right," he muttered. "He hid here and watched all that happened and then decided to lie low and wait until he was sure that the way was clear and no one would see him." In this Jimmy was partly right and partly wrong, as you and I know.

He stared down the long dark doorway a minute. Then he made up his mind. "I'll go down and make Peter a call, and I won't bother to knock," he chuckled, and poked his head inside the doorway. But that was as far as Jimmy Skunk went. Yes, Sir, that was just as far as Jimmy Skunk went. You see, no sooner did he start to enter that old house of Johnny Chuck's than he was met by a lot of those Yellow Jackets, and they were in a very bad temper.

Jimmy Skunk knows all about Yellow Jackets and the sharp little lances they carry in their tails; he has the greatest respect for them. He backed out in a hurry and actually hurried away to a safe distance. Then he sat down to think. After a little he began to chuckle again. "I know what happened," said he, talking to himself. "Peter Rabbit popped into that doorway. Those Yellow Jackets just naturally got after him. He didn't dare come out for fear of Reddy Fox and me, and so he went on down to Jimmy Chuck's old bedroom, and he's down there now, wondering how ever he is to get out without getting stung. I reckon I don't need to scare Peter to pay him for that joke. I reckon he's been punished already."

Day 70

1. Read chapter 10 of *The Adventures of Jimmy Skunk*.
2. How did Peter try to get out of Johnny Chuck's house? (Answers)
3. What did Jimmy Skunk say to Peter to get him back? (Answers)
4. Tell someone the story of the book so far.

Chapter X   Peter Rabbit Is Most Uncomfortable

If ever any one was sorry for having played pranks on other folks, that one was Peter Rabbit. I am afraid it wasn't quite the right kind of sorrow. You see, he wasn't sorry because of what had happened to Jimmy Skunk and Reddy Fox, but because of what had happened to himself. There he was, down in the bedroom of Johnny Chuck's old house, smarting and aching all over from the sharp little lances of the Yellow Jackets who had driven him down there before he had had a chance to see what happened to Reddy Fox. That was bad enough, but what troubled Peter more was the thought that he couldn't get out without once again facing those hot-tempered Yellow Jackets. Peter wished with all his might that he had known about their home in Johnny Chuck's old house before ever he thought of hiding there.

But wishes of that kind are about the most useless things in the world. They wouldn't help him now. He had so many aches and smarts that he didn't see how he could stand a single one more, and yet he couldn't see how he was going to get out without receiving several more. All at once he had a comforting thought. He remembered that Johnny Chuck usually has a back door. If that were the case here, he would be all right. He would find out. Cautiously he poked his head out of the snug bedroom. There was the long hall down which he had come. And there yes, Sir, there was another hall! It must be the way to the back door. Carefully Peter crept up it.

"Funny," thought he, "that I don't see any light ahead of me."

And then he bumped his nose. Yes, Sir, Peter bumped his nose against the end of that hall. You see, it was an old house, and like most old houses it was rather a tumble-down affair. Anyway, the back door had been blocked with a great stone, and the walls of the back hall had fallen in. There was no way out there. Sadly Peter backed out to the little bedroom. He would wait until night, and perhaps then the Yellow Jackets would be asleep, and he could steal out the front way without getting any more stings. Meanwhile he would try to get a nap and forget his aches and pains.

Hardly had Peter curled up for that nap when he heard a voice. It sounded as if it came from a long way off, but he knew just where it came from. It came from the doorway of that old house. He knew, too, whose voice it was. It was Jimmy Skunk's voice.

"I know where you are, Peter Rabbit," said the voice. "And I know why you are hiding down there. I know, too, how it happened that I was rolled down hill in that barrel. I'm just giving you a little warning, Peter. There are a lot of very angry Yellow Jackets up here, as you will find out if you try to come out before dark. I'm going away now, but

I'm going to come back about dark to wait for you. I may want to play a little joke on you to pay you back for the one you played on me."

That put an end to Peter's hope of a nap. He shivered as he thought of what might happen to him if Jimmy Skunk should catch him. What with his aches and pains from the stings of the Yellow Jackets, and fear of being caught by Jimmy Skunk, it was quite impossible to sleep. He was almost ready to face those Yellow Jackets rather than wait and meet Jimmy Skunk. Twice he started up the long hall, but turned back. He just couldn't stand any more stings. He was miserable. Yes, Sir, he was miserable and most uncomfortable in both body and mind.

"I wish I'd never thought of that joke," he half sobbed. "I thought it was a great joke, but it wasn't. It was a horrid, mean joke. Why, oh, why did I ever think of it?"

Meanwhile Jimmy Skunk had gone off, chuckling.

Day 71

1. Read chapter 11 of *The Adventures of Jimmy Skunk.*
2. What does it mean that Jimmy Skunk "kept his word." (Answers)

Chapter XI   Jimmy Skunk Keeps His Word

Keep your word, whate'er you do,
  And to your inmost self be true.

When Jimmy Skunk shouted down the hall of Johnny Chuck's old house to Peter Rabbit that he would come back at dark, he was half joking. He did it to make Peter uneasy and to worry him. The truth is, Jimmy was no longer angry at all. He had quite recovered his good nature and was very much inclined to laugh himself over Peter's trick. But he felt that it wouldn't do to let Peter off without some kind of punishment, and so he decided to frighten Peter a little. He knew that Peter wouldn't dare come out during the daytime because of the Yellow Jackets whose home was just inside the doorway of that old house; and he knew that Peter wouldn't dare face him, for he would be afraid of being treated as Reddy Fox had been. So that is why he told Peter that he was coming back at dark. He felt that if Peter was kept a prisoner in there for a while, all the time worrying about how he was to get out, he would be very slow to try such a trick again.

As Jimmy ambled away to look for some beetles, he chuckled and chuckled and chuckled. "I guess that by this time Peter wishes he hadn't thought of that joke on Reddy Fox and myself," said he. "Perhaps I'll go back there tonight and perhaps I won't. He won't know whether I do or not, and he won't dare come out."

Then he stopped and scratched his head thoughtfully. Then he sighed. Then he scratched his head again and once more sighed. "I really don't want to go back there tonight," he muttered, "but I guess I'll have to. I said I would, and so I'll have to do it. I believe in keeping my word. If I shouldn't and some day he should find it out, he wouldn't believe me the next time I happened to say I would do a thing. Yes, Sir, I'll have to go back. There is nothing like making people believe that when you say a thing you mean it. There is nothing like keeping your word to make people respect you."

Being naturally rather lazy, Jimmy decided not to go any farther than the edge of the Old Orchard, which was only a little way above Johnny Chuck's old house, where Peter was a prisoner. There Jimmy found a warm, sunny spot and curled up for a nap. In fact, he spent all the day there. When jolly, round, red Mr. Sun went to bed behind the Purple Hills, and the Black Shadows came trooping across the Green Meadows, Jimmy got up, yawned, chuckled, and then slowly ambled down to Johnny Chuck's old house. A look at the footprints in the sand on the doorstep told him that Peter had not come out. Jimmy sat down and waited until it was quite dark. Then he poked his head in at the doorway. The Yellow Jackets had gone to bed for the night.

"Come out, Peter. I'm waiting for you!" he called down the hall, and made his voice sound as angry as he could. But inside he was chuckling. Then Jimmy Skunk calmly turned and went about his business. He had kept his word.

As for Peter Rabbit, that had been one of the very worst days he could recall. He had ached and smarted from the stings of the Yellow Jackets; he had worried all day about what would happen to him if he did meet Jimmy Skunk, and he was hungry. He had had just a little bit of hope, and this was that Jimmy Skunk wouldn't come back when it grew dark. He had crept part way up the hall at the first hint of night and stretched himself out to wait until he could be sure that those dreadful Yellow Jackets had gone to sleep. He had just about made up his mind that it was safe for him to scamper out when Jimmy Skunk's voice came down the hall to him. Poor Peter! The sound of that voice almost broke his heart.

"He has come back. He's kept his word," he half sobbed as he once more went back to Johnny Chuck's old bedroom.

There he stayed nearly all the rest of the night, though his stomach was so empty it ached. Just before it was time for Mr. Sun to rise, Peter ventured to dash out of Johnny Chuck's old house. He got past the home of the Yellow Jackets safely, for they were not yet awake. With his heart in his mouth, he sprang out of the doorway. Jimmy Skunk wasn't there. With a sigh of relief, Peter started for the dear, safe Old Briar-patch, lipperty-lipperty-lip, as fast as he could go.

"I'll never, never play another joke," he said, over and over again as he ran.

Day 72

1. Here is a sentence from the chapter:
   o Unc' Billy grinned. "Good mo'nin', Brer Skunk," he replied. "Ah can't
      rightly say Ah have. Ah had it on *mah* mind to ask *yo'* the same thing."
   o Here is what it says: Uncle Billy grinned. "Good morning, Brother Skunk," he
      replied. "I can't rightly say I have. I had it on my mind to ask you the same
      thing."
   o He speaks with a kind of accent. He's what we call a country bumpkin; it's
      like in the poem about the frost on the "punkin."
   o Do a little acting. Read the sentence out loud like Unc' Billy would.
   o Anytime you aren't sure what he is saying, read it out loud to help you.
2. Read chapter 12 of *The Adventures of Jimmy Skunk.*
3. What happened in the chapter?

Chapter XII   Jimmy Skunk and Unc' Billy Possum

Jimmy Skunk ambled along down the Lone Little Path through the Green Forest. He
didn't hurry. Jimmy never does hurry. Hurrying and worrying are two things he leaves
for his neighbors. Now and then Jimmy stopped to turn over a bit of bark or a stick,
hoping to find some fat beetles. But it was plain to see that he had something besides
fat beetles on his mind.

Up the Lone Little Path through the Green Forest shuffled Unc' Billy Possum. He didn't
hurry. It was too warm to hurry. Unlike Jimmy Skunk, he does hurry sometimes, does
Unc' Billy, especially when he suspects that Bowser the Hound is about.   And
sometimes Unc' Billy does worry. You see, there are people who think that Unc' Billy
would make a very good dinner. Unc' Billy doesn't think he would. Anyway, he has
no desire to have the experiment tried. So occasionally, when he discovers one of these
people who think he would make a good dinner, he worries a little.

But just now Unc' Billy was neither hurrying nor worrying. There was no need of doing
either, and Unc' Billy never does anything that there is no need of doing. So Unc' Billy
shuffled up the Lone Little Path, and Jimmy Skunk ambled down the Lone Little Path,
and right at a bend in the Lone Little Path they met.

Jimmy Skunk grinned. "Hello, Unc' Billy!" said he. "Have you seen any fat beetles this morning?"

Unc' Billy grinned. "Good mo'nin', Brer Skunk," he replied. "Ah can't rightly say Ah have. Ah had it on *mah* mind to ask *yo'* the same thing."

Jimmy sat down and looked at Unc' Billy with twinkling eyes. His grin grew broader and became a chuckle. "Unc' Billy," said he, "have you ever in your life combed your hair or brushed your coat?" You know Unc' Billy usually looks as if every hair was trying to point in a different direction from every other hair, while Jimmy Skunk always appears as neat as if he spent half his time brushing and smoothing his handsome black and white coat.

Unc' Billy's eyes twinkled. "Ah reckons Ah did such a thing once or twice when Ah was very small, Brer Skunk," said he, without a trace of a smile. "But it seems to me a powerful waste of time. Ah have mo' important things to worry about. By the way, Brer Skunk, did *yo'* ever run away from anybody in all your life?"

Jimmy looked surprised at the question. He scratched his head thoughtfully. "Not that I remember of," said he after a little. "Most folks run away from me," he added with a little throaty chuckle. "Those who don't run away always are polite and step aside. It may be that when I was a very little fellow and didn't know much about the Great World and the people who live in it, I might have run away from some one, but if I did, I can't remember it. Why do you ask, Unc' Billy?"

"Oh, no reason in particular, Brer Skunk. No reason in particular. Only Ah wonder sometimes if *yo'* ever realize how lucky *yo'* are. If Ah never had to worry about *mah* hungry neighbors, Ah reckons perhaps Ah might brush *mah* coat oftener." Unc' Billy's eyes twinkled more than ever.

"Worry," replied Jimmy Skunk sagely, "is the result of being unprepared. Anybody who is prepared has no occasion to worry. Just think it over, Unc' Billy."

It was Unc' Billy's turn to scratch his head thoughtfully. "Ah fear Ah don't quite get your meaning, Brer Skunk," said he.

"Sit down, Unc' Billy, and I'll explain," replied Jimmy.

Day 73

1. Read chapter 13 of *The Adventures of Jimmy Skunk.*
2. Jimmy Skunk can spray a stinky perfume. Who else has a "weapon" to keep others from attacking him? (Answers)

Vocabulary

1. **defence** – when you stop an attacker
2. **offence** – when you attack
3. What does the sentence below mean?
    - Prickly Porky and I are armed for *defence*, but we never use our weapons for *offence*. (Answers)

Chapter XIII   Jimmy Skunk Explains

You'll find this true where'er you go
  That those prepared few troubles know.

"To begin with, I am not such a very big fellow, am I?" said Jimmy.

"Ah reckons Ah knows a right smart lot of folks bigger than *yo'*, Brer Skunk," replied Unc' Billy, with a grin. You know Jimmy Skunk really is a little fellow compared with some of his neighbors.

"And I haven't very long claws or very big teeth, have I?" continued Jimmy.

"Ah reckons mine are about as long and about as big," returned Unc' Billy, looking more puzzled than ever.

"But you never see anybody bothering me, do you?" went on Jimmy.

"No," replied Unc' Billy.

"And it's the same way with Prickly Porky the Porcupine. You never see anybody bothering him or offering to do him any harm, do you?" persisted Jimmy.

"No," replied Unc' Billy once more.

"Why?" demanded Jimmy.

Unc' Billy grinned broadly. "Ah reckons, Brer Skunk," said he, "that there isn't anybody wants to go fo' to meddle with *yo'* and Brer Porky. Ah reckons most folks knows what would happen if they did, and that *yo'* and Brer Porky are folks it's a sight mo' comfortable to leave alone. Leastways, Ah does. Ah ain't aiming fo' trouble with either of *yo'*. That li'l bag of scent *yo'* carry is cert'nly most powerful, Brer Skunk, and Ah isn't hankering to brush against those little spears Brer Porky is so free with. Ah knows when Ah's well off, and Ah reckons most folks feel the same way."

Jimmy Skunk chuckled. "One more question, Unc' Billy," said he. "Did you ever know me to pick a quarrel and use that bag of scent without being attacked?"

Unc' Billy considered for a few minutes. "Ah can't say Ah ever did," he replied.

"And you never knew Prickly Porky to go hunting trouble either," declared Jimmy. "We don't either of us go hunting trouble, and trouble never comes hunting us, and the reason is that we both are always prepared for trouble and everybody knows it. Buster Bear could squash me by just stepping on me, but he doesn't try it. You notice he always is very polite when we meet. Prickly Porky and I are armed for *defence*, but we never use our weapons for *offence*. Nobody bothers us, and we bother nobody. That's the beauty of being prepared."

Unc' Billy thought it over for a few minutes. Then he sighed and sighed again.

"Ah reckons *yo'* and Brer Porky are about the luckiest people Ah knows," said he. "Yes, Sah, Ah reckons *yo'* is just that. Ah don't fear anybody *mah* own size, but Ah cert'nly does have some mighty scary times when Ah meets some people Ah might mention. Ah wish *Ol'* Mother Nature had done gone and given me something fo' to make people as scary of me as they are of *yo'*. Ah cert'nly believes in preparedness after seein' *yo'*, Brer Skunk. Ah cert'nly does just that very thing. Have *yo'* found any nice fresh aiggs lately?"

Day 74

1. Read chapter 14 of *The Adventures of Jimmy Skunk.*
2. What are two different views about eggs? (Answers)

Chapter XIV   A Little Something About Eggs

"An egg," says Jimmy Skunk, "is good;
   It's very good indeed to eat."
 "An egg," says Mrs. Grouse, "is dear;
   'Twill hatch into a baby sweet."

So in the matter of eggs, as in a great many other matters, it all depends on the point of view. To Jimmy Skunk and Unc' Billy Possum eggs are looked on from the viewpoint of something to eat. Their stomachs prompt them to think of eggs. Eggs are good to fill empty stomachs. The mere thought of eggs will make Jimmy and Unc' Billy smack their lips. They say they "love" eggs, but they don't. They "like" them, which is quite different.

But Mrs. Grouse and most of the other feathered people of the Green Forest and the Green Meadows and the Old Orchard really do "love" eggs. It is the heart instead of the stomach that responds to the thought of eggs. To them eggs are almost as precious as babies, because they know that some day, some day very soon, those eggs will become babies. There are a few feathered folks, I am sorry to say, who "love" their own eggs, but "like" the eggs of other people like them just as Jimmy Skunk and Unc' Billy Possum do, to eat. Blacky the Crow is one and his cousin, Sammy Jay, is another.

So in the springtime there is always a great deal of matching of wits between the little people of the Green Forest and the Green Meadows and the Old Orchard. Those who have eggs try to keep them a secret or to build the nests that hold them where none who like to eat them can get them; and those who have an appetite for eggs try to find them.

When Unc' Billy Possum suddenly changed the subject by asking Jimmy Skunk if he had found any nice fresh eggs lately, he touched a subject very close to Jimmy's heart. I should have said, rather, his stomach. To tell the truth, it was a longing for some eggs that had brought Jimmy to the Green Forest. He knew that somewhere there Mrs. Grouse must be hiding a nestful of the very nicest of eggs, and it was to hunt for these that he had come.

"No," replied Jimmy, "I haven't had any luck at all this spring. I've almost forgotten what an egg tastes like. Either I'm growing dull and stupid, or some folks are smarter than they used to be. By the way, have you seen Mrs. Grouse lately?" Jimmy looked very innocent as he asked this.

Unc' Billy chuckled until his sides shook. "*Do yo*' suppose Ah'd tell *yo*' if Ah had?" he demanded. "Ah reckons Mrs. Grouse hasn't got any mo' aiggs than Ah could comfortably take care of mahself, not to mention Mrs. Possum." Here Unc' Billy looked back over his shoulder to make sure that old Mrs. Possum wasn't within hearing, and Jimmy Skunk chuckled. "Seems to me, Brer Skunk, *yo'* might better do your aigg hunting on the Green Meadows and leave the Green Forest to me," continued Unc' Billy. "That would be no mo' than fair. Yo' know Ah never did hanker fo' to get far away from trees, but *yo'* don't mind. Besides there are mo' aiggs for *yo'* to find on the Green Meadows than there are fo' me to find in the Green Forest. A right smart lot of birds make their nests on the ground there. There is Brer Bob White and Brer Meadowlark and Brer Bobolink and Brer Field Sparrow and Brer--"

"Never mind any more, Unc' Billy," interrupted Jimmy Skunk. "I know all about them. That is, I know all about them I want to know, except where their eggs are. Didn't I just tell you I haven't had any luck at all? That's why I'm over here."

"Well, *yo'* won't have any mo' luck here unless *yo'* are a right smart lot sharper than your Unc' Billy, and when it comes to hunting aiggs, Ah don't take *mah* hat off to anybody, not even to *yo'*, Brer Skunk," replied Unc' Billy.

Day 75

1. Read chapter 15 of *The Adventures of Jimmy Skunk.*
2. What are Jimmy Skunk and Uncle Billy both thinking about? (Answers)
3. Do you think they are going to get the eggs?

Chapter XV   A Second Meeting

Jimmy Skunk couldn't think of anything but eggs. The more he thought of them, the more he wanted some. After parting from Unc' Billy Possum in the Green Forest he went back to the Green Meadows and prowled about, hunting for the nests of his feathered neighbors who build on the ground, and having no more luck than he had had before.

Unc' Billy Possum was faring about the same way. He couldn't, for the life of him, stop thinking about those eggs that belonged to Mrs. Grouse. The more he tried to forget about them, the more he thought about them.

"Ah feels it in *mah* bones that there isn't the least bit of use in huntin' fo' them," said he to himself, as he watched Jimmy Skunk amble out of sight up the Lone Little Path. "No, Sah, there isn't the least bit of use. Ah done look every place Ah can think of already. Still, Ah haven't got anything else special on *mah* mind, and those aiggs cert'nly would taste good. Ah reckons it must be Ah needs those aiggs, or Ah wouldn't have them on *mah* mind so much. Ah finds it rather painful to carry aiggs on *mah* mind all the time, but Ah would enjoy carrying them in *mah* stomach. Ah cert'nly would." Unc' Billy grinned and started to ramble about aimlessly, hoping that chance would lead him to the nest of Mrs. Grouse.

Do what he would, Unc' Billy couldn't get the thought of eggs off his mind, and the more he thought about them the more he wanted some. And that led him to think of Farmer Brown's henhouse. He had long ago resolved never again to go there, but the longing for a taste of eggs was too much for his good resolutions, and as soon as jolly, round, red Mr. Sun sank to rest behind the Purple Hills, and the Black Shadows came creeping across the Green Meadows and through the Green Forest, Unc' Billy slipped away, taking pains that old Mrs. Possum shouldn't suspect where he was going.

Out from the Green Forest, keeping among the Black Shadows along by the old stone wall on the edge of the Old Orchard, he stole, and so at last he reached Farmer Brown's henhouse. He stopped to listen. There was no sign of Bowser the Hound, and Unc' Billy sighed gently. It was a sigh of relief. Then he crept around a corner of the henhouse towards a certain hole under it he remembered well. Just as he reached it, he saw something white. It moved. It was coming towards him from the other end of the henhouse. Unc' Billy stopped right where he was. He was undecided whether to run or stay. Then he heard a little grunt and decided to stay. He even grinned. A few seconds later up came Jimmy Skunk. It was a white stripe on Jimmy's coat that Unc' Billy had seen.

Jimmy gave a little snort of surprise when he almost bumped into Unc' Billy.

"What are you doing here?" he demanded.

"Just taking a li'l walk fo' the good of *mah* appetite," replied Unc' Billy, grinning more broadly than ever. "What are *yo'* doing here, Brer Skunk?"

"The same thing," replied Jimmy. Then he chuckled. "This is an unexpected meeting. I guess you must have had the same thing on your mind all day that I have," he added.

"Ah reckon so," replied Unc' Billy, and both grinned.

Day 76

1. Read chapter 16 of *The Adventures of Jimmy Skunk.*
2. Why does Uncle Billy want Jimmy to go first? (Answers)
3. Why does Jimmy want Uncle Billy to go first? (Answers)
4. Review your "City Zoo" vocabulary by going to Day 25 or looking for it under Level 2 on the Review Games page of the Easy Peasy All-in-One Homeschool site.

Chapter XVI   A Matter of Politeness

It costs not much to be polite
  And, furthermore, it's always right.

Unc' Billy Possum and Jimmy Skunk, facing each other among the Black Shadows close by a hole that led under Farmer Brown's henhouse, chuckled as each thought of what had brought the other there. It is queer how a like thought often brings people together. Unc' Billy had the same longing in his stomach that Jimmy Skunk had, and Jimmy Skunk had the same thing on his mind that Unc' Billy had. More than this, it was the second time that day that they had met. They had met in the morning in the Green Forest and now they had met again among the Black Shadows of the evening at Farmer Brown's henhouse. And it was all on account of eggs. Yes, Sir, it was all on account of eggs.

"Are you just coming out, or are you just going in?" Jimmy inquired politely.

"Ah was just going in, but Ah'll follow *yo'*, Brer Skunk," replied Unc' Billy just as politely.

"Nothing of the kind," returned Jimmy. "I wouldn't for a minute think of going before you. I hope I know my manners better than that."

"Yo' cert'nly are most polite, Brer Skunk. Yo' cert'nly are most polite. Yo' are a credit to your bringing up, but politeness always did run in your family. There is a saying that han'some is as han'some does, and your politeness is as fine as *yo'* are han'some, Brer Skunk. Ah'll just step one side and let*yo'* go first just to show that Ah sho'ly does appreciate your friendship," said Unc' Billy.

Jimmy Skunk chuckled. "I guess you've forgotten that other old saying, 'Age before beauty,' Unc' Billy," said he. "So you go first. You know you are older than I. I couldn't think of being so impolite as to go first. I really couldn't think of such a thing."

And so they argued and argued, each insisting in the most polite way that the other should go first. If the truth were known, neither of them was insisting out of politeness at all. No, Sir, politeness had nothing to do with it Jimmy Skunk wanted Unc' Billy to go first because Jimmy believes in safety first, and it had popped into Jimmy's head that there might, there just might, happen to be a trap inside that hole. If there was, he much preferred that Unc' Billy should be the one to find it out. Yes, Sir, that is why Jimmy Skunk was so very polite.

Unc' Billy wanted Jimmy to go first because he always feels safer behind Jimmy than in front of him. He has great respect for that little bag of scent that Jimmy carries, and he knows that when Jimmy makes use of it, he always throws it in front and never behind him. Jimmy seldom uses it, but sometimes he does if he happens to be startled and thinks danger near. So Unc' Billy preferred that Jimmy should go first. It wasn't politeness at all on the part of Unc' Billy. In both cases it was a kind of selfishness. Each was thinking of self.

How long they would have continued to argue and try to appear polite if something hadn't happened, nobody knows. But something did happen. There was a sudden loud sniff just around the corner of the henhouse. It was from Bowser the Hound. Right then and there Unc' Billy Possum and Jimmy Skunk forgot all about politeness, and both tried to get through that hole at the same time. They couldn't, because it wasn't big enough, but, they tried hard. Bowser sniffed again, and this time Unc' Billy managed to squeeze Jimmy aside and slip through. Jimmy was right at his heels.

Day 77

1. Read chapter 17 of *The Adventures of Jimmy Skunk.*
2. What hit Jimmy on the head so that he "saw stars"? (Answers)

Chapter XVII   Jimmy Skunk Gets a Bump

Hardly had Jimmy Skunk entered the hole under Farmer Brown's henhouse, following close on the heels of Unc' Billy Possum, than along came Bowser the Hound, sniffing and sniffing in a way that made Unc' Billy nervous. When Bowser reached that hole, of course he smelled the tracks of Unc' Billy and Jimmy, and right away he became excited. He began to dig. Goodness, how he did make the dirt fly! All the time he whined with eagerness.

Unc' Billy wasted no time in squeezing through a hole in the floor way over in one corner, a hole that Farmer Brown's boy had intended to nail a board over long before. Unc' Billy knew that Bowser couldn't get through that, even if he did manage to dig his way under the henhouse. Once through that and fairly in the henhouse, Unc' Billy drew a long breath. He felt safe for the time being, anyway, and he didn't propose to worry over the future.

Jimmy Skunk hurried after Unc' Billy. It wasn't fear that caused Jimmy to hurry. No, indeed, it wasn't fear. He had been startled by the unexpectedness of Bowser's appearance. It was this that had caused him to struggle to be first through that hole under the henhouse. But once through, he had felt a bit ashamed that he had been so undignified. He wasn't afraid of Bowser. He was sorely tempted to turn around and send Bowser about his business, as he knew he very well could. But he thought better of it. Besides, Unc' Billy was already through that hole in the floor, and Jimmy didn't for a minute forget what had brought him there. He had come for eggs, and so had Unc' Billy. It would never do to let Unc' Billy be alone up there for long. So Jimmy Skunk did what he very seldom does hurried. Yes, Sir, he hurried after Unc' Billy Possum. He meant to make sure of his share of the eggs he was certain were up there.

There was a row of nesting boxes along one side close to the floor. Above these was another row and above these a third row. Jimmy doesn't climb, but Unc' Billy is a famous climber.

"I'll take these lower nests," said Jimmy, and lifted his tail in a way that made Unc' Billy nervous.

"All right," replied Unc' Billy promptly. "All right, Brer Skunk. It's just as *yo'* say."

With this, Unc' Billy scrambled up to the next row of nests. Jimmy grinned and started to look in the lower nests. He took his time about it, for that is Jimmy's way. There was nothing in the first one and nothing in the second one and nothing in the third one. This was disappointing, to say the least, and Jimmy began to move a little faster. Meanwhile Unc' Billy had hurried from one nest to another in the second row with no better success. By the time Jimmy was half-way along his row Unc' Billy bad begun on the upper row, and the only eggs he had found were hard china nest-eggs put there by Farmer Brown's boy to tempt the hens to lay in those particular nests. Disappointment was making Unc' Billy lose his temper. Each time he peeped in a nest and saw one of those china eggs, he hoped it was a real egg, and each time when he found it wasn't he grew angrier.

At last he so lost his temper that when he found another of those eggs he angrily kicked it out of the nest. Now it happened that Jimmy Skunk was just underneath. Down fell that hard china egg squarely on Jimmy Skunk's head. For just a minute Jimmy saw stars. At least, he thought he did. Then he saw the egg, and knew that Unc' Billy had knocked it down, and that it was this that had hit him. Jimmy was sore at heart because he had found no eggs, and now he had a bump on the head that also was sore. Jimmy Skunk lost his temper, a thing he rarely does.

Day 78

1. Read chapter 18 of *The Adventures of Jimmy Skunk.*
2. Why did they have bad tempers? (Why were they in a bad mood?) (hint: It tells you in the last paragraph, at the very end of the chapter.) (Answers)

Chapter XVIII   A Sad, Sad, Quarrel

Jimmy Skunk sat on the floor of Farmer Brown's henhouse, rubbing his head and glaring up at the upper row of nests with eyes red with anger. Of course it was dark in the henhouse, for it was night, but Jimmy can see in the dark, just as so many other little people who wear fur can. What he saw was the anxious looking face of Unc' Billy Possum staring down at him.

"You did that purposely!" snapped Jimmy. "You did that purposely, and you needn't tell me you didn't."

"*On mah* honor Ah didn't," protested Unc' Billy. "It was an accident, just a sho' 'nuff accident, and Ah'm right sorry fo' it."

"That sounds very nice, but I don't believe a word of it. You did it purposely, and you can't make me believe anything else. Come down here and fight. I dare you to!" Jimmy was getting more and more angry every minute.

Unc' Billy began to grow angry. Of course, it was wholly his fault that that egg had fallen, but it wasn't his fault that Jimmy had happened to be just beneath. He hadn't known that Jimmy was there. He had apologized, and he felt that no one could do more than that. Jimmy Skunk had doubted his word, had refused to believe him, and that made him angry. His little eyes glowed with rage.

"If *yo'* want to fight, come up here. I'll wait fo' *yo'* right where Ah am," he sputtered.

This made Jimmy angrier than ever. He couldn't climb up there, and he knew that Unc' Billy knew it. Unc' Billy was perfectly safe in promising to wait for him.

"You're a coward, just a plain no-account coward!" snapped Jimmy. "I'm not going to climb up there, but I'll tell you what I am going to do; I'm going to wait right down here until you come down, if it isn't until next year. Nobody can drop things on my head and not get paid back. I thought you were a friend, but now I know better."

"Wait as long as *yo'* please. Ah reckons Ah can stay as long as *yo' can*," retorted Unc' Billy, grinding and snapping his teeth.

"Suit yourself," retorted Jimmy. "I'm going to pay you up for that bump on my head or know the reason why."

And so they kept on quarreling and calling each other names, for the time being quite forgetting that they were where they had no business to be, either of them. It really was dreadful. And it was all because both had been sadly disappointed. They had found no eggs where they had been sure they would find plenty. You see, Farmer Brown's boy had gathered every egg when he shut the biddies up for the night. Did you ever notice what a bad thing for the temper disappointment often is?

Day 79

1. Read chapter 19 of *The Adventures of Jimmy Skunk.*
2. Why do you think Jimmy Skunk is not afraid of Farmer Brown's boy? (Answers)

Chapter XIX   Jimmy Skunk Is True to His Word

Unc' Billy Possum was having a bad night of it. When he had grown tired of quarreling with Jimmy Skunk, he had tried to take a nap. He had tried first one nest and then another, but none just suited him. This was partly because he wasn't sleepy. He was hungry and not at all sleepy. He wished with all his heart that he hadn't foolishly yielded to that fit of temper which had resulted in kicking that china nest-egg out of a nest and down on the head of Jimmy Skunk, making Jimmy so thoroughly angry.

Unc' Billy had no intention of going down while Jimmy was there. He thought that Jimmy would soon grow tired of waiting and go away. So for quite awhile Unc' Billy didn't worry. But as it began to get towards morning he began to grow anxious. Unc' Billy had no desire to be found in that henhouse when Farmer Brown's boy came to feed the biddies.

Then, too, he was hungry. He had counted on a good meal of eggs, and not one had he found. Now he wanted to get out to look for something else to eat, but he couldn't without facing Jimmy Skunk, and it was better to go hungry than to do that. Yes, Sir, it was a great deal better to go hungry. Several times, when he thought Jimmy was asleep, he tried to steal down. He was just as careful not to make a sound as he could be, but every time Jimmy knew and was waiting for him. Unc' Billy wished that there was no such place as Farmer Brown's henhouse. He wished he had never thought of eggs. He wished many other foolish wishes, but most of all he wished that he hadn't lost his temper and kicked that egg down on Jimmy Skunk's head. When the first light stole in under the door and the biddies began to stir uneasily on their roosts Unc' Billy's anxiety would allow him to keep still no longer.

"*Don' yo'* think we-*uns* better make up and get out of here, Brer Skunk?" he ventured.

"I don't mind staying here; it's very comfortable," replied Jimmy, looking up at Unc' Billy in a way that made him most *uncomfortable*. It was plain to see that Jimmy hadn't forgiven him.

For some time Unc' Billy said no more, but he grew more and more restless. You see, he knew it would soon be time for Farmer Brown's boy to come to let the hens out and feed them. At last he ventured to speak again.

"Ah reckons *yo'* done forget something," said he.

"What is that?" asked Jimmy.

"Ah reckons *yo'* done fo'get that it's most time fo' Farmer Brown's boy to come, and it won't do fo' we-*uns* to be found in here," replied Unc' Billy.

"I'm not worrying about Farmer Brown's boy. He can come as soon as he pleases," retorted Jimmy Skunk, and grinned.

That sounded like boasting, but it wasn't. No, Sir, it wasn't, and Unc' Billy knew it. He knew that Jimmy meant it. Unc' Billy was in despair. He didn't dare stay, and he didn't dare go down and face Jimmy Skunk, and there he was. It certainly had been a bad night for Unc' Billy Possum.

Day 80

1. Read chapter 20 of *The Adventures of Jimmy Skunk*.
2. Tell someone about the chapter and explain what the vocabulary words mean.

Vocabulary

1. **impudent** – not showing respect to someone who deserves respect
2. **acquaintance** – someone you know, but not really well

Chapter XX Farmer Brown's Boy Arrives

The light crept farther under the door of Farmer Brown's henhouse, and by this time the hens were all awake. Furthermore, they had discovered Jimmy Skunk down below and were making a great fuss. They were cackling so that Unc' Billy was sure Farmer Brown's boy would soon hear them and hurry out to find out what the noise was all about.

"If *yo'* would just get out of sight, Brer Skunk, Ah reckons those fool hens would keep quiet," Unc' Billy ventured.

"I don't mind their noise. It doesn't trouble me a bit," replied Jimmy Skunk, and grinned. It was plain enough to Unc' Billy that Jimmy was enjoying the situation.

But Unc' Billy wasn't. He was so anxious that he couldn't keep still. He paced back and forth along the shelf in front of the upper row of nests and tried to make up his mind whether it would be better to go down and face Jimmy Skunk or to try to hide under the hay in one of the nests, and all the time he kept listening and listening and listening for the footsteps of Farmer Brown's boy.

At last he heard them, and he knew by the sound that Farmer Brown's boy was coming in a hurry. He had heard the noise of the hens and was coming to find out what it was all about. Unc' Billy hoped that now Jimmy Skunk would retreat through the hole in the floor and give him a chance to escape.

"He's coming! Farmer Brown's boy is coming, Brer Skunk! Yo' better get away while *yo' can*!" whispered Unc' Billy.

"I hear him," replied Jimmy calmly. "I'm waiting for him to open the door for me to go out. It will be much easier than squeezing through that hole."

Unc' Billy gasped. He knew, of course, that it was Jimmy Skunk's boast that he feared no one, but it was hard to believe that Jimmy really intended to face Farmer Brown's boy right in his own henhouse where Jimmy had no business to be. He hoped that at last Jimmy's boldness would get him into trouble. Yes, he did. You see, that might give him a chance to slip away himself. Otherwise, he would be in a bad fix.

The latch on the door rattled. Unc' Billy crept into one of the nests, but frightened as he was, he couldn't keep from peeping over the edge to see what would happen. The door swung open, letting in a flood of light. The hens stopped their noise. Farmer Brown's boy stood in the doorway and looked in. Jimmy Skunk lifted his big plume of a tail just a bit higher than usual and calmly and without the least sign of being in a hurry walked straight towards the open door. Of course Farmer Brown's boy saw him at once.

"So it's you, you black and white rascal!" he exclaimed. "I suppose you expect me to step out of your way, and I suppose I will do just that very thing. You are the most impudent and independent fellow of my acquaintance. That's what you are. You didn't get any eggs, because I gathered all of them last night. And you didn't get a chicken because they were wise enough to stay on their roosts, so I don't know as I have any quarrel with you, and I'm sure I don't want any. Come along out of there, you rascal."

Farmer Brown's boy stepped aside, and Jimmy Skunk calmly and without the least sign of hurry or worry walked out, stopped for a drink at the pan of water in the henyard, walked through the henyard gate, and turned towards the stone wall along the edge of the Old Orchard.

Day 81

1. Read chapter 21 of *The Adventures of Jimmy Skunk.*
2. Tell someone about the chapter.

Vocabulary

1. Farmer Brown's boy says to Uncle Billy, "Never lose your temper over trifles."
2. The word **trifle** (say it try-full) appears at the end as well:
   * It had seemed a trifle, kicking that egg out of that nest, but see what the results were. Truly, little things often are not so little as they seem.
3. The last sentence is our clue as to what **trifle** means. It calls them "little things."
4. What do you think **trifle** means? Does it mean things that are small? No, that's not it. What do you think those sentences are saying? (Answers)

5. Today's a good day to practice your vocabulary. You can look back in your book to Day 46 or play the vocabulary review game on the Review Games page on EP's website.

Chapter XXI The Nest Egg Gives Unc' Billy Away

'Tis little things that often seem
  Scarce worth a passing thought
 Which in the end may prove that they
  With big results are fraught.

Farmer Brown's boy watched Jimmy Skunk calmly and peacefully go his way and grinned as he watched him. He scratched his head thoughtfully. "I suppose," said he, "that that is as perfect an example of the value of preparedness as there is. Jimmy knew he was all ready for trouble if I chose to make it, and that because of that I wouldn't make it. So he has calmly gone his way as if he were as much bigger than I as I am bigger than he. There certainly is nothing like being prepared if you want to avoid trouble."

Then Farmer Brown's boy once more turned to the henhouse and entered it. He looked to make sure that no hen had been foolish enough to go to sleep where Jimmy could have caught her, and satisfied of this, he would have gone about his usual morning work of feeding the hens but for one thing. That one thing was the china nest-egg on the floor.

"Hello!" exclaimed Farmer Brown's boy when he saw it. "Now how did that come there? It must be that Jimmy Skunk pulled it out of one of those lower nests."

Now he knew just which nests had contained nest-eggs, and it didn't take but a minute to find that none was missing in any of the lower nests. "That's queer," he muttered. "That egg must have come from one of the upper nests. Jimmy couldn't have got up to those. None of the hens could have kicked it out last night, because they were all on the roosts when I shut them up. They certainly didn't do it this morning, because they wouldn't have dared leave the roosts with Jimmy Skunk here. I'll have to look into this."

So he began with the second row of nests and looked in each. Then he started on the upper row, and so he came to the nest in which Unc' Billy Possum was hiding under the hay and holding his breath. Now Unc' Billy had covered himself up pretty well with the hay, but he had forgotten one thing; he had forgotten his tail. Yes, Sir, Unc' Billy had forgotten his tail, and it hung just over the edge of the nest. Of course, Farmer Brown's boy saw it. He couldn't help but see it.

"Ho, ho!" he exclaimed right away. "Ho, ho! So there was more than one visitor here last night. This henhouse seems to be a very popular place. I see that the first thing for me to do after breakfast is to nail a board over that hole in the floor. So it was you, Unc' Billy Possum, who kicked that nest-egg out. Found it a little hard for your teeth, didn't you? Lost your temper and kicked it out, didn't you? That was foolish, Unc' Billy, very foolish indeed. Never lose your temper over trifles. It doesn't pay. Now I wonder what I'd better do with you."

All this time Unc' Billy hadn't moved. Of course, he couldn't understand what Farmer Brown's boy was saying. Nor could he see what Farmer Brown's boy was doing. So he held his breath and hoped and hoped that he hadn't been discovered. And perhaps he wouldn't have been but for that telltale nest-egg on the floor. That was the cause of all his troubles. First it had angered Jimmy Skunk because as you remember, it had fallen on Jimmy's head. Then it had led Farmer Brown's boy to look in all the nests. It had seemed a trifle, kicking that egg out of that nest, but see what the results were. Truly, little things often are not so little as they seem.

Day 82

1. Read chapter 22 of *The Adventures of Jimmy Skunk.*
2. What trick did Uncle Billy do to try and get out of trouble? (Answers)
3. Did he fool Farmer Brown's boy? Did he think the possum was dead? (Answers)

Chapter XXII   Uncle Billy Possum Tries His Old Trick

The first knowledge Unc' Billy Possum had that he was discovered came to him through his tail. Yes, Sir, it came to him through his tail. Farmer Brown's boy pinched it. It was rather a mean thing to do, but Farmer Brown's boy was curious. He wanted to see what Unc' Billy would do. And he didn't pinch very hard, not hard enough to really hurt. Farmer Brown's boy is too good-hearted to hurt any one if he can help it.

Now any other of the Green Forest and Green Meadows people would promptly have pulled their tail away had they been in Unc' Billy's place. But Unc' Billy didn't. No, Sir, Unc' Billy didn't. That tail might have belonged to any one but him so far as he made any sign. Of course, he felt like pulling it away. Any one would have in his place. But he didn't move it the tiniest bit, which goes to show that Unc' Billy has great self-control when he wishes.

Farmer Brown's boy pinched again, just a little harder, but still Unc' Billy made no sign. Farmer Brown's boy chuckled and began to pull on that tail. He pulled and pulled until finally he had pulled Unc' Billy out of his hiding-place, and he swung by his tail from the hand of Farmer Brown's boy. There wasn't the least sign of life about Unc' Billy. He looked as if he were dead, and he acted as if he were dead. Any one not knowing Unc' Billy would have supposed that he *was* dead.

Farmer Brown's boy dropped Unc' Billy on the floor. He lay just as he fell. Farmer Brown's boy rolled him over with his foot, but there wasn't a sign of life in Unc' Billy. He hoped that Farmer Brown's boy really did think him dead. That was what he wanted. Farmer Brown's boy picked him up again and laid him on a box, first putting a board over the hole in the floor and closing the henhouse door. Then he went about his work of cleaning out the henhouse and measuring out the grain for the biddies.

Unc' Billy lay there on the box, and he certainly was pathetic looking. A dead animal or bird is always pathetic looking, and none was ever more so than Unc' Billy Possum as he lay on that box. His hair was all rumpled up, as it usually is. It was filled with dust from the floor and bits of straw. His lips were drawn back and his mouth partly open. His eyes seemed to be closed. As a matter of fact, they were open just a teeny, weeny bit, just enough for Unc' Billy to watch Farmer Brown's boy. But to have looked at him you would have thought him as dead as the deadest thing that ever was.

As he went about his work Farmer Brown's boy kept an eye on Unc' Billy and chuckled. "You old fraud," said he. "You think you are fooling me, but I know you. Possums don't die of nothing in hens' nests. You certainly are a clever old rascal, and the best actor I've ever seen. I wonder how long you will keep it up. I wish I had half as much self-control."

When he had finished his work he picked Unc' Billy up by the tail once more, opened the door, and started for the house with Unc' Billy swinging from his hand and bumping against his legs. Still Unc' Billy gave no sign of life. He wondered where he was being taken to. He was terribly frightened. But he stuck to his old trick of playing dead which had served him so well more than once before.

Day 83

1. Read chapter 23 of *The Adventures of Jimmy Skunk.*

2. How did Farmer Brown's boy get Uncle Billy to stop pretending? (Answers)

Chapter XXIII   Unc' Billy Gives Himself Away

If ever had Unc' Billy Possum played that old trick of his better than he was playing it now. Farmer Brown's boy knew that Unc' Billy was only pretending to be dead, yet so well did Unc' Billy pretend that it was hard work for Farmer Brown's boy to believe what he knew was the truth that Unc' Billy was very much alive and only waiting for a chance to slip away.

They were half-way from the henyard to the house when Bowser the Hound came to meet his master. "Now we shall see what we shall see," said Farmer Brown's boy, as Bowser came trotting up. "If Unc' Billy can stand this test, I'll take off my hat to him every time we meet hereafter." He held Unc' Billy out to Bowser, and Bowser sniffed him all over.

Just imagine that! Just think of being nosed and sniffed at by one of whom you were terribly afraid and not so much as twitching an ear! Farmer Brown's boy dropped Unc' Billy on the ground, and Bowser rolled him over and sniffed at him and then looked up at his master, as much as to say: "This fellow doesn't interest me. He's dead. He must be the fellow I saw go under the henhouse last night. How did you kill him?"

Farmer Brown's boy laughed and picked Unc' Billy up by the tail again. "He's fooled you all right, old fellow, and you don't know it," said he to Bowser, as the latter pranced on ahead to the house. The mother of Farmer Brown's boy was in the doorway, watching them approach.

"What have you got there?" she demanded. "I declare if it isn't a Possum! Where did you kill him? Was he the cause of all that racket among the chickens?"

Farmer Brown's boy took Unc' Billy into the kitchen and dropped him on a chair. Mrs. Brown came over to look at him closer. "Poor little fellow," said she. "Poor little fellow. It was too bad he got into mischief and had to be killed. I don't suppose he knew any better. Somehow it always seems wrong to me to kill these little creatures just because they get into mischief when all the time they don't know that they are in mischief." She stroked Unc' Billy gently.

The eyes of Farmer Brown's boy twinkled. He went over to a corner and pulled a straw from his mother's broom. Then he returned to Unc' Billy and began to tickle Unc' Billy's nose. Mrs. Brown looked puzzled. She was puzzled.

"What are you doing that for?" she asked.

"Just for fun," replied Farmer Brown's boy and kept on tickling Unc' Billy's nose. Now Unc' Billy could stand having his tail pinched, and being carried head down, and being dropped on the ground, but this was too much for him; he wanted to sneeze. He had *got* to sneeze. He did sneeze. He couldn't help it, though it were to cost him his life.

"Land of love!" exclaimed Mrs. Brown, jumping back and clutching her skirts in both hands as if she expected Unc' Billy would try to take refuge behind them. "Do you mean to say that that Possum is alive?"

"Seems that way," replied Farmer Brown's boy as Unc' Billy sneezed again, for that straw was still tickling his nose. "I should certainly say it seems that way. The old sinner is no more dead than I am. He's just pretending. He fooled you all right, Mother, but he didn't fool me. I haven't hurt a hair of him. You ought to know me well enough by this time to know that I wouldn't hurt him."

He looked at his mother reproachfully, and she hastened to apologize. "But what could I think?" she demanded. "If he isn't a dead-looking creature, I never have seen one. What are you going to do with him, son?"

"Take him over to the Green Forest after breakfast and let him go," replied Farmer Brown's boy.

This is just what he did do, and Unc' Billy wasted no time in getting home. It was a long time before he met Jimmy Skunk again. When he did, Jimmy was his usual good-natured self, and Unc' Billy was wise enough not to refer to eggs.

Day 84

1. Write a book review. Write the author's name, the title of the book, where the story took place, who and what it was about, and what you liked about the book.
2. Save this in your portfolio.

Day 85

1. Read the first part of *King John and Prince Arthur.*

I. THERE was once a king of England whose name was John. He was a trifling, worthless fellow, and as mean a man as ever wore a crown.

He was not the rightful king of England; for by the English law the crown ought to have gone to his nephew, Prince Arthur. But the prince was only a child, and in those rude, rough times the young and the weak had but little chance against the wicked and the strong. It was an easy matter for John to push the lad aside, take possession of his castles and treasures, and then proclaim himself king.

He allowed Arthur to go to Brittany in France, and there the little prince lived for some time in a castle which had been his mother's. John himself often went to France; for in those days a large part of that country was ruled by the English king.

The French king, Philip, was very jealous of John, and there was nothing that he wanted so much as to drive him out of his possessions and take them for his own. But he was a great coward, and although he was always talking about making war upon King John, it was seldom that he found courage enough to do anything. One day as he was thinking about the matter, it occurred to him that it would be a good plan to persuade Prince Arthur to help him. So he invited the boy to come and see him at Paris.

"My dear young prince," he said, "how would you like to be king of England?"

"I should like it above all things," answered the boy, "for indeed it is my right. Had not my uncle taken that which belongs to me, I should even now be wearing the English crown."

"How many fighting men do you think you could muster in case of war?" was King Philip's next question.
"From my own castle, perhaps five hundred," said Arthur.

"Well, then," said Philip, "it will be an easy thing for you to win back your kingdom of England. Only do as I say, and all will be well."

And then he told the prince how he should arm his men and lead them out to fight against the soldiers of King John.

"When the country people see that you are in earnest they will all hasten to help you," said he. "Soon you will have a large army, and all your uncle's castles in France will fall before you. In the meanwhile I will cross the English Channel with my French army, and will attack King John in his own country. He cannot withstand both of us. He will give up everything that he has taken from you. And then you shall be king of England."

Prince Arthur was delighted with the plan, and he promised Philip that he would do what he could. But it is doubtful if he would have done anything had it not been for wicked men who wished to use him for their own selfish purposes.

Day 86

1. Read part 2 of *King John and Prince Arthur*.

II. It was a proud day for Arthur when he rode out at the head of his little army and marched away to fight for the crown of which he had been so wrongfully deprived. It was a foolish undertaking, and hopeless from the start; and the men who were with the little prince ought to have told him so. But, no doubt, they had their own selfish ends to gain, and were willing that he should be deceived.

He had never been happier than when he rode through the meadows that morning, the sunlight flashing from his bright armor, the tall grass rustling in the breeze, the birds singing by the roadside. Alas, he was never to be so happy again.

The people did not join him on the road as he expected, and King Philip seemed to be in no hurry to send him help. But the little prince was brave and hopeful, and he led his army straight across the country to a small town where King John's mother was staying.

"If you can capture the king's mother," said some of his advisers, "the king will give up everything for her sake." But he ought to have known that John had no such love as that for anybody.

The town was easily captured by the prince's followers; but all the great people shut themselves up in the castle that stood close by, and dared their enemies to come near them.

While Prince Arthur and his knights were besieging the castle and trying to find some way to get inside of it, King John himself came to the rescue with an army many times larger than the prince's.

What could the prince do? Some of his men turned against him and went over to the king's army. With the rest he shut himself up in the town, and there, for several days, he defended himself like a young hero. But one night, when a dreadful storm was raging, a number of the king's soldiers climbed over the walls and got into the town. Before the alarm could be given, they were masters of the place. The prince was seized upon while he was in bed. Some of his knights were killed while trying to defend him. Others were made prisoners and afterwards thrown into dark dungeons, where they died.

"Come to my arms, my dear nephew," said King John when Arthur was led before him. "Right glad I am to hold your hand again. You have played a lively game with your loving uncle, and your uncle will reward you as you deserve." And with that he sent the prince to the castle of Falaise, to be kept there until further orders.

"I'll tell you what, Hubert," said he to his head officer, "that boy is the very bane of my life. I can do nothing, think of nothing, but that he is always in my way. Do you understand me, Hubert? You are his keeper."

"Yes," said Hubert, "and I'll keep him so well that he shall never trouble you again."

But Hubert was a gentle knight and had no intention of doing the boy any harm. He gave him the best room in the castle of Falaise and treated him as tenderly as though he were his own son. The prince, however, was very unhappy. He spent much of his time looking out of the narrow windows of his prison and wishing that he could once more see his dear old home in Brittany.

Day 87

1. Read part 3 of *King John and Prince Arthur*.

III. The king had hoped that Hubert would find means to put Arthur to death, and when he learned that the lad was still alive he was more troubled than before. He called some of his friends together—men who were as wicked and worthless as himself—and asked their advice.

"What shall we do with that boy?" he asked. "He is the torment of my life. So long as he is alive there will be men to plot and plan to make him king. How shall we be rid of him?"

"Put his eyes out," said one.

"Send some one with a dagger to visit him," said another.

"Throw him into the river to be king of the fishes," said a third.

King John liked the idea of the dagger. He told William de Bray, a Norman knight, that if he would stab the young prince he should be richly rewarded with lands and gold. But Sir William turned on his heel and left the king, saying, "I am a gentleman and not a murderer."

Then the king thought of putting out the boy's eyes. He found two ruffians who were willing to do the deed for pay, and sent them down to Falaise. They took with them the king's order, which they gave to Hubert:—

"You are commanded to burn the boy's eyes out with red-hot irons. See that you fail not. The men who carry this to you will do your bidding in the matter."

Hubert read it and then showed it to the prince.

"Arthur," he said, "I have a message from you uncle. I pray you look it over and tell me what you think of it;" and then he turned away while the prince read.

"Hubert!" said Arthur.

"Well, my prince!"

"Shall I tell you what I think of it? I think that you will not burn out my eyes."

"But the king commands, and I must obey. He will take my life if I refuse."

"Then do it, dear Hubert, to save yourself. But how can you? These eyes never harmed you. They never so much as frowned upon you, nor never shall they. Is there no other way?"

Hubert made no answer, but motioned to the ruffians to come in. They came, with the red-hot irons in their hands. The prince ran to Hubert and clasped him about the knees.

"Oh, save me, Hubert! save me!" he cried, "If it must be done, do it yourself; but send these men away. I promise that I will be very still. I will not flinch when the iron burns me; I will not cry out. But do it yourself, kind Hubert."

The child's distress and terror were more than the tender-hearted Hubert could endure. He sent the ruffians away. "Give me the irons," he said, "I will do it myself." And they, to tell the truth, were glad enough to be off without doing the barbarous deed.

Hubert led Arthur to another part of the castle, into a room that was seldom visited. "I would not harm your eyes for all the treasure that your uncle owns," he said. "But no one must know that I have saved you. The men must carry back false reports, and you must stay here in hiding. I have taken great risks in disobeying your uncle."

When the ruffians went back to the king and said that his orders had been carried out, he was very much pleased. He felt sure now that the prince was out of the way and would give him no more trouble; and for a time all went well with him.

Day 88

1. Read part 4 of *King John and Prince Arthur*.

IV. At length Hubert was called away to fight in distant lands; and Arthur was left in the lonely castle, not daring to stir out or to show himself beyond the walls. One day a wicked talebearer who had been entertained and fed at Falaise Castle carried the news to the king that the prince was still alive and well.

King John was furious. "Hubert shall die for this!" he cried. Then he sent men to Falaise to find Arthur's hiding place. They carried the boy far away to one of the king's castles on the

Seine River. There he was put in charge of a very cruel keeper. He was shut up in a narrow room above the river, where the only sounds to be heard were the lapping of the waves and the sighing of the wind.

One night the prince was wakened from his sleep by his keeper, who told him that friends were waiting for him at the water gate. He hastened to dress himself, and then followed the keeper down the narrow stairway to the door that opened out upon the river. The night was dark; and he wondered if Hubert had come to rescue him from his prison. He could see near the door the dim shadow of a boat with two men in it. They were muffled in long cloaks and were sitting very quietly.

"Step into the boat," whispered the keeper.

The prince obeyed, and sat down in the stern. Then the man who held the oars pushed the boat off into the stream, and it was soon floating swiftly far away from the castle.

"Is that you, Hubert?" whispered the prince to the man who sat in front of him. The man loosened his cloak and lifted his face. Then, as the moon peeped out from behind a cloud, Arthur saw that it was his uncle and that he held a dagger in his hand.

In the morning while the gray mists were still hanging above the river, King John and his boatman were seen floating down the river towards the place where the king's army was encamped. But Prince Arthur was not in the boat; nor did any one ever see him again.

Day 89

   1. Read the first part of *King John and the Magna Carta.*

KING JOHN was so selfish and cruel that all the people in his kingdom both feared and hated him.

One by one he lost the dominions in France which the former kings of England had held. Men called him Lackland, because in the end he had neither lands nor castles that he could rightfully call his own.

He robbed his people. He quarreled with his knights and barons. He offended all good men. He formed a plan for making war against King Philip of France, and called upon his barons to join him. When some of them refused, he burned their castles and destroyed their fields.

At last the barons met together at a place called St. Edmundsbury to talk about their grievances. "Why should we submit to be ruled by such a king?" said some of the boldest. But most of them were afraid to speak their minds.

Stephen Langton, the Archbishop of Canterbury, was with them, and there was no bolder friend of liberty than he. He made a stirring speech that gave courage even to the most cowardly.

"Are you men?" he said. "Why then do you submit to this false-hearted king? Stand up and declare your freedom. Refuse to be the slaves of this man. Demand the rights and privileges that belong to you as free men. Put this demand in writing—in the form of a great charter—and require the king to sign it. So shall it be to you and your children a safeguard forever against the injustice of unworthy rulers."

The barons were astonished at the boldness of this speech. Some of them shrank back in fear, but the bravest among them showed by their looks and gestures that they were ready to make a bold stand for liberty.

"Come forward!" cried Stephen Langton. "Come, and swear that you will never rest until King John has given you the rights that are yours. Swear that you will have the charter from his hand, or that you will wage war upon him to the very death."

Never before had Englishmen heard such a speech. The barons took the oath which Stephen Langton prescribed. Then they gathered their fighting men together and marched upon London. The cowardly king was frightened.

Day 90

1. Read the last half of *King John and the Magna Carta*.
2. I'll start with a little reminder of where you were.

Never before had Englishmen heard such a speech. The barons took the oath which Stephen Langton prescribed. Then they gathered their fighting men together and marched upon London. The cowardly king was frightened.

"What do these men want?" he asked.

They sent him word that they wanted their rights as Englishmen, and that they would never rest until he had given them a charter of liberties signed by his own hand.

"Oh, well! If that is all, you shall surely have it," he said.

But he put them off with one excuse and another. He sent a messenger to Rome to ask the Pope to help him. He tried, by fine promises, to persuade Stephen Langton to abandon the cause he had undertaken. But no one knew the falseness of his heart better than the Pope and the Archbishop of Canterbury.

The people from all parts of the country now came and joined the army of the barons. Of all the knights in England, only seven remained true to the king.

The barons made out a list of their demands; and Stephen Langton carried it to the king.

"These things we will have," they said; "and there shall be no peace until you grant them."

Oh, how angry was King John! He raved like a wild beast; he clenched his fists; he stamped upon the floor. But he saw that he was helpless. At last he said that he would sign the charter at such time and place as the barons might name.

"Let the time be the 15th of June," they said, "and let the place be Runnymede."

Now Runnymede was a green meadow not far from the city of London, and thither the king went with his few followers. There he was met by the barons, with an army of determined men behind them.

The charter which Stephen Langton and his friends had drawn up was spread out before the king. He was not a scholar, and so it was read to him, line by line. It was a promise that the people should not be oppressed; that the rights of the cities and boroughs should be respected; that no man should be imprisoned without a fair trial; that justice should not be delayed or denied to any one.

Pale with anger, the king signed the charter, and then rode back to his castle at Windsor. As soon as he was in his own chamber he began to rave like a madman. He rolled on the floor; he beat the air with his fists; he gnawed sticks and straws; he foamed at the mouth; he cursed the barons and the people for treating their king so badly.

But he was helpless. The charter was signed—the MAGNA CHARTA, to which Englishmen still point as the first safeguard of their rights and liberties.

As might have been expected, it was not long before John tried to break all his promises. The barons made war upon him, and never again did he see a peaceful day. His anger and anxiety caused him to fall into a fever which nothing could cure. At last, despised and shunned as he deserved to be, he died. I doubt if there was an eye in England that wept for him.

Day 91

1. Your new book you will begin reading is called, *Fifty Famous Stories*.
2. Read the first story. There are words with hyphens (hy–phens) in them. It's supposed to help you read the words by separating them into parts.
3. What country is Alfred the king of? (Answers)
4. Who was his army fighting against? (Answers)
5. When King Alfred fled from a battle, where did he end up? (Answers)
6. What did King Alfred forget to do? (Answers)
7. What was the lady's reaction? (Answers)

KING ALFRED AND THE CAKES

Many years ago there lived in Eng-land a wise and good king whose name was Al-fred. No other man ever did so much for his country as he; and people now, all over the world, speak of him as Alfred the Great.

In those days a king did not have a very easy life. There was war almost all the time, and no one else could lead his army into battle so well as he. And so, between ruling and fighting, he had a busy time of it indeed.

A fierce, rude people, called the Danes, had come from over the sea, and were fighting the Eng-lish. There were so many of them, and they were so bold and strong, that for a long time they gained every battle. If they kept on, they would soon be the masters of the whole country.

At last, after a great battle, the English army was broken up and scat-tered. Every man had to save himself in the best way he could. King Alfred fled alone, in great haste, through the woods and swamps.

Late in the day the king came to the hut of a wood-cut-ter. He was very tired and hungry, and he begged the wood-cut-ter's wife to give him something to eat and a place to sleep in her hut.

The wom-an was baking some cakes upon the hearth, and she looked with pity upon the poor, ragged fellow who seemed so hungry. She had no thought that he was the king.

"Yes," she said, "I will give you some supper if you will watch these cakes. I want to go out and milk the cow; and you must see that they do not burn while I am gone."

King Alfred was very willing to watch the cakes, but he had far greater things to think about. How was he going to get his army to-geth-er again? And how was he going to drive the fierce Danes out of the land? He forgot his hunger; he forgot the cakes; he forgot that he was in the woodcutter's hut. His mind was busy making plans for to-mor-row.

In a little while the wom-an came back. The cakes were smoking on the hearth. They were burned to a crisp. Ah, how angry she was!

"You lazy fellow!" she cried. "See what you have done! You want some-thing to eat, but you do not want to work!"

I have been told that she even struck the king with a stick; but I can hardly be-lieve that she was so ill-na-tured.

The king must have laughed to himself at the thought of being scolded in this way; and he was so hungry that he did not mind the woman's angry words half so much as the loss of the cakes.

I do not know whether he had any-thing to eat that night, or whether he had to go to bed without his supper. But it was not many days until he had gath-ered his men to-geth-er again, and had beaten the Danes in a great battle.

Day 92

1. Read the second story, about the beggar.
2. Tell the story to someone.

KING ALFRED AND THE BEGGAR

At one time the Danes drove King Alfred from his kingdom, and he had to lie hidden for a long time on a little is-land in a river.

One day, all who were on the is-land, except the king and queen and one servant, went out to fish. It was a very lonely place, and no one could get to it except by a boat. About noon a ragged beggar came to the king's door, and asked for food.

The king called the servant, and asked, "How much food have we in the house?"

"My lord," said the servant, "we have only one loaf and a little wine."

Then the king gave thanks to God, and said, "Give half of the loaf and half of the wine to this poor man."

The servant did as he was bidden. The beggar thanked the king for his kindness, and went on his way.

In the after-noon the men who had gone out to fish came back. They had three boats full of fish, and they said, "We have caught more fish today than in all the other days that we have been on this island."

The king was glad, and he and his people were more hopeful than they had ever been before.

When night came, the king lay awake for a long time, and thought about the things that had happened that day. At last he fancied that he saw a great light like the sun; and in the midst of the light there stood an old man with black hair, holding an open book in his hand.

It may all have been a dream, and yet to the king it seemed very real indeed. He looked and wondered, but was not afraid.

"Who are you?" he asked of the old man.

"Alfred, my son, be brave," said the man; "for I am the one to whom you gave this day the half of all the food that you had. Be strong and joyful of heart, and listen to what I say. Rise up early in the morning and blow your horn three times, so loudly that the Danes may hear it. By nine o'clock, five hundred men will be around you ready to be led into battle. Go forth bravely, and within seven days your en-e-mies shall be beaten, and you shall go back to your kingdom to reign in peace."

Then the light went out, and the man was seen no more.

In the morning the king arose early, and crossed over to the mainland. Then he blew his horn three times very loudly; and when his friends heard it they were glad, but the Danes were filled with fear.

At nine o'clock, five hundred of his bravest soldiers stood around him ready for battle. He spoke, and told them what he had seen and heard in his dream; and when he had fin-ished, they all cheered loudly, and said that they would follow him and fight for him so long as they had strength.

So they went out bravely to battle; and they beat the Danes, and drove them back into their own place. And King Alfred ruled wisely and well over all his people for the rest of his days.

Day 93

1. Read the story about the seashore.
2. Tell the story to someone.

KING CANUTE ON THE SEASHORE

A hundred years or more after the time of Alfred the Great there was a king of England named Ca-nuté. King Canute was a Dane; but the Danes were not so fierce and cruel then as they had been when they were at war with King Alfred.

The great men and of-fi-cers who were around King Canute were always praising him.

"You are the greatest man that ever lived," one would say.

Then an-oth-er would say, "O king! there can never be an-oth-er man so mighty as you."

And another would say, "Great Canute, there is nothing in the world that dares to dis-o-bey you."

The king was a man of sense, and he grew very tired of hearing such foolish speeches.

One day he was by the sea-shore, and his of-fi-cers were with him. They were praising him, as they were in the habit of doing. He thought that now he would teach them a lesson, and so he bade them set his chair on the beach close by the edge of the water.

"Am I the greatest man in the world?" he asked.

"O king!" they cried, "there is no one so mighty as you."

"Do all things obey me?" he asked.

"There is nothing that dares to dis-o-bey you, O king!" they said. "The world bows before you, and gives you honor."

"Will the sea obey me?" he asked; and he looked down at the little waves which were lapping the sand at his feet.

The foolish officers were puzzled, but they did not dare to say "No."

"Command it, O king! and it will obey," said one.

"Sea," cried Canute, "I command you to come no farther! Waves, stop your rolling, and do not dare to touch my feet!"

But the tide came in, just as it always did. The water rose higher and higher. It came up around the king's chair, and wet not only his feet, but also his robe. His officers stood about him, alarmed, and won-der-ing whether he was not mad.

Then Canute took off his crown, and threw it down upon the sand.

"I shall never wear it again," he said. "And do you, my men, learn a lesson from what you have seen. There is only one King who is all-powerful; and it is he who rules the sea, and holds the ocean in the hollow of his hand. It is he whom you ought to praise and serve above all others."

Day 94

1. Read about William.
2. Tell the story to someone.

THE SONS OF WILLIAM THE CONQUEROR

There was once a great king of England who was called Wil-liam the Con-quer-or, and he had three sons.

One day King Wil-liam seemed to be thinking of something that made him feel very sad; and the wise men who were about him asked him what was the matter.

"I am thinking," he said, "of what my sons may do after I am dead. For, unless they are wise and strong, they cannot keep the kingdom which I have won for them. Indeed, I am at a loss to know which one of the three ought to be the king when I am gone."

"O king!" said the wise men, "if we only knew what things your sons admire the most, we might then be able to tell what kind of men they will be. Perhaps, by asking each one of them a few ques-tions, we can find out which one of them will be best fitted to rule in your place."

"The plan is well worth trying, at least," said the king. "Have the boys come before you, and then ask them what you please."

The wise men talked with one another for a little while, and then agreed that the young princes should be brought in, one at a time, and that the same ques-tions should be put to each.

The first who came into the room was Robert. He was a tall, willful lad, and was nick-named Short Stocking.

"Fair sir," said one of the men, "answer me this question: If, instead of being a boy, it had pleased God that you should be a bird, what kind of a bird would you rather be?"

"A hawk," answered Robert. "I would rather be a hawk, for no other bird reminds one so much of a bold and gallant knight."

The next who came was young William, his father's name-sake and pet. His face was jolly and round, and because he had red hair he was nicknamed Rufus, or the Red.

"Fair sir," said the wise man, "answer me this question: If, instead of being a boy, it had pleased God that you should be a bird, what kind of a bird would you rather be?"

"An eagle," answered William. "I would rather be an eagle, because it is strong and brave. It is feared by all other birds, and is there-fore the king of them all."

Lastly came the youngest brother, Henry, with quiet steps and a sober, thought-ful look. He had been taught to read and write, and for that reason he was nick-named Beau-clerc, or the Hand-some Schol-ar.

"Fair sir," said the wise man, "answer me this question: If, instead of being a boy, it had pleased God that you should be a bird, what kind of a bird would you rather be?"

"A star-ling," said Henry. "I would rather be a star-ling, because it is good-mannered and kind and a joy to every one who sees it, and it never tries to rob or abuse its neigh-bor."

Then the wise men talked with one another for a little while, and when they had agreed among themselves, they spoke to the king.

"We find," said they, "that your eldest son, Robert, will be bold and gallant. He will do some great deeds, and make a name for himself; but in the end he will be over-come by his foes, and will die in prison.

"The second son, William, will be as brave and strong as the eagle; but he will be feared and hated for his cruel deeds. He will lead a wicked life, and will die a shameful death.

"The youngest son, Henry, will be wise and prudent and peaceful. He will go to war only when he is forced to do so by his enemies. He will be loved at home, and re-spect-ed abroad; and he will die in peace after having gained great pos-ses-sions."

Years passed by, and the three boys had grown up to be men. King William lay upon his death-bed, and again he thought of what would become of his sons when he was gone. Then he re-mem-bered what the wise men had told him; and so he de-clared that Robert should have the lands which he held in France, that William should be the King of England, and that Henry should have no land at all, but only a chest of gold.

So it hap-pened in the end very much as the wise men had fore-told. Robert, the Short Stocking, was bold and reckless, like the hawk which he so much admired. He lost all the lands that his father had left him, and was at last shut up in prison, where he was kept until he died.

William Rufus was so over-bear-ing and cruel that he was feared and hated by all his people. He led a wicked life, and was killed by one of his own men while hunting in the forest.

And Henry, the Handsome Scholar, had not only the chest of gold for his own, but he became by and by the King of England and the ruler of all the lands that his father had had in France.

Day 95

1. Read about the white ship.
2. Tell someone about the story.

THE WHITE SHIP

King Henry, the Handsome Scholar, had one son, named William, whom he dearly loved. The young man was noble and brave, and every-body hoped that he would some day be the King of England.

One summer Prince William went with his father across the sea to look after their lands in France. They were wel-comed with joy by all their people there, and the young prince was so gallant and kind, that he won the love of all who saw him.

But at last the time came for them to go back to England. The king, with his wise men and brave knights, set sail early in the day; but Prince William with his younger friends waited a little while. They had had so joyous a time in France that they were in no great haste to tear them-selves away.

Then they went on board of the ship which was waiting to carry them home. It was a beau-ti-ful ship with white sails and white masts, and it had been fitted up on purpose for this voyage.

The sea was smooth, the winds were fair, and no one thought of danger. On the ship, every-thing had been ar-ranged to make the trip a pleasant one. There was music and dancing, and everybody was merry and glad.

The sun had gone down before the white-winged vessel was fairly out of the bay. But what of that? The moon was at its full, and it would give light enough; and before the dawn of the morrow, the narrow sea would be crossed. And so the prince, and the young people who were with him, gave themselves up to mer-ri-ment and feasting and joy.

The ear-li-er hours of the night passed by; and then there was a cry of alarm on deck. A moment after-ward there was a great crash. The ship had struck upon a rock. The water rushed in. She was sinking. Ah, where now were those who had lately been so heart-free and glad?

Every heart was full of fear. No one knew what to do. A small boat was quickly launched, and the prince with a few of his bravest friends leaped into it. They pushed off just as the ship was be-gin-ning to settle beneath the waves. Would they be saved?

They had rowed hardly ten yards from the ship, when there was a cry from among those that were left behind.

"Row back!" cried the prince. "It is my little sister. She must be saved!"

The men did not dare to disobey. The boat was again brought along-side of the sinking vessel. The prince stood up, and held out his arms for his sister. At that moment the ship gave a great lurch forward into the waves. One shriek of terror was heard, and then all was still save the sound of the moaning waters.

Ship and boat, prince and prin-cess, and all the gay com-pa-ny that had set sail from France, went down to the bottom together. One man clung to a floating plank, and was saved the next day. He was the only person left alive to tell the sad story.

When King Henry heard of the death of his son his grief was more than he could bear. His heart was broken. He had no more joy in life; and men say that no one ever saw him smile again.

Day 96

1. Read *King John and the Abbot.*
2. Tell the story to someone.

KING JOHN AND THE ABBOT

I. THE THREE QUESTIONS

There was once a king of England whose name was John. He was a bad king; for he was harsh and cruel to his people, and so long as he could have his own way, he did not care what became of other folks. He was the worst king that England ever had.

Now, there was in the town of Can-ter-bur-y a rich old abbot who lived in grand style in a great house called the Abbey. Every day a hundred noble men sat down with him to dine; and fifty brave knights, in fine velvet coats and gold chains, waited upon him at his table.

When King John heard of the way in which the abbot lived, he made up his mind to put a stop to it. So he sent for the old man to come and see him.

"How now, my good abbot?" he said. "I hear that you keep a far better house than I. How dare you do such a thing? Don't you know that no man in the land ought to live better than the king? And I tell you that no man shall."

"O king!" said the abbot, "I beg to say that I am spending nothing but what is my own. I hope that you will not think ill of me for making things pleasant for my friends and the brave knights who are with me."

"Think ill of you?" said the king. "How can I help but think ill of you? All that there is in this broad land is mine by right; and how do you dare to put me to shame by living in grander style than I? One would think that you were trying to be king in my place."

"Oh, do not say so!" said the abbot "For I"—

"Not another word!" cried the king. "Your fault is plain, and unless you can answer me three questions, your head shall be cut off, and all your riches shall be mine."

"I will try to answer them, O king!" said the abbot.

"Well, then," said King John, "as I sit here with my crown of gold on my head, you must tell me to within a day just how long I shall live. Sec-ond-ly, you must tell me how soon I shall ride round the whole world; and lastly, you shall tell me what I think."

"O king!" said the abbot, "these are deep, hard questions, and I cannot answer them just now. But if you will give me two weeks to think about them, I will do the best that I can."

"Two weeks you shall have," said the king; "but if then you fail to answer me, you shall lose your head, and all your lands shall be mine."

The abbot went away very sad and in great fear. He first rode to Oxford. Here was a great school, called a u-ni-ver-si-ty, and he wanted to see if any of the wise pro-fess-ors could help him. But they shook their heads, and said that there was nothing about King John in any of their books.

Then the abbot rode down to Cam-bridge, where there was another u-ni-ver-si-ty. But not one of the teachers in that great school could help him.

At last, sad and sor-row-ful, he rode toward home to bid his friends and his brave knights good-by. For now he had not a week to live.

II. THE THREE ANSWERS

As the abbot was riding up the lane which led to his grand house, he met his shep-herd going to the fields.

"Welcome home, good master!" cried the shepherd. "What news do you bring us from great King John?"

"Sad news, sad news," said the abbot; and then he told him all that had happened.

"Cheer up, cheer up, good master," said the shepherd. "Have you never yet heard that a fool may teach a wise man wit? I think I can help you out of your trouble."

"You help me!" cried the abbot "How? how?"

"Well," answered the shepherd, "you know that everybody says that I look just like you, and that I have some-times been mis-tak-en for you. So, lend me your servants and your horse and your gown, and I will go up to London and see the king. If nothing else can be done, I can at least die in your place."

"My good shepherd," said the abbot, "you are very, very kind; and I have a mind to let you try your plan. But if the worst comes to the worst, you shall not die for me. I will die for myself."

So the shepherd got ready to go at once. He dressed himself with great care. Over his shepherd's coat he threw the abbot's long gown, and he bor-rowed the abbot's cap and golden staff. When all was ready, no one in the world would have thought that he was not the great man himself. Then he mounted his horse, and with a great train of servants set out for London.

Of course the king did not know him.

"Welcome, Sir Abbot!" he said. "It is a good thing that you have come back. But, prompt as you are, if you fail to answer my three questions, you shall lose your head."

"I am ready to answer them, O king!" said the shepherd.

"Indeed, indeed!" said the king, and he laughed to himself. "Well, then, answer my first question: How long shall I live? Come, you must tell me to the very day."

"You shall live," said the shepherd, "until the day that you die, and not one day longer. And you shall die when you take your last breath, and not one moment before."

The king laughed.

"You are witty, I see," he said. "But we will let that pass, and say that your answer is right. And now tell me how soon I may ride round the world."

"You must rise with the sun," said the shepherd, "and you must ride with the sun until it rises again the next morning. As soon as you do that, you will find that you have ridden round the world in twenty-four hours."

The king laughed again. "Indeed," he said, "I did not think that it could be done so soon. You are not only witty, but you are wise, and we will let this answer pass. And now comes my third and last question: What do I think?"

"That is an easy question," said the shepherd. "You think that I am the Abbot of Can-ter-bur-y. But, to tell you the truth, I am only his poor shepherd, and I have come to beg your pardon for him and for me." And with that, he threw off his long gown.

The king laughed loud and long.

"A merry fellow you are," said he, "and you shall be the Abbot of Canterbury in your master's place."

"O king! that cannot be," said the shepherd; "for I can neither read nor write."

"Very well, then," said the king, "I will give you something else to pay you for this merry joke. I will give you four pieces of silver every week as long as you live. And when you get home, you may tell the old abbot that you have brought him a free pardon from King John."

Day 97

1. Read *A Story of Robin Hood*.
2. In front of an audience (can be your family on the couch), tell them the story and read to them the poem at the end of the story.

A STORY OF ROBIN HOOD

In the rude days of King Rich-ard and King John there were many great woods in England. The most famous of these was Sher-wood forest, where the king often went to hunt deer. In this forest there lived a band of daring men called out-laws.

They had done something that was against the laws of the land, and had been forced to hide themselves in the woods to save their lives. There they spent their time in roaming about among the trees, in hunting the king's deer, and in robbing rich trav-el-ers that came that way.

There were nearly a hundred of these outlaws, and their leader was a bold fellow called Robin Hood. They were dressed in suits of green, and armed with bows and arrows; and sometimes they carried long wooden lances and broad-swords, which they knew how to handle well. When-ever they had taken anything, it was brought and laid at the feet of Robin Hood, whom they called their king. He then di-vid-ed it fairly among them, giving to each man his just share.

Robin never allowed his men to harm any-body but the rich men who lived in great houses and did no work. He was always kind to the poor, and he often sent help to them; and for that reason the common people looked upon him as their friend.

Long after he was dead, men liked to talk about his deeds. Some praised him, and some blamed him. He was, indeed, a rude, lawless fellow; but at that time, people did not think of right and wrong as they do now.

A great many songs were made up about Robin Hood, and these songs were sung in the cot-ta-ges and huts all over the land for hundreds of years after-ward.

Here is a little story that is told in one of those songs:—

Robin Hood was standing one day under a green tree by the road-side. While he was lis-ten-ing to the birds among the leaves, he saw a young man passing by. This young man was dressed in a fine suit of bright red cloth; and, as he tripped gayly along the road, he seemed to be as happy as the day.

"I will not trou-ble him," said Robin Hood, "for I think he is on his way to his wedding."

The next day Robin stood in the same place. He had not been there long when he saw the same young man coming down the road. But he did not seem to be so happy this time. He had left his scarlet coat at home, and at every step he sighed and groaned.

"Ah the sad day! the sad day!" he kept saying to himself.

Then Robin Hood stepped out from under the tree, and said,—

"I say, young man! Have you any money to spare for my merry men and me?"

"I have nothing at all," said the young man, "but five shil-lings and a ring."

"A gold ring?" asked Robin.

"Yes?" said the young man, "it is a gold ring. Here it is."

"Ah, I see!" said Robin: "it is a wedding ring."

"I have kept it these seven years," said the young man; "I have kept it to give to my bride on our wedding day. We were going to be married yes-ter-day. But her father has prom-ised her to a rich old man whom she never saw. And now my heart is broken."

"What is your name?" asked Robin.

"My name is Allin-a-Dale," said the young man.

"What will you give me, in gold or fee," said Robin, "if I will help you win your bride again in spite of the rich old man to whom she has been promised?"

"I have no money," said Allin, "but I will promise to be your servant."

"How many miles is it to the place where the maiden lives?" asked Robin.

"It is not far," said Allin. "But she is to be married this very day, and the church is five miles away."

Then Robin made haste to dress himself as a harper; and in the after-noon he stood in the door of the church.

"Who are you?" said the bishop, "and what are you doing here?"

"I am a bold harper," said Robin, "the best in the north country."

"I am glad you have come," said the bishop kindly. "There is no music that I like so well as that of the harp. Come in, and play for us."

"I will go in," said Robin Hood; "but I will not give you any music until I see the bride and bridegroom."

Just then an old man came in. He was dressed in rich clothing, but was bent with age, and was feeble and gray. By his side walked a fair young girl. Her cheeks were very pale, and her eyes were full of tears.

"This is no match," said Robin. "Let the bride choose for herself."

Then he put his horn to his lips, and blew three times. The very next minute, four and twenty men, all dressed in green, and car-ry-ing long bows in their hands, came running across the fields. And as they marched into the church, all in a row, the fore-most among them was Allin-a-Dale.

"Now whom do you choose?" said Robin to the maiden.

"I choose Allin-a-Dale," she said, blushing.

"And Allin-a-Dale you shall have," said Robin; "and he that takes you from Allin-a-Dale shall find that he has Robin Hood to deal with."

And so the fair maiden and Allin-a-Dale were married then and there, and the rich old man went home in a great rage.

"And thus having ended this merry wedding,
The bride looked like a queen:
And so they re-turned to the merry green wood,
Amongst the leaves so green."

Day 98

1. Read *Bruce and the Spider.*
2. Tell the story to someone.
3. If you are able, go online and play the vocabulary review game on the second level of the Review Games page on the Easy Peasy website, or you can review the vocabulary on Day 46.

BRUCE AND THE SPIDER

There was once a king of Scot-land whose name was Robert Bruce. He had need to be both brave and wise, for the times in which he lived were wild and rude. The King of England was at war with him, and had led a great army into Scotland to drive him out of the land.

Battle after battle had been fought. Six times had Bruce led his brave little army against his foes; and six times had his men been beaten, and driven into flight. At last his army was scat-tered, and he was forced to hide himself in the woods and in lonely places among the moun-tains.

One rainy day, Bruce lay on the ground under a rude shed, lis-ten-ing to the patter of the drops on the roof above him. He was tired and sick at heart, and ready to give up all hope. It seemed to him that there was no use for him to try to do anything more.

As he lay thinking, he saw a spider over his head, making ready to weave her web. He watched her as she toiled slowly and with great care. Six times she tried to throw her frail thread from one beam to another, and six times it fell short.

"Poor thing!" said Bruce: "you, too, know what it is to fail."

But the spider did not lose hope with the sixth failure. With still more care, she made ready to try for the seventh time. Bruce almost forgot his own troubles as he watched her swing herself out upon the slender line. Would she fail again? No! The thread was carried safely to the beam, and fas-tened there.

"I, too, will try a seventh time!" cried Bruce.

He arose and called his men together. He told them of his plans, and sent them out with mes-sa-ges of cheer to his dis-heart-ened people. Soon there was an army of brave Scotch-men around him. Another battle was fought, and the King of England was glad to go back into his own country.

I have heard it said, that, after that day, no one by the name of Bruce would ever hurt a spider. The lesson which the little crea-ture had taught the king was never for-got-ten.

Day 99

1. Read *The Black Douglas.*
2. Tell the story to someone.

THE BLACK DOUGLAS

In Scotland, in the time of King Robert Bruce, there lived a brave man whose name was Doug-las. His hair and beard were black and long, and his face was tanned and dark; and for this reason people nicknamed him the Black Douglas. He was a good friend of the king, and one of his strongest helpers.

In the war with the English, who were trying to drive Bruce from Scotland, the Black Douglas did many brave deeds; and the English people became very much afraid of him.

By and by the fear of him spread all through the land. Nothing could frighten an English lad more than to tell him that the Black Douglas was not far away. Women would tell their chil-dren, when they were naughty, that the Black Douglas would get them; and this would make them very quiet and good.

There was a large cas-tle in Scotland which the English had taken early in the war. The Scot-tish soldiers wanted very much to take it again, and the Black Douglas and his men went one day to see what they could do. It happened to be a hol-i-day, and most of the English soldiers in the cas-tle were eating and drinking and having a merry time. But they had left watch-men on the wall to see that the Scottish soldiers did not come upon them un-a-wares; and so they felt quite safe.

In the e-ven-ing, when it was growing dark, the wife of one of the soldiers went up on the wall with her child in her arms. As she looked over into the fields below the castle, she saw some dark objects moving toward the foot of the wall. In the dusk she could not make out what they were, and so she pointed them out to one of the watch-men.

"Pooh, pooh!" said the watchman. "Those are nothing to frighten us. They are the farmer's cattle, trying to find their way home. The farmer himself is en-joy-ing the hol-i-day, and he has forgotten to bring them in. If the Douglas should happen this way before morning, he will be sorry for his care-less-ness."

But the dark objects were not cattle. They were the Black Douglas and his men, creeping on hands and feet toward the foot of the castle wall. Some of them were dragging ladders behind them through the grass. They would soon be climbing to the top of the wall. None of the English soldiers dreamed that they were within many miles of the place.

The woman watched them until the last one had passed around a corner out of sight. She was not afraid, for in the dark-en-ing twi-light they looked indeed like cattle. After a little while she began to sing to her child:—

"Hush ye, hush ye, little pet ye, Hush ye, hush ye, do not fret ye, The Black Douglas shall not get ye."

All at once a gruff voice was heard behind her, saying, "Don't be so sure about that!"

She looked around, and there stood the Black Douglas himself. At the same moment a Scottish soldier climbed off a ladder and leaped upon the wall; and then there came another and another and another, until the wall was covered with them. Soon there was hot fighting in every part of the castle. But the English were so taken by surprise that they could not do much. Many of them were killed, and in a little while the Black Douglas and his men were the masters of the castle, which by right be-longed to them.

As for the woman and her child, the Black Douglas would not suffer any one to harm them. After a while they went back to England; and whether the mother made up any more songs about the Black Douglas I cannot tell.

Day 100

1. Read *Three Men of Gotham.*
2. Tell the story to someone.

THREE MEN OF GOTHAM

There is a town in England called Go-tham, and many merry stories are told of the queer people who used to live there.

One day two men of Go-tham met on a bridge. Hodge was coming from the market, and Peter was going to the market.

"Where are you going?" said Hodge.

"I am going to the market to buy sheep," said Peter.

"Buy sheep?" said Hodge. "And which way will you bring them home?"

"I shall bring them over this bridge," said Peter.

"No, you shall not," said Hodge.

"Yes, but I will," said Peter.

"You shall not," said Hodge.

"I will," said Peter.

Then they beat with their sticks on the ground as though there had been a hundred sheep between them.

"Take care!" cried Peter. "Look out that my sheep don't jump on the bridge."

"I care not where they jump," said Hodge; "but they shall not go over it."

"But they shall," said Peter.

"Have a care," said Hodge; "for if you say too much, I will put my fingers in your mouth."

"Will you?" said Peter.

Just then another man of Gotham came from the market with a sack of meal on his horse. He heard his neigh-bors quar-rel-ing about sheep; but he could see no sheep between them, and so he stopped and spoke to them.

"Ah, you foolish fellows!" he cried. "It is strange that you will never learn wisdom.—Come here, Peter, and help me lay my sack on my shoul-der."

Peter did so, and the man carried his meal to the side of the bridge.

"Now look at me," he said, "and learn a lesson." And he opened the mouth of the sack, and poured all the meal into the river.

"Now, neighbors," he said, "can you tell how much meal is in my sack?"

"There is none at all!" cried Hodge and Peter together.

"You are right," said the man; "and you that stand here and quarrel about nothing, have no more sense in your heads than I have meal in my sack!"

Day 101

1. Read *Other Wise Men of Gotham.*
2. Tell the story to someone.

OTHER WISE MEN OF GOTHAM

One day, news was brought to Gotham that the king was coming that way, and that he would pass through the town. This did not please the men of Gotham at all. They hated the king, for they knew that he was a cruel, bad man. If he came to their town, they would have to find food and lodg-ing for him and his men; and if he saw anything that pleased him, he would be sure to take it for his own. What should they do?

They met together to talk the matter over.

"Let us chop down the big trees in the woods, so that they will block up all the roads that lead into the town," said one of the wise men.

"Good!" said all the rest.

So they went out with their axes, and soon all the roads and paths to the town were filled with logs and brush. The king's horse-men would have a hard time of it getting into Gotham. They would either have to make a new road, or give up the plan al-to-geth-er, and go on to some other place.

When the king came, and saw that the road had been blocked up, he was very angry.

"Who chopped those trees down in my way?" he asked of two country lads that were passing by.

"The men of Gotham," said the lads.

"Well," said the king, "go and tell the men of Gotham that I shall send my sher-iff into their town, and have all their noses cut off."

The two lads ran to the town as fast as they could, and made known what the king had said.

Every-body was in great fright. The men ran from house to house, carrying the news, and asking one another what they should do.

"Our wits have kept the king out of the town," said one; "and so now our wits must save our noses."

"True, true!" said the others. "But what shall we do?"

Then one, whose name was Dobbin, and who was thought to be the wisest of them all, said, "Let me tell you something. Many a man has been punished because he was wise, but I have never heard of any one being harmed because he was a fool. So, when the king's sher-iff comes, let us all act like fools."

"Good, good!" cried the others. "We will all act like fools."

It was no easy thing for the king's men to open the roads; and while they were doing it, the king grew tired of waiting, and went back to London. But very early one morning, the sheriff with a party of fierce soldiers rode through the woods, and between the fields, toward Gotham. Just before they reached the town, they saw a queer sight. The old men were rolling big stones up the hill, and all the young men were looking on, and grunting very loudly.

The sheriff stopped his horses, and asked what they were doing.

"We are rolling stones up-hill to make the sun rise," said one of the old men.

"You foolish fellow!" said the sheriff. "Don't you know that the sun will rise without any help?"

"Ah! will it?" said the old man. "Well, I never thought of that. How wise you are!"

"And what are *you* doing?" said the sheriff to the young men.

"Oh, we do the grunting while our fathers do the working," they answered.

"I see," said the sheriff. "Well, that is the way the world goes every-where." And he rode on toward the town.

He soon came to a field where a number of men were building a stone wall.

"What are you doing?" he asked.

"Why, master," they answered, "there is a cuck-oo in this field, and we are building a wall around it so as to keep the bird from straying away."

"You foolish fellows!" said the sheriff. "Don't you know that the bird will fly over the top of your wall, no matter how high you build it?"

"Why, no," they said. "We never thought of that. How very wise you are!"

The sheriff next met a man who was carrying a door on his back.

"What are you doing?" he asked.

"I have just started on a long jour-ney," said the man.

"But why do you carry that door?" asked the sheriff.

"I left my money at home."

"Then why didn't you leave the door at home too?"

"I was afraid of thieves; and you see, if I have the door with me, they can't break it open and get in."

"You foolish fellow!" said the sheriff. "It would be safer to leave the door at home, and carry the money with you."

"Ah, would it, though?" said the man. "Now, I never thought of that. You are the wisest man that I ever saw."

Then the sheriff rode on with his men; but every one that they met was doing some silly thing.

"Truly I believe that the people of Gotham are all fools," said one of the horsemen.

"That is true," said another. "It would be a shame to harm such simple people."

"Let us ride back to London, and tell the king all about them," said the sheriff.

"Yes, let us do so," said the horsemen.

So they went back, and told the king that Gotham was a town of fools; and the king laughed, and said that if that was the case, he would not harm them, but would let them keep their noses.

Day 102

1. Read *The Miller of the Dee.*
2. Tell someone about the story.

THE MILLER OF THE DEE

Once upon a time there lived on the banks of the River Dee a miller, who was the hap-pi-est man in England. He was always busy from morning till night, and he was always singing as merrily as any lark. He was so cheerful that he made everybody else cheerful; and people all over the land liked to talk about his pleasant ways. At last the king heard about him.

"I will go down and talk with this won-der-ful miller," he said. "Perhaps he can tell me how to be happy."

As soon as he stepped inside of the mill, he heard the miller singing:—

"I envy no-body—no, not I!—For I am as happy as I can be; And nobody envies me."

"You're wrong, my friend," said the king. "You're wrong as wrong can be. I envy you; and I would gladly change places with you, if I could only be as light-hearted as you are."

The miller smiled, and bowed to the king.

"I am sure I could not think of changing places with you, sir," he said.

"Now tell me," said the king, "what makes you so cheerful and glad here in your dusty mill, while I, who am king, am sad and in trouble every day."

The miller smiled again, and said, "I do not know why you are sad, but I can eas-i-ly tell why I am glad. I earn my own bread; I love my wife and my children; I love my friends, and they love me; and I owe not a penny to any man. Why should I not be happy? For here is the River Dee, and every day it turns my mill; and the mill grinds the corn that feeds my wife, my babes, and me."

"Say no more," said the king. "Stay where you are, and be happy still. But I envy you. Your dusty cap is worth more than my golden crown. Your mill does more for you than my kingdom can do for me. If there were more such men as you, what a good place this world would be! Good-by, my friend!"

The king turned about, and walked sadly away; and the miller went back to his work singing:—

"Oh, I'm as happy as happy can be,
For I live by the side of the River Dee!"

Day 103

1. Read *Sir Philip Sidney.*
2. Tell someone about the story.

SIR PHILIP SIDNEY

A cruel battle was being fought. The ground was covered with dead and dying men. The air was hot and stifling. The sun shone down without pity on the wounded soldiers lying in the blood and dust.

One of these soldiers was a no-ble-man, whom everybody loved for his gen-tle-ness and kindness. Yet now he was no better off than the poorest man in the field. He had been wounded, and would die; and he was suf-fer-ing much with pain and thirst.

When the battle was over, his friends hurried to his aid. A soldier came running with a cup in his hand.

"Here, Sir Philip," he said, "I have brought you some clear, cool water from the brook. I will raise your head so that you can drink."

The cup was placed to Sir Philip's lips. How thank-ful-ly he looked at the man who had brought it! Then his eyes met those of a dying soldier who was lying on the ground close by. The wist-ful look in the poor man's face spoke plainer than words.

"Give the water to that man," said Sir Philip quickly; and then, pushing the cup toward him, he said, "Here, my comrade, take this. Thy need is greater than mine."

What a brave, noble man he was! The name of Sir Philip Sidney will never be for-got-ten; for it was the name of a Chris-tian gen-tle-man who always had the good of others in his mind. Was it any wonder that everybody wept when it was heard that he was dead?

It is said, that, on the day when he was carried to the grave, every eye in the land was filled with tears. Rich and poor, high and low, all felt that they had lost a friend; all mourned the death of the kindest, gentlest man that they had ever known.

Day 104

1. Read *The Ungrateful Soldier.*
2. Tell someone about the story.

THE UNGRATEFUL SOLDIER

Here is another story of the bat-tle-field, and it is much like the one which I have just told you.

Not quite a hundred years after the time of Sir Philip Sidney there was a war between the Swedes and the Danes. One day a great battle was fought, and the Swedes were beaten, and driven from the field. A soldier of the Danes who had been slightly wounded was sitting on the ground. He was about to take a drink from a flask. All at once he heard some one say,—

"O sir! give me a drink, for I am dying."

It was a wounded Swede who spoke. He was lying on the ground only a little way off. The Dane went to him at once. He knelt down by the side of his fallen foe, and pressed the flask to his lips.

"Drink," said he, "for thy need is greater than mine."

Hardly had he spoken these words, when the Swede raised himself on his elbow. He pulled a pistol from his pocket, and shot at the man who would have be-friend-ed him. The bullet grazed the Dane's shoulder, but did not do him much harm.

"Ah, you rascal!" he cried. "I was going to befriend you, and you repay me by trying to kill me. Now I will punish you. I would have given you all the water, but now you shall have only half." And with that he drank the half of it, and then gave the rest to the Swede.

When the King of the Danes heard about this, he sent for the soldier and had him tell the story just as it was.

"Why did you spare the life of the Swede after he had tried to kill you?" asked the king.

"Because, sir," said the soldier, "I could never kill a wounded enemy."

"Then you deserve to be a no-ble-man," said the king. And he re-ward-ed him by making him a knight, and giving him a noble title.

Day 105

1. Read *Sir Humphrey Gilbert.*
2. Tell someone about the story.

SIR HUMPHREY GILBERT

More than three hundred years ago there lived in England a brave man whose name was Sir Humphrey Gil-bert. At that time there were no white people in this country of ours. The land was covered with forests; and where there are now great cities and fine farms there were only trees and swamps among which roamed wild In-di-ans and wild beasts.

Sir Hum-phrey Gilbert was one of the first men who tried to make a set-tle-ment in A-mer-i-ca. Twice did he bring men and ships over the sea, and twice did he fail, and sail back for England. The second time, he was on a little ship called the "Squirrel." Another ship, called the "Golden Hind," was not far away. When they were three days from land, the wind failed, and the ships lay floating on the waves. Then at night the air grew very cold. A breeze sprang up from the east. Great white ice-bergs came drifting around them. In the morning the little ships were almost lost among the floating mountains of ice. The men on the "Hind" saw Sir Humphrey sitting on the deck of the "Squirrel" with an open book in his hand. He called to them and said,—

"Be brave, my friends! We are as near heaven on the sea as on the land."

Night came again. It was a stormy night, with mist and rain. All at once the men on the "Hind" saw the lights on board of the "Squirrel" go out. The little vessel, with brave Sir Humphrey and all his brave men, was swal-lowed up by the waves.

Day 106

1. Read about Sir Walter Raleigh. The "leigh" part of the name is pronounced–LEE.
2. Tell someone about the story. Where did he travel from England to? (Answers)

SIR WALTER RALEIGH

There once lived in England a brave and noble man whose name was Walter Ra-leigh. He was not only brave and noble, but he was also handsome and polite; and for that reason the queen made him a knight, and called him Sir Walter Ra-leigh.

I will tell you about it.

When Raleigh was a young man, he was one day walking along a street in London. At that time the streets were not paved, and there were no sidewalks. Raleigh was dressed in very fine style, and he wore a beau-ti-ful scar-let cloak thrown over his shoulders.

As he passed along, he found it hard work to keep from stepping in the mud, and soiling his hand-some new shoes. Soon he came to a puddle of muddy water which reached from one side of the street to the other. He could not step across. Perhaps he could jump over it.

As he was thinking what he should do, he happened to look up. Who was it coming down the street, on the other side of the puddle?

It was E-liz-a-beth, the Queen of England, with her train of gen-tle-wom-en and waiting maids. She saw the dirty puddle in the street. She saw the handsome young man with the scar-let cloak, stand-ing by the side of it. How was she to get across?

Young Raleigh, when he saw who was coming, forgot about himself. He thought only of helping the queen. There was only one thing that he could do, and no other man would have thought of that.

He took off his scarlet cloak, and spread it across the puddle. The queen could step on it now, as on a beautiful carpet.

She walked across. She was safely over the ugly puddle, and her feet had not touched the mud. She paused a moment, and thanked the young man.

As she walked onward with her train, she asked one of the gen-tle-wom-en, "Who is that brave gen-tle-man who helped us so handsomely?"

"His name is Walter Raleigh," said the gentle-woman.

"He shall have his reward," said the queen.

Not long after that, she sent for Raleigh to come to her pal-ace.

The young man went, but he had no scarlet cloak to wear. Then, while all the great men and fine ladies of England stood around, the queen made him a knight. And from that time he was known as Sir Walter Raleigh, the queen's favorite.

Sir Walter Raleigh and Sir Humphrey Gilbert about whom I have already told you, were half-broth-ers.

When Sir Humphrey made his first voy-age to America, Sir Walter was with him. After that, Sir Walter tried sev-er-al times to send men to this country to make a set-tle-ment.

But those whom he sent found only great forests, and wild beasts, and sav-age In-di-ans. Some of them went back to England; some of them died for want of food; and some of them were lost in the woods. At last Sir Walter gave up trying to get people to come to America.

But he found two things in this country which the people of England knew very little about. One was the po-ta-to, the other was to-bac-co.

If you should ever go to Ireland, you may be shown the place where Sir Walter planted the few po-ta-toes which he carried over from America. He told his friends how the Indians used them for food; and he proved that they would grow in the Old World as well as in the New.

Sir Walter had seen the Indians smoking the leaves of the to-bac-co plant. He thought that he would do the same, and he carried some of the leaves to England. Englishmen had never used tobacco before that time; and all who saw Sir Walter puff-ing away at a roll of leaves thought that it was a strange sight.

One day as he was sitting in his chair and smoking, his servant came into the room. The man saw the smoke curling over his master's head, and he thought that he was on fire.

He ran out for some water. He found a pail that was quite full. He hurried back, and threw the water into Sir Walter's face. Of course the fire was all put out.

After that a great many men learned to smoke. And now tobacco is used in all countries of the world. It would have been well if Sir Walter Raleigh had let it alone.

Day 107

1. Read about Pocahontas.
2. Tell someone about Pocahontas. What brave thing did she do to save a man's life? (Answers)

POCAHONTAS

There was once a very brave man whose name was John Smith. He came to this country many years ago, when there were great woods everywhere, and many wild beasts and Indians. Many tales are told of his ad-ven-tures, some of them true and some of them untrue. The most famous of all these is the fol-low-ing:—

One day when Smith was in the woods, some Indians came upon him, and made him their pris-on-er. They led him to their king, and in a short time they made ready to put him to death.

A large stone was brought in, and Smith was made to lie down with his head on it. Then two tall Indians with big clubs in their hands came forward. The king and all his great men stood around to see. The Indians raised their clubs. In another moment they would fall on Smith's head.

But just then a little Indian girl rushed in. She was the daugh-ter of the king, and her name was Po-ca-hon-tas. She ran and threw herself between Smith and the up-lift-ed clubs. She clasped Smith's head with her arms. She laid her own head upon his.

"O father!" she cried, "spare this man's life. I am sure he has done you no harm, and we ought to be his friends."

The men with the clubs could not strike, for they did not want to hurt the child. The king at first did not know what to do. Then he spoke to some of his war-riors, and they lifted Smith from the ground. They untied the cords from his wrists and feet, and set him free.

The next day the king sent Smith home; and several Indians went with him to protect him from harm.

After that, as long as she lived, Po-ca-hon-tas was the friend of the white men, and she did a great many things to help them.

Day 108

1. Read about George Washington and the famous story about the cherry tree.
2. Tell someone about the story. What did he do wrong? What did he do right? (Answers)

GEORGE WASHINGTON AND HIS HATCHET

When George Wash-ing-ton was quite a little boy, his father gave him a hatchet. It was bright and new, and George took great delight in going about and chopping things with it.

He ran into the garden, and there he saw a tree which seemed to say to him, "Come and cut me down!"

George had often seen his father's men chop down the great trees in the forest, and he thought that it would be fine sport to see this tree fall with a crash to the ground. So he set to work with his little hatchet, and, as the tree was a very small one, it did not take long to lay it low.

Soon after that, his father came home.

"Who has been cutting my fine young cherry tree?" he cried. "It was the only tree of its kind in this country, and it cost me a great deal of money."

He was very angry when he came into the house.

"If I only knew who killed that cherry tree," he cried, "I would—yes, I would"—

"Father!" cried little George. "I will tell you the truth about it. I chopped the tree down with my hatchet."

His father forgot his anger.

"George," he said, and he took the little fellow in his arms, "George, I am glad that you told me about it. I would rather lose a dozen cherry trees than that you should tell one false-hood."

Day 109

1. Read *Grace Darling.*
2. Tell someone about the story. What brave thing did she do? (Answers)

GRACE DARLING

It was a dark Sep-tem-ber morning. There was a storm at sea. A ship had been driven on a low rock off the shores of the Farne Islands. It had been broken in two by the waves, and half of it had been washed away. The other half lay yet on the rock, and those of the crew who were still alive were cling-ing to it. But the waves were dashing over it, and in a little while it too would be carried to the bottom.

Could any one save the poor, half-drowned men who were there?

On one of the islands was a light-house; and there, all through that stormy night, Grace Darling had listened to the storm.

Grace was the daughter of the light-house keeper, and she had lived by the sea as long as she could re-mem-ber.

In the darkness of the night, above the noise of the winds and waves, she heard screams and wild cries. When day-light came, she could see the wreck, a mile away, with the angry waters all around it. She could see the men clinging to the masts.

"We must try to save them!" she cried. "Let us go out in the boat at once!"

"It is of no use, Grace," said her father. "We cannot reach them."

He was an old man, and he knew the force of the mighty waves.

"We cannot stay here and see them die," said Grace. "We must at least try to save them."

Her father could not say, "No."

In a few minutes they were ready. They set off in the heavy lighthouse boat. Grace pulled one oar, and her father the other, and they made straight toward the wreck. But it was hard rowing against such a sea, and it seemed as though they would never reach the place.

At last they were close to the rock, and now they were in greater danger than before. The fierce waves broke against the boat, and it would have been dashed in pieces, had it not been for the strength and skill of the brave girl.

But after many trials, Grace's father climbed upon the wreck, while Grace herself held the boat. Then one by one the worn-out crew were helped on board. It was all that the girl could do to keep the frail boat from being drifted away, or broken upon the sharp edges of the rock.

Then her father clam-bered back into his place. Strong hands grasped the oars, and by and by all were safe in the lighthouse. There Grace proved to be no less tender as a nurse than she had been brave as a sailor. She cared most kindly for the ship-wrecked men until the storm had died away and they were strong enough to go to their own homes.

All this happened a long time ago, but the name of Grace Darling will never be forgotten. She lies buried now in a little church-yard by the sea, not far from her old home. Every year many people go there to see her grave; and there a mon-u-ment has been placed in honor of the brave girl. It is not a large mon-u-ment, but it is one that speaks of the noble deed which made Grace Darling famous. It is a figure carved in stone of a woman lying at rest, with a boat's oar held fast in her right hand.

Day 110

1. Read about William Tell. A **tyrant** is a bad leader who acts mean and makes everyone do whatever he wants.
2. Tell someone about the story. What test of his skill did Tell have to perform? (Answers)

THE STORY OF WILLIAM TELL

The people of Swit-zer-land were not always free and happy as they are to-day. Many years ago a proud tyrant, whose name was Gessler, ruled over them, and made their lot a bitter one indeed.

One day this tyrant set up a tall pole in the public square, and put his own cap on the top of it; and then he gave orders that every man who came into the town should bow down before it. But there was one man, named William Tell, who would not do this. He stood up straight with folded arms, and laughed at the swinging cap. He would not bow down to Gessler himself.

When Gessler heard of this, he was very angry. He was afraid that other men would disobey, and that soon the whole country would rebel against him. So he made up his mind to punish the bold man.

William Tell's home was among the mountains, and he was a famous hunter. No one in all the land could shoot with bow and arrow so well as he. Gessler knew this, and so he thought of a cruel plan to make the hunter's own skill bring him to grief. He ordered that Tell's little boy should be made to stand up in the public square with an apple on his head; and then he bade Tell shoot the apple with one of his arrows.

Tell begged the tyrant not to have him make this test of his skill. What if the boy should move? What if the bow-man's hand should tremble? What if the arrow should not carry true?

"Will you make me kill my boy?" he said.

"Say no more," said Gessler. "You must hit the apple with your one arrow. If you fail, my sol-diers shall kill the boy before your eyes."

Then, without another word, Tell fitted the arrow to his bow. He took aim, and let it fly. The boy stood firm and still. He was not afraid, for he had all faith in his father's skill.

The arrow whistled through the air. It struck the apple fairly in the center, and carried it away. The people who saw it shouted with joy.

As Tell was turning away from the place, an arrow which he had hidden under his coat dropped to the ground.

"Fellow!" cried Gessler, "what mean you with this second arrow?"

"Tyrant!" was Tell's proud answer, "this arrow was for your heart if I had hurt my child."

And there is an old story, that, not long after this, Tell did shoot the tyrant with one of his arrows; and thus he set his country free.

Day 111

1. Read the story of *The Bell of Atri.*
2. Who rang the bell? Did he really ring it to let people know he had been wronged? (Answers)
3. What had been done wrong to him and how was it fixed? (Answers)

THE BELL OF ATRI

A-tri is the name of a little town in It-a-ly. It is a very old town, and is built half-way up the side of a steep hill.

A long time ago, the King of Atri bought a fine large bell, and had it hung up in a tower in the market place. A long rope that reached almost to the ground was fas-tened to the bell. The smallest child could ring the bell by pulling upon this rope.

"It is the bell of justice," said the king.

When at last everything was ready, the people of Atri had a great holiday. All the men and women and children came down to the market place to look at the bell of justice. It was a very pretty bell, and was, pol-ished until it looked almost as bright and yellow as the sun.

"How we should like to hear it ring!" they said.

Then the king came down the street.

"Perhaps he will ring it," said the people; and everybody stood very still, and waited to see what he would do.

But he did not ring the bell. He did not even take the rope in his hands. When he came to the foot of the tower, he stopped, and raised his hand.

"My people," he said, "do you see this beautiful bell? It is your bell; but it must never be rung except in case of need. If any one of you is wronged at any time, he may come and ring the bell; and then the judges shall come together at once, and hear his case, and give him justice. Rich and poor, old and young, all alike may come; but no one must touch the rope unless he knows that he has been wronged."

Many years passed by after this. Many times did the bell in the market place ring out to call the judges together. Many wrongs were righted, many ill-doers were punished. At last the hempen rope was almost worn out. The lower part of it was un-twist-ed; some of the strands were broken; it became so short that only a tall man could reach it.

"This will never do," said the judges one day. "What if a child should be wronged? It could not ring the bell to let us know it."

They gave orders that a new rope should be put upon the bell at once,—a rope that should hang down to the ground, so that the smallest child could reach it. But there was not a rope to be found in all Atri. They would have to send across the mountains for one, and it would be many days before it could be brought. What if some great wrong should be done before it came? How could the judges know about it, if the in-jured one could not reach the old rope?

"Let me fix it for you," said a man who stood by.

He ran into his garden, which was not far away, and soon came back with a long grape-vine in his hands.

"This will do for a rope," he said; and he climbed up, and fastened it to the bell. The slender vine, with its leaves and ten-drils still upon it, trailed to the ground.

"Yes," said the judges, "it is a very good rope. Let it be as it is."

Now, on the hill-side above the village, there lived a man who had once been a brave knight. In his youth he had ridden through many lands, and he had fought in many a battle. His best friend through all that time had been his horse,—a strong, noble steed that had borne him safe through many a danger.

But the knight, when he grew older, cared no more to ride into battle; he cared no more to do brave deeds; he thought of nothing but gold; he became a miser. At last he sold all that he had, except his horse, and went to live in a little hut on the hill-side. Day after day he sat among his money bags, and planned how he might get more gold; and day after day his horse stood in his bare stall, half-starved, and shiv-er-ing with cold.

"What is the use of keeping that lazy steed?" said the miser to himself one morning. "Every week it costs me more to keep him than he is worth. I might sell him; but there is not a man that wants him. I cannot even give him away. I will turn him out to shift for himself, and pick grass by the roadside. If he starves to death, so much the better."

So the brave old horse was turned out to find what he could among the rocks on the barren hill-side. Lame and sick, he strolled along the dusty roads, glad to find a blade of grass or a thistle. The boys threw stones at him, the dogs barked at him, and in all the world there was no one to pity him.

One hot afternoon, when no one was upon the street, the horse chanced to wander into the market place. Not a man nor child was there, for the heat of the sun had driven them all indoors. The gates were wide open; the poor beast could roam where he pleased. He saw the grape-vine rope that hung from the bell of justice. The leaves and tendrils upon it were still fresh and green, for it had not been there long. What a fine dinner they would be for a starving horse!

He stretched his thin neck, and took one of the tempting morsels in his mouth. It was hard to break it from the vine. He pulled at it, and the great bell above him began to ring. All the people in Atri heard it. It seemed to say,—

> "Some one   has done   me wrong!
> Some one   has done   me wrong!
> Oh! come   and judge   my case!
> Oh! come   and judge   my case!
> For I've   been   wronged!"

The judges heard it. They put on their robes, and went out through the hot streets to the market place. They wondered who it could be who would ring the bell at such a time. When they passed through the gate, they saw the old horse nibbling at the vine.

"Ha!" cried one, "it is the miser's steed. He has come to call for justice; for his master, as everybody knows, has treated him most shame-ful-ly."

"He pleads his cause as well as any dumb brute can," said another.

"And he shall have justice!" said the third.

Mean-while a crowd of men and women and children had come into the market place, eager to learn what cause the judges were about to try. When they saw the horse, all stood still in wonder. Then every one was ready to tell how they had seen him wan-der-ing on the hills, unfed, un-cared for, while his master sat at home counting his bags of gold.

"Go bring the miser before us," said the judges.

And when he came, they bade him stand and hear their judg-ment.

"This horse has served you well for many a year," they said. "He has saved you from many a peril. He has helped you gain your wealth. Therefore we order that one half of all your gold shall be set aside to buy him shelter and food, a green pasture where he may graze, and a warm stall to comfort him in his old age."

The miser hung his head, and grieved to lose his gold; but the people shouted with joy, and the horse was led away to his new stall and a dinner such as he had not had in many a day.

Day 112

1. Read about Napoleon crossing the Alps.
2. If a man has made up his mind to win, what word will he never say? (Answers)
3. Today review the vocabulary words from the story, *The City Zoo*, either by going to Day 25 or by going online to the Review Games page on the Easy Peasy website.

HOW NAPOLEON CROSSED THE ALPS

About a hundred years ago there lived a great gen-er-al whose name was Na-po-le-on Bo-na-parte. He was the leader of the French army; and France was at war with nearly all the countries around. He wanted very much to take his soldiers into It-a-ly; but between France and Italy there are high mountains called the Alps, the tops of which are covered with snow.

"Is it pos-si-ble to cross the Alps?" said Na-po-le-on.

The men who had been sent to look at the passes over the mountains shook their heads. Then one of them said, "It may be possible, but"—

"Let me hear no more," said Napoleon. "Forward to Italy!"

People laughed at the thought of an army of sixty thousand men crossing the Alps where there was no road. But Napoleon waited only to see that everything was in good order, and then he gave the order to march.

The long line of soldiers and horses and cannon stretched for twenty miles. When they came to a steep place where there seemed to be no way to go farther, the trum-pets sounded "Charge!" Then every man did his best, and the whole army moved right onward.

Soon they were safe over the Alps. In four days they were marching on the plains of Italy.

"The man who has made up his mind to win," said Napoleon, "will never say 'Im-pos-si-ble.'"

Day 113

1. Read about *Cincinnatus.*
2. Why did everyone trust him? (Answers)

THE STORY OF CINCINNATUS

There was a man named Cin-cin-na-tus who lived on a little farm not far from the city of Rome. He had once been rich, and had held the highest office in the land; but in one way or another he had lost all his wealth. He was now so poor that he had to do all the work on his farm with his own hands. But in those days it was thought to be a noble thing to till the soil.

Cin-cin-na-tus was so wise and just that every-body trusted him, and asked his advice; and when any one was in trouble, and did not know what to do, his neighbors would say,—

"Go and tell Cincinnatus. He will help you."

Now there lived among the mountains, not far away, a tribe of fierce, half-wild men, who were at war with the Roman people. They per-suad-ed another tribe of bold war-riors to help them, and then marched toward the city, plun-der-ing and robbing as they came. They boasted that they would tear down the walls of Rome, and burn the houses, and kill all the men, and make slaves of the women and children.

At first the Romans, who were very proud and brave, did not think there was much danger. Every man in Rome was a soldier, and the army which went out to fight the robbers was the finest in the world. No one staid at home with the women and children and boys but the white-haired "Fathers," as they were called, who made the laws for the city, and a small company of men who guarded the walls. Everybody thought that it would be an easy thing to drive the men of the mountains back to the place where they belonged.

But one morning five horsemen came riding down the road from the mountains. They rode with great speed; and both men and horses were covered with dust and blood. The watchman at the gate knew them, and shouted to them as they gal-loped in. Why did they ride thus? and what had happened to the Roman army?

They did not answer him, but rode into the city and along the quiet streets; and everybody ran after them, eager to find out what was the matter. Rome was not a large city at that time; and soon they reached the market place where the white-haired Fathers were sitting. Then they leaped from their horses, and told their story.

"Only yes-ter-day," they said, "our army was marching through a narrow valley between two steep mountains. All at once a thou-sand sav-age men sprang out from among the rocks before us and above us. They had blocked up the way; and the pass was so narrow that we could not fight. We tried to come back; but they had blocked up the way on this side of us too. The fierce men of the mountains were before us and behind us, and they were throwing rocks down upon us from above. We had been caught in a trap. Then ten of us set spurs to our horses; and five of us forced our way through, but the other five fell before the spears of the mountain men. And now, O Roman Fathers! send help to our army at once, or every man will be slain, and our city will be taken."

"What shall we do?" said the white-haired Fathers. "Whom can we send but the guards and the boys? and who is wise enough to lead them, and thus save Rome?"

All shook their heads and were very grave; for it seemed as if there was no hope. Then one said, "Send for Cincinnatus. He will help us."

Cincinnatus was in the field plowing when the men who had been sent to him came in great haste. He stopped and greeted them kindly, and waited for them to speak.

"Put on your cloak, Cincinnatus," they said, "and hear the words of the Roman people."

Then Cincinnatus wondered what they could mean. "Is all well with Rome?" he asked; and he called to his wife to bring him his cloak.

She brought the cloak; and Cincinnatus wiped the dust from his hands and arms, and threw it over his shoulders. Then the men told their errand.

They told him how the army with all the noblest men of Rome had been en-trapped in the mountain pass. They told him about the great danger the city was in. Then they said, "The people of Rome make you their ruler and the ruler of their city, to do with everything as you choose; and the Fathers bid you come at once and go out against our enemies, the fierce men of the mountains."

So Cincinnatus left his plow standing where it was, and hurried to the city. When he passed through the streets, and gave orders as to what should be done, some of the people were afraid, for they knew that he had all power in Rome to do what he pleased. But he armed the guards and the boys, and went out at their head to fight the fierce mountain men, and free the Roman army from the trap into which it had fallen.

A few days afterward there was great joy in Rome. There was good news from Cincinnatus. The men of the mountains had been beaten with great loss. They had been driven back into their own place.

And now the Roman army, with the boys and the guards, was coming home with banners flying, and shouts of vic-to-ry; and at their head rode Cincinnatus. He had saved Rome.

Cincinnatus might then have made himself king; for his word was law, and no man dared lift a finger against him. But, before the people could thank him enough for what he had done, he gave back the power to the white-haired Roman Fathers, and went again to his little farm and his plow.

He had been the ruler of Rome for sixteen days.

Day 114

1. Read *Cornelia's Jewels*.
2. What were Cornelia's jewels? (Answers)

CORNELIA'S JEWELS

It was a bright morning in the old city of Rome many hundred years ago. In a vine-covered summer-house in a beautiful garden, two boys were standing. They were looking at their mother and her friend, who were walking among the flowers and trees.

"Did you ever see so handsome a lady as our mother's friend?" asked the younger boy, holding his tall brother's hand. "She looks like a queen."

"Yet she is not so beautiful as our mother," said the elder boy. "She has a fine dress, it is true; but her face is not noble and kind. It is our mother who is like a queen."

"That is true," said the other. "There is no woman in Rome so much like a queen as our own dear mother."

Soon Cor-ne-li-a, their mother, came down the walk to speak with them. She was simply dressed in a plain white robe. Her arms and feet were bare, as was the custom in those days; and no rings nor chains glit-tered about her hands and neck. For her only crown, long braids of soft brown hair were coiled about her head; and a tender smile lit up her noble face as she looked into her sons' proud eyes.

"Boys," she said, "I have something to tell you."

They bowed before her, as Roman lads were taught to do, and said, "What is it, mother?"

"You are to dine with us to-day, here in the garden; and then our friend is going to show us that wonderful casket of jewels of which you have heard so much."

The brothers looked shyly at their mother's friend. Was it possible that she had still other rings besides those on her fingers? Could she have other gems besides those which sparkled in the chains about her neck?

When the simple out-door meal was over, a servant brought the casket from the house. The lady opened it. Ah, how those jewels dazzled the eyes of the wondering boys! There were ropes of pearls, white as milk, and smooth as satin; heaps of shining rubies, red as the glowing coals; sap-phires as blue as the sky that summer day; and di-a-monds that flashed and sparkled like the sunlight.

The brothers looked long at the gems.

"Ah!" whis-pered the younger; "if our mother could only have such beautiful things!"

At last, how-ever, the casket was closed and carried care-ful-ly away.

"Is it true, Cor-ne-li-a, that you have no jewels?" asked her friend. "Is it true, as I have heard it whis-pered, that you are poor?"

"No, I am not poor," answered Cornelia, and as she spoke she drew her two boys to her side; "for here are my jewels. They are worth more than all your gems."

I am sure that the boys never forgot their mother's pride and love and care; and in after years, when they had become great men in Rome, they often thought of this scene in the garden. And the world still likes to hear the story of Cornelia's jewels.

Day 115

1. Read about the slave and the lion.
2. How did the slave help the lion? (Answers)
3. How did that save the slave's life? (Answers)

ANDROCLUS AND THE LION

In Rome there was once a poor slave whose name was An-dro-clus. His master was a cruel man, and so unkind to him that at last An-dro-clus ran away.

He hid himself in a wild wood for many days; but there was no food to be found, and he grew so weak and sick that he thought he should die. So one day he crept into a cave and lay down, and soon he was fast asleep.

After a while a great noise woke him up. A lion had come into the cave, and was roaring loudly. Androclus was very much afraid, for he felt sure that the beast would kill him. Soon, however, he saw that the lion was not angry, but that he limped as though his foot hurt him.

Then Androclus grew so bold that he took hold of the lion's lame paw to see what was the matter. The lion stood quite still, and rubbed his head against the man's shoulder. He seemed to say,—

"I know that you will help me."

Androclus lifted the paw from the ground, and saw that it was a long, sharp thorn which hurt the lion so much. He took the end of the thorn in his fingers; then he gave a strong, quick pull, and out it came. The lion was full of joy. He jumped about like a dog, and licked the hands and feet of his new friend.

Androclus was not at all afraid after this; and when night came, he and the lion lay down and slept side by side.

For a long time, the lion brought food to Androclus every day; and the two became such good friends, that Androclus found his new life a very happy one.

One day some soldiers who were passing through the wood found Androclus in the cave. They knew who he was, and so took him back to Rome.

It was the law at that time that every slave who ran away from his master should be made to fight a hungry lion. So a fierce lion was shut up for a while without food, and a time was set for the fight.

When the day came, thousands of people crowded to see the sport. They went to such places at that time very much as people now-a-days go to see a circus show or a game of base-ball.

The door opened, and poor Androclus was brought in. He was almost dead with fear, for the roars of the lion could al-read-y be heard. He looked up, and saw that there was no pity in the thou-sands of faces around him.

Then the hungry lion rushed in. With a single bound he reached the poor slave. Androclus gave a great cry, not of fear, but of gladness. It was his old friend, the lion of the cave.

The people, who had ex-pect-ed to see the man killed by the lion, were filled with wonder. They saw Androclus put his arms around the lion's neck; they saw the lion lie down at his feet, and lick them lov-ing-ly; they saw the great beast rub his head against the slave's face as though he wanted to be petted. They could not un-der-stand what it all meant.

After a while they asked Androclus to tell them about it. So he stood up before them, and, with his arm around the lion's neck, told how he and the beast had lived together in the cave.

"I am a man," he said; "but no man has ever befriended me. This poor lion alone has been kind to me; and we love each other as brothers."

The people were not so bad that they could be cruel to the poor slave now. "Live and be free!" they cried. "Live and be free!"

Others cried, "Let the lion go free too! Give both of them their liberty!"

And so Androclus was set free, and the lion was given to him for his own. And they lived together in Rome for many years.

Day 116

1. Read about *Horatius.*
2. How did he save the Roman city? (Answers)

HORATIUS AT THE BRIDGE

Once there was a war between the Roman people and the E-trus-cans who lived in the towns on the other side of the Ti-ber River. Por-se-na, the King of the E-trus-cans, raised a great army, and marched toward Rome. The city had never been in so great danger.

The Romans did not have very many fighting men at that time, and they knew that they were not strong enough to meet the Etruscans in open battle. So they kept themselves inside of their walls, and set guards to watch the roads.

One morning the army of Por-se-na was seen coming over the hills from the north. There were thousands of horsemen and footmen, and they were marching straight toward the wooden bridge which spanned the river at Rome.

"What shall we do?" said the white-haired Fathers who made the laws for the Roman people. "If they once gain the bridge, we cannot hinder them from crossing; and then what hope will there be for the town?"

Now, among the guards at the bridge, there was a brave man named Ho-ra-ti-us. He was on the farther side of the river, and when he saw that the Etruscans were so near, he called out to the Romans who were behind him.

"Hew down the bridge with all the speed that you can!" he cried. "I, with the two men who stand by me, will keep the foe at bay."

Then, with their shields before them, and their long spears in their hands, the three brave men stood in the road, and kept back the horsemen whom Porsena had sent to take the bridge.

On the bridge the Romans hewed away at the beams and posts. Their axes rang, the chips flew fast; and soon it trembled, and was ready to fall.

"Come back! come back, and save your lives!" they cried to Ho-ra-ti-us and the two who were with him.

But just then Porsena's horsemen dashed toward them again.

"Run for your lives!" said Horatius to his friends. "I will keep the road."

They turned, and ran back across the bridge. They had hardly reached the other side when there was a crashing of beams and timbers. The bridge toppled over to one side, and then fell with a great splash into the water.

When Horatius heard the sound, he knew that the city was safe. With his face still toward Porsena's men, he moved slowly back-ward till he stood on the river's bank. A dart thrown by one of Porsena's soldiers put out his left eye; but he did not falter. He cast his spear at the fore-most horseman, and then he turned quickly around. He saw the white porch of his own home among the trees on the other side of the stream;

"And he spake to the noble river that rolls by the walls of Rome: O Tiber! father Tiber! To whom the Romans pray, a Roman's life, a Roman's arms, take thou in charge to-day.'"

He leaped into the deep, swift stream. He still had his heavy armor on; and when he sank out of sight, no one thought that he would ever be seen again. But he was a strong man, and the best swimmer in Rome. The next minute he rose. He was half-way across the river, and safe from the spears and darts which Porsena's soldiers hurled after him.

Soon he reached the farther side, where his friends stood ready to help him. Shout after shout greeted him as he climbed upon the bank. Then Porsena's men shouted also, for they had never seen a man so brave and strong as Horatius. He had kept them out of Rome, but he had done a deed which they could not help but praise.

As for the Romans, they were very grateful to Horatius for having saved their city. They called him Horatius Co-cles, which meant the "one-eyed Horatius," because he had lost an eye in defending the bridge; they caused a fine statue of brass to be made in his honor; and they gave him as much land as he could plow around in a day. And for hundreds of years afterwards—

"With weeping and with laugh-ter, still was the story told, how well Horatius kept the bridge in the brave days of old."

Day 117

1. Read about Julius Caesar.
2. He was a ruler where?   (Answers)
3. Today review your words from the book, *The Adventures of Old Mr. Toad.* You can either go to Day 46 or to the Review Games page on the Easy Peasy website.

JULIUS CAESAR

Nearly two thousand years ago there lived in Rome a man whose name was Julius Cae-sar. He was the greatest of all the Romans.

Why was he so great?

He was a brave warrior, and had con-quered many countries for Rome. He was wise in planning and in doing. He knew how to make men both love and fear him.

At last he made himself the ruler of Rome. Some said that he wished to become its king. But the Romans at that time did not believe in kings.

Once when Cae-sar was passing through a little country village, all the men, women, and children of the place came out to see him. There were not more than fifty of them, all together, and they were led by their may-or, who told each one what to do.

These simple people stood by the roadside and watched Caesar pass. The may-or looked very proud and happy; for was he not the ruler of this village? He felt that he was almost as great a man as Caesar himself.

Some of the fine of-fi-cers who were with Caesar laughed. They said, "See how that fellow struts at the head of his little flock!"

"Laugh as you will," said Caesar, "he has reason to be proud. I would rather be the head man of a village than the second man in Rome!"

At an-oth-er time, Caesar was crossing a narrow sea in a boat. Before he was halfway to the farther shore, a storm overtook him. The wind blew hard; the waves dashed high; the lightning flashed; the thunder rolled.

It seemed every minute as though the boat would sink. The captain was in great fright. He had crossed the sea many times, but never in such a storm as this. He trembled with fear; he could not guide the boat; he fell down upon his knees; he moaned, "All is lost! all is lost!"

But Caesar was not afraid. He bade the man get up and take his oars again.

"Why should you be afraid?" he said. "The boat will not be lost; for you have Caesar on board."

Day 118

1. Read *The Sword of Damocles.*
2. Who are not as happy as they seem? (Answers)

THE SWORD OF DAMOCLES

There was once a king whose name was Di-o-nys-i-us. He was so unjust and cruel that he won for himself the name of tyrant. He knew that almost everybody hated him, and so he was always in dread lest some one should take his life.

But he was very rich, and he lived in a fine palace where there were many beautiful and costly things, and he was waited upon by a host of servants who were always ready to do his bidding. One day a friend of his, whose name was Dam-o-cles, said to him,—

"How happy you must be! You have here everything that any man could wish."

"Perhaps you would like to change places with me," said the tyrant.

"No, not that, O king!" said Dam-o-cles; "but I think, that, if I could only have your riches and your pleas-ures for one day, I should not want any greater hap-pi-ness."

"Very well," said the tyrant. "You shall have them."

And so, the next day, Damocles was led into the palace, and all the servants were bidden to treat him as their master. He sat down at a table in the banquet hall, and rich foods were placed before him. Nothing was wanting that could give him pleasure. There were costly wines, and beautiful flowers, and rare perfumes, and de-light-ful music. He rested himself among soft cushions, and felt that he was the happiest man in all the world.

Then he chanced to raise his eyes toward the ceiling. What was it that was dangling above him, with its point almost touching his head? It was a sharp sword, and it was hung by only a single horse-hair. What if the hair should break? There was danger every moment that it would do so.

The smile faded from the lips of Damocles. His face became ashy pale. His hands trembled. He wanted no more food; he could drink no more wine; he took no more delight in the music. He longed to be out of the palace, and away, he cared not where.

"What is the matter?" said the tyrant.

"That sword! that sword!" cried Damocles. He was so badly frightened that he dared not move.

"Yes," said Di-o-nys-i-us, "I know there is a sword above your head, and that it may fall at any moment. But why should that trouble you? I have a sword over my head all the time. I am every moment in dread lest something may cause me to lose my life."

"Let me go," said Damocles. "I now see that I was mis-tak-en, and that the rich and pow-er-ful are not so happy as they seem. Let me go back to my old home in the poor little cot-tage among the mountains."

And so long as he lived, he never again wanted to be rich, or to change places, even for a moment, with the king.

Day 119

1. Read about two friends.
2. Damon offered to be in prison instead of his friend and to even take his punishment of death if Pythias didn't come back from visiting his family.
3. What did the tyrant do when he saw how faithful and trusting the friends were? (Answers)

DAMON AND PYTHIAS

A young man whose name was Pyth-i-as had done something which the tyrant Dionysius did not like. For this offense he was dragged to prison, and a day was set when he should be put to death. His home was far away, and he wanted very much to see his father and mother and friends before he died.

"Only give me leave to go home and say good-by to those whom I love," he said, "and then I will come back and give up my life."

The tyrant laughed at him.

"How can I know that you will keep your promise?" he said. "You only want to cheat me, and save your-self."

Then a young man whose name was Da-mon spoke and said,—

"O king! put me in prison in place of my friend Pyth-i-as, and let him go to his own country to put his affairs in order, and to bid his friends fare-well. I know that he will come back as he promised, for he is a man who has never broken his word. But if he is not here on the day which you have set, then I will die in his stead."

The tyrant was sur-prised that anybody should make such an offer. He at last agreed to let Pythias go, and gave orders that the young man Da-mon should be shut up in prison.

Time passed, and by and by the day drew near which had been set for Pythias to die; and he had not come back. The tyrant ordered the jailer to keep close watch upon Damon, and not let him escape. But Damon did not try to escape. He still had faith in the truth and honor of his friend. He said, "If Pythias does not come back in time, it will not be his fault. It will be because he is hin-dered against his will."

At last the day came, and then the very hour. Damon was ready to die. His trust in his friend was as firm as ever; and he said that he did not grieve at having to suffer for one whom he loved so much.

Then the jailer came to lead him to his death; but at the same moment Pythias stood in the door. He had been de-layed by storms and ship-wreck, and he had feared that he was too late. He greeted Damon kindly, and then gave himself into the hands of the jailer. He was happy because he thought that he had come in time, even though it was at the last moment.

The tyrant was not so bad but that he could see good in others. He felt that men who loved and trusted each other, as did Damon and Pythias, ought not to suffer un-just-ly. And so he set them both free.

"I would give all my wealth to have one such friend," he said.

Day 120

1. Read *A Laconic Answer.* You read it, luh – con – ick.
2. What is a laconic answer? (Answers)
3. At dinner tell all the big people in your home what a laconic answer is and they will be impressed.

A LACONIC ANSWER

Many miles beyond Rome there was a famous country which we call Greece. The people of Greece were not u-nit-ed like the Romans; but instead there were sev-er-al states, each of which had its own rulers.

Some of the people in the southern part of the country were called Spar-tans, and they were noted for their simple habits and their brav-er-y. The name of their land was La-co-ni-a, and so they were sometimes called La-cons.

One of the strange rules which the Spartans had, was that they should speak briefly, and never use more words than were needed. And so a short answer is often spoken of as being *la-con-ic*; that is, as being such an answer as a Lacon would be likely to give.

There was in the northern part of Greece a land called Mac-e-don; and this land was at one time ruled over by a war-like king named Philip.

Philip of Mac-e-don wanted to become the master of all Greece. So he raised a great army, and made war upon the other states, until nearly all of them were forced to call him their king. Then he sent a letter to the Spartans in La-co-ni-a, and said, "If I go down into your country, I will level your great city to the ground."

In a few days, an answer was brought back to him. When he opened the letter, he found only one word written there.

That word was "IF."

It was as much as to say, "We are not afraid of you so long as the little word 'if' stands in your way."

Day 121

1. Read *The Ungrateful Guest.*
2. Who was the ungrateful guest? (Answers)
3. A base deed is a bad deed. He did something very wrong. If you are building something out of blocks, you start with a base. The base is the bottom, so a base deed is a low down, dirty deed. It's the lowest thing you could do.

THE UNGRATEFUL GUEST

Among the soldiers of King Philip there was a poor man who had done some brave deeds. He had pleased the king in more ways than one, and so the king put a good deal of trust in him.

One day this soldier was on board of a ship at sea when a great storm came up. The winds drove the ship upon the rocks, and it was wrecked. The soldier was cast half-drowned upon the shore; and he would have died there, had it not been for the kind care of a farmer who lived close by.

When the soldier was well enough to go home, he thanked the farmer for what he had done, and promised that he would repay him for his kindness.

But he did not mean to keep his promise. He did not tell King Philip about the man who had saved his life. He only said that there was a fine farm by the seashore, and that he would like very much to have it for his own. Would the king give it to him?

"Who owns the farm now?" asked Philip.

"Only a churlish farmer, who has never done anything for his country," said the soldier.

"Very well, then," said Philip. "You have served me for a long time, and you shall have your wish. Go and take the farm for yourself."

And so the soldier made haste to drive the farmer from his house and home. He took the farm for his own.

The poor farmer was stung to the heart by such treat-ment. He went boldly to the king, and told the whole story from beginning to end. King Philip was very angry when he learned that the man whom he had trusted had done so base a deed. He sent for the soldier in great haste; and when he had come, he caused these words to be burned in his forehead:—

"THE UNGRATEFUL GUEST."

Thus all the world was made to know of the mean act by which the soldier had tried to enrich himself; and from that day until he died all men shunned and hated him.

Day 122

1. Read about Alexander taming a horse.
2. Tell the story to someone.

3. Who spoke scornfully in the story? What does that mean? (Answers)
4. If you are able, review your vocabulary by using the Jimmy Skunk vocabulary link on the Review Games page on the Easy Peasy website. Otherwise, you can start at Day 62 and review the bold (dark) words in the assignments from that book.

ALEXANDER AND BUCEPHALUS

One day King Philip bought a fine horse called Bu-ceph-a-lus. He was a noble an-i-mal, and the king paid a very high price for him. But he was wild and savage, and no man could mount him, or do anything at all with him.

They tried to whip him, but that only made him worse. At last the king bade his servants take him away.

"It is a pity to ruin so fine a horse as that," said Al-ex-an-der, the king's young son. "Those men do not know how to treat him."

"Perhaps you can do better than they," said his father scorn-ful-ly.

"I know," said Al-ex-an-der, "that, if you would only give me leave to try, I could manage this horse better than any one else."

"And if you fail to do so, what then?" asked Philip.

"I will pay you the price of the horse," said the lad.

While everybody was laughing, Alexander ran up to Bu-ceph-a-lus, and turned his head toward the sun. He had noticed that the horse was afraid of his own shadow.

He then spoke gently to the horse, and patted him with his hand. When he had qui-et-ed him a little, he made a quick spring, and leaped upon the horse's back.

Everybody expected to see the boy killed outright. But he kept his place, and let the horse run as fast as he would. By and by, when Bucephalus had become tired, Alexander reined him in, and rode back to the place where his father was standing.

All the men who were there shouted when they saw that the boy had proved himself to be the master of the horse.

He leaped to the ground, and his father ran and kissed him.

"My son," said the king, "Macedon is too small a place for you. You must seek a larger kingdom that will be worthy of you."

After that, Alexander and Bucephalus were the best of friends. They were said to be always together, for when one of them was seen, the other was sure to be not far away. But the horse would never allow any one to mount him but his master.

Alexander became the most famous king and warrior that was ever known; and for that reason he is always called Alexander the Great. Bucephalus carried him through many countries and in many fierce battles, and more than once did he save his master's life.

Day 123

1. Read about Socrates. You read his name, sock – ruh – tees.

SOCRATES AND HIS HOUSE

There once lived in Greece a very wise man whose name was Soc-ra-tes. Young men from all parts of the land went to him to learn wisdom from him; and he said so many pleasant things, and said them in so delightful a way, that no one ever grew tired of listening to him.

One summer he built himself a house, but it was so small that his neighbors wondered how he could be content with it.

"What is the reason," said they, "that you, who are so great a man, should build such a little box as this for your dwelling house?"

"Indeed, there may be little reason," said he; "but, small as the place is, I shall think myself happy if I can fill even it with true friends."

Day 124

1. Read about Genghis Khan.
2. How did the hawk save his life? (Answers)

THE KING AND HIS HAWK

Gen-ghis Khan was a great king and war-rior.

He led his army into China and Persia, and he con-quered many lands. In every country, men told about his daring deeds; and they said that since Alexander the Great there had been no king like him.

One morning when he was home from the wars, he rode out into the woods to have a day's sport. Many of his friends were with him. They rode out gayly, carrying their bows and arrows. Behind them came the servants with the hounds.

It was a merry hunting party. The woods rang with their shouts and laughter. They expected to carry much game home in the evening.

On the king's wrist sat his favorite hawk; for in those days hawks were trained to hunt. At a word from their masters they would fly high up into the air, and look around for prey. If they chanced to see a deer or a rabbit, they would swoop down upon it swift as any arrow.

All day long Gen-ghis Khan and his huntsmen rode through the woods. But they did not find as much game as they expected.

Toward evening they started for home. The king had often ridden through the woods, and he knew all the paths. So while the rest of the party took the nearest way, he went by a longer road through a valley between two mountains.

The day had been warm, and the king was very thirsty. His pet hawk had left his wrist and flown away. It would be sure to find its way home.

The king rode slowly along. He had once seen a spring of clear water near this path-way. If he could only find it now! But the hot days of summer had dried up all the moun-tain brooks.

At last, to his joy, he saw some water tric-kling down over the edge of a rock. He knew that there was a spring farther up. In the wet season, a swift stream of water always poured down here; but now it came only one drop at a time.

The king leaped from his horse. He took a little silver cup from his hunting bag. He held it so as to catch the slowly falling drops.

It took a long time to fill the cup; and the king was so thirsty that he could hardly wait. At last it was nearly full. He put the cup to his lips, and was about to drink.

All at once there was a whir-ring sound in the air, and the cup was knocked from his hands. The water was all spilled upon the ground.

The king looked up to see who had done this thing. It was his pet hawk.

The hawk flew back and forth a few times, and then alighted among the rocks by the spring.

The king picked up the cup, and again held it to catch the tric-kling drops.

This time he did not wait so long. When the cup was half full, he lifted it toward his mouth. But before it had touched his lips, the hawk swooped down again, and knocked it from his hands.

And now the king began to grow angry. He tried again; and for the third time the hawk kept him from drinking.

The king was now very angry indeed.

"How do you dare to act so?" he cried. "If I had you in my hands, I would wring your neck!"

Then he filled the cup again. But before he tried to drink, he drew his sword.

"Now, Sir Hawk," he said, "this is the last time."

He had hardly spoken, before the hawk swooped down and knocked the cup from his hand. But the king was looking for this. With a quick sweep of the sword he struck the bird as it passed.

The next moment the poor hawk lay bleeding and dying at its master's feet.

"That is what you get for your pains," said Genghis Khan.

But when he looked for his cup, he found that it had fallen between two rocks, where he could not reach it.

"At any rate, I will have a drink from that spring," he said to himself.

With that he began to climb the steep bank to the place from which the water trickled. It was hard work, and the higher he climbed, the thirst-i-er he became.

At last he reached the place. There indeed was a pool of water; but what was that lying in the pool, and almost filling it? It was a huge, dead snake of the most poi-son-ous kind.

The king stopped. He forgot his thirst. He thought only of the poor dead bird lying on the ground below him.

"The hawk saved my life!" he cried; "and how did I repay him? He was my best friend, and I have killed him."

He clam-bered down the bank. He took the bird up gently, and laid it in his hunting bag. Then he mounted his horse and rode swiftly home. He said to himself,—

"I have learned a sad lesson to-day; and that is, never to do any-thing in anger."

Day 125

1. This is your reading assignment, but it's writing. Forgive me, okay? Did you know that the best way to become a better writer is to read good writing?
2. Write the fifty–first famous story. You could write anything, but a lot of these stories are about real life people from history. Is there anyone you learned about in history that you could tell a story about? You can type your story. It can be short, but tell the story. If you like your story a lot, you could send it to me, and I will post it for other kids to read.

Day 126

1. Read *Doctor Goldsmith.*
2. What was the "medicine?" (Answers)
3. It says that Doctor Goldsmith gave all his "ready money," all the money he had ready. What do you think that means? (Answers)
   - "I don't know" is not an answer. It's okay to be wrong, but it's not okay to not try.

DOCTOR GOLDSMITH

There was once a kind man whose name was Oliver Gold-smith. He wrote many de-light-ful books, some of which you will read when you are older.

He had a gentle heart. He was always ready to help others and to share with them anything that he had. He gave away so much to the poor that he was always poor himself.

He was some-times called Doctor Goldsmith; for he had studied to be a phy-si-cian.

One day a poor woman asked Doctor Goldsmith to go and see her husband, who was sick and could not eat.

Goldsmith did so. He found that the family was in great need. The man had not had work for a long time. He was not sick, but in distress; and, as for eating, there was no food in the house.

"Call at my room this evening," said Goldsmith to the woman, "and I will give you some med-i-cine for your husband."

In the evening the woman called. Goldsmith gave her a little paper box that was very heavy.

"Here is the med-i-cine," he said. "Use it faith-ful-ly, and I think it will do your husband a great deal of good. But don't open the box until you reach home."

"What are the di-rec-tions for taking it?" asked the woman.

"You will find them inside of the box," he answered.

When the woman reached her home, she sat down by her husband's side, and they opened the box; What do you think they found in it?

It was full of pieces of money. And on the top were the di-rec-tions:—

"TO BE TAKEN AS OFTEN AS NE-CES-SI-TY REQUIRES."

Goldsmith had given them all the ready money that he had.

Day 127

1. Read *The Kingdoms.* In this story it talks about the vegetable kingdom, mineral kingdom and the animal kingdom. Kingdom is a word that is used to describe the whole collection of each type of thing.
2. When the king says, "so be it," he means amen, please let it be so. What kingdom does the king want to belong to? (Answers)

3. If you are able, you could play a vocabulary review game on level 2 of the Review Games page on the Easy Peasy website, or you could go to Day 25 and review those words. Do you still remember what they mean?

THE KINGDOMS

There was once a king of Prussia whose name was Frederick William.

On a fine morning in June he went out alone to walk in the green woods. He was tired of the noise of the city, and he was glad to get away from it.

So, as he walked among the trees, he often stopped to listen to the singing birds, or to look at the wild flowers that grew on every side. Now and then he stooped to pluck a violet, or a primrose, or a yellow but-ter-cup. Soon his hands were full of pretty blossoms.

After a while he came to a little meadow in the midst of the wood. Some children were playing there. They were running here and there, and gathering the cow-slips that were blooming among the grass.

It made the king glad to see the happy children, and hear their merry voices. He stood still for some time, and watched them as they played.

Then he called them around him, and all sat down to-geth-er in the pleasant shade. The children did not know who the strange gentleman was; but they liked his kind face and gentle manners.

"Now, my little folks," said the king, "I want to ask you some ques-tions, and the child who gives the best answer shall have a prize."

Then he held up an orange so that all the children could see.

"You know that we all live in the king-dom of Prussia," he said; "but tell me, to what king-dom does this orange belong?"

The children were puz-zled. They looked at one another, and sat very still for a little while. Then a brave, bright boy spoke up and said,—

"It belongs to the veg-e-ta-ble kingdom, sir."

"Why so, my lad?" asked the king.

"It is the fruit of a plant, and all plants belong to that kingdom," said the boy.

The king was pleased. "You are quite right," he said; "and you shall have the orange for your prize."

He tossed it gayly to the boy. "Catch it if you can!" he said.

Then he took a yellow gold piece from his pocket, and held it up so that it glit-tered in the sunlight.

"Now to what kingdom does this belong?" he asked.

Another bright boy answered quick-ly, "To the min-er-al kingdom, sir! All metals belong to that kingdom."

"That is a good answer," said the king. "The gold piece is your prize."

The children were de-light-ed. With eager faces they waited to hear what the stranger would say next.

"I will ask you only one more question," said the king, "and it is an easy one." Then he stood up, and said, "Tell me, my little folks, to what kingdom do I belong?"

The bright boys were puz-zled now. Some thought of saying, "To the kingdom of Prussia." Some wanted to say, "To the animal kingdom." But they were a little afraid, and all kept still.

At last a tiny blue-eyed child looked up into the king's smiling face, and said in her simple way,—

"I think to the kingdom of heaven."

King Frederick William stooped down and lifted the little maiden in his arms. Tears were in his eyes as he kissed her, and said, "So be it, my child! So be it."

Day 128

1. Read *The Endless Tale.* A granary is a storage place for grain.
2. What was the endless tale?   (Answers)

THE ENDLESS TALE

In the Far East there was a great king who had no work to do. Every day, and all day long, he sat on soft cush-ions and lis-tened to stories. And no matter what the story was about, he never grew tired of hearing it, even though it was very long.

"There is only one fault that I find with your story," he often said: "it is too short."

All the story-tellers in the world were in-vit-ed to his palace; and some of them told tales that were very long indeed. But the king was always sad when a story was ended.

At last he sent word into every city and town and country place, offering a prize to any one who should tell him an endless tale. He said,—

"To the man that will tell me a story which shall last forever, I will give my fairest daugh-ter for his wife; and I will make him my heir, and he shall be king after me."

But this was not all. He added a very hard con-di-tion. "If any man shall try to tell such a story and then fail, he shall have his head cut off."

The king's daughter was very pretty, and there were many young men in that country who were willing to do anything to win her. But none of them wanted to lose their heads, and so only a few tried for the prize.

One young man invented a story that lasted three months; but at the end of that time, he could think of nothing more. His fate was a warning to others, and it was a long time before another story-teller was so rash as to try the king's patience.

But one day a stran-ger from the South came into the palace.

"Great king," he said, "is it true that you offer a prize to the man who can tell a story that has no end?"

"It is true," said the king.

"And shall this man have your fairest daughter for his wife, and shall he be your heir?"

"Yes, if he suc-ceeds," said the king. "But if he fails, he shall lose his head."

"Very well, then," said the stran-ger. "I have a pleasant story about locusts which I would like to relate."

"Tell it," said the king. "I will listen to you."

The story-teller began his tale.

"Once upon a time a certain king seized upon all the corn in his country, and stored it away in a strong gran-a-ry. But a swarm of locusts came over the land and saw where the grain had been put. After search-ing for many days they found on the east side of the gran-a-ry a crev-ice that was just large enough for one locust to pass through at a time. So one locust went in and carried away a grain of corn; then another locust went in and carried away a grain of corn; then another locust went in and carried away a grain of corn."

Day after day, week after week, the man kept on saying, "Then another locust went in and carried away a grain of corn."

A month passed; a year passed. At the end of two years, the king said,—

"How much longer will the locusts be going in and carrying away corn?"

"O king!" said the story-teller, "they have as yet cleared only one cubit; and there are many thousand cubits in the granary."

"Man, man!" cried the king, "you will drive me mad. I can listen to it no longer. Take my daughter; be my heir; rule my kingdom. But do not let me hear another word about those horrible locusts!"

And so the strange story-teller married the king's daughter. And he lived happily in the land for many years. But his father-in-law, the king, did not care to listen to any more stories.

Day 129

1. Read *The Blind Men and the Elephant.*
2. Why did the blind men argue? What had happened to make them think the elephant looked like so many different things? (Answers)

THE BLIND MEN AND THE ELEPHANT

There were once six blind men who stood by the road-side every day, and begged from the people who passed. They had often heard of el-e-phants, but they had never seen one; for, being blind, how could they?

It so happened one morning that an el-e-phant was driven down the road where they stood. When they were told that the great beast was before them, they asked the driver to let him stop so that they might see him.

Of course they could not see him with their eyes; but they thought that by touching him they could learn just what kind of animal he was.

The first one happened to put his hand on the elephant's side. "Well, well!" he said, "now I know all about this beast. He is ex-act-ly like a wall."

The second felt only of the elephant's tusk. "My brother," he said, "you are mistaken. He is not at all like a wall. He is round and smooth and sharp. He is more like a spear than anything else."

The third happened to take hold of the elephant's trunk. "Both of you are wrong," he said. "Anybody who knows anything can see that this elephant is like a snake."

The fourth reached out his arms, and grasped one of the elephant's legs. "Oh, how blind you are!" he said. "It is very plain to me that he is round and tall like a tree."

The fifth was a very tall man, and he chanced to take hold of the elephant's ear. "The blind-est man ought to know that this beast is not like any of the things that you name," he said. "He is ex-act-ly like a huge fan."

The sixth was very blind indeed, and it was some time before he could find the elephant at all. At last he seized the animal's tail. "O foolish fellows!" he cried. "You surely have lost your senses. This elephant is not like a wall, or a spear, or a snake, or a tree; neither is he like a fan. But any man with a par-ti-cle of sense can see that he is exactly like a rope."

Then the elephant moved on, and the six blind men sat by the roadside all day, and quar-reled about him. Each believed that he knew just how the animal looked; and each called the others hard names because they did not agree with him. People who have eyes sometimes act as foolishly.

Day 130

1. Read about the king and the gooseherd (someone who herds, or watches, geese-like a shepherd watches sheep).
2. What can't the king do? (Answers)
3. How many pieces of gold does the boy get? (Answers)

MAXIMILIAN AND THE GOOSE BOY

One summer day King Max-i-mil-ian of Ba-va-ri-a was walking in the country. The sun shone hot, and he stopped under a tree to rest.

It was very pleasant in the cool shade. The king lay down on the soft grass, and looked up at the white clouds sailing across the sky. Then he took a little book from his pocket and tried to read.

But the king could not keep his mind on his book. Soon his eyes closed, and he was fast asleep.

It was past noon when he awoke. He got up from his grassy bed, and looked around. Then he took his cane in his hand, and started for home.

When he had walked a mile or more, he happened to think of his book. He felt for it in his pocket. It was not there. He had left it under the tree.

The king was already quite tired, and he did not like to walk back so far. But he did not wish to lose the book. What should he do?

If there was only some one to send for it!

While he was thinking, he happened to see a little bare-foot-ed boy in the open field near the road. He was tending a large flock of geese that were picking the short grass, and wading in a shallow brook.

The king went toward the boy. He held a gold piece in his hand.

"My boy," he said, "how would you like to have this piece of money?"

"I would like it," said the boy; "but I never hope to have so much."

"You shall have it if you will run back to the oak tree at the second turning of the road, and fetch me the book that I left there."

The king thought that the boy would be pleased. But not so. He turned away, and said, "I am not so silly as you think."

"What do you mean?" said the king. "Who says that you are silly?"

"Well," said the boy, "you think that I am silly enough to believe that you will give me that gold piece for running a mile, and fetch-ing you a book. You can't catch me."

"But if I give it to you now, perhaps you will believe me," said the king; and he put the gold piece into the little fellow's hand.

The boy's eyes spar-kled; but he did not move.

"What is the matter now?" said the king. "Won't you go?"

The boy said, "I would like to go; but I can't leave the geese. They will stray away, and then I shall be blamed for it."

"Oh, I will tend them while you are away," said the king.

The boy laughed. "I should like to see you tending them!" he said. "Why, they would run away from you in a minute."

"Only let me try," said the king.

At last the boy gave the king his whip, and started off. He had gone but a little way, when he turned and came back.

"What is the matter now?" said Max-i-mil-ian.

"Crack the whip!"

The king tried to do as he was bidden, but he could not make a sound.

"I thought as much," said the boy. "You don't know how to do anything."

Then he took the whip, and gave the king lessons in whip cracking. "Now you see how it is done," he said, as he handed it back. "If the geese try to run away, crack it loud."

The king laughed. He did his best to learn his lesson; and soon the boy again started off on his errand.

Maximilian sat down on a stone, and laughed at the thought of being a goose-herd. But the geese missed their master at once. With a great cac-kling and hissing they went, half flying, half running, across the meadow.

The king ran after them, but he could not run fast. He tried to crack the whip, but it was of no use. The geese were soon far away. What was worse, they had gotten into a garden, and were feeding on the tender veg-e-ta-bles.

A few minutes after-ward, the goose boy came back with the book.

"Just as I thought," he said. "I have found the book, and you have lost the geese."

"Never mind," said the king, "I will help you get them again."

"Well, then, run around that way, and stand by the brook while I drive them out of the garden."

The king did as he was told. The boy ran forward with his whip, and after a great deal of shouting and scolding, the geese were driven back into the meadow.

"I hope you will pardon me for not being a better goose-herd," said Maximilian; "but, as I am a king, I am not used to such work."

"A king, indeed!" said the boy. "I was very silly to leave the geese with you. But I am not so silly as to believe that you are a king."

"Very well," said Maximilian, with a smile; "here is another gold piece, and now let us be friends."

The boy took the gold, and thanked the giver. He looked up into the king's face and said,—

"You are a very kind man, and I think you might be a good king; but if you were to try all your life, you would never be a good gooseherd."

Day 131

1. Read *The Inchcape Rock.*
2. What did the abbot do to protect ships from crashing into the Inchcape Rock? (Answers)
3. What mean thing did the robbers do? (Answers)
4. Who crashed into the rock? (Answers)

THE INCHCAPE ROCK

In the North Sea there is a great rock called the Inch-cape Rock. It is twelve miles from any land, and is covered most of the time with water.

Many boats and ships have been wrecked on that rock; for it is so near the top of the water that no vessel can sail over it without striking it.

More than a hundred years ago there lived not far away a kind-heart-ed man who was called the Abbot of Ab-er-broth-ock.

"It is a pity," he said, "that so many brave sailors should lose their lives on that hidden rock."

So the abbot caused a buoy to be fastened to the rock. The buoy floated back and forth in the shallow water. A strong chain kept it from floating away.

On the top of the buoy the abbot placed a bell; and when the waves dashed against it, the bell would ring out loud and clear.

Sailors, now, were no longer afraid to cross the sea at that place. When they heard the bell ringing, they knew just where the rock was, and they steered their vessels around it.

"God bless the good Abbot of Ab-er-broth-ock!" they all said.

One calm summer day, a ship with a black flag happened to sail not far from the Inch-cape Rock. The ship belonged to a sea robber called Ralph the Rover; and she was a terror to all honest people both on sea and shore.

There was but little wind that day, and the sea was as smooth as glass. The ship stood almost still; there was hardly a breath of air to fill her sails.

Ralph the Rover was walking on the deck. He looked out upon the glassy sea. He saw the buoy floating above the Inchcape Rock. It looked like a big black speck upon the water. But the bell was not ringing that day. There were no waves to set it in motion.

"Boys!" cried Ralph the Rover; "put out the boat, and row me to the Inchcape Rock. We will play a trick on the old abbot."

The boat was low-ered. Strong arms soon rowed it to the Inchcape Rock. Then the robber, with a heavy ax, broke the chain that held the buoy.

He cut the fas-ten-ings of the bell. It fell into the water. There was a gur-gling sound as it sank out of sight.

"The next one that comes this way will not bless the abbot," said Ralph the Rover.

Soon a breeze sprang up, and the black ship sailed away. The sea robber laughed as he looked back and saw that there was nothing to mark the place of the hidden rock.

For many days, Ralph the Rover scoured the seas, and many were the ships that he plun-dered. At last he chanced to sail back toward the place from which he had started.

The wind had blown hard all day. The waves rolled high. The ship was moving swiftly. But in the evening the wind died away, and a thick fog came on.

Ralph the Rover walked the deck. He could not see where the ship was going. "If the fog would only clear away!" he said.

"I thought I heard the roar of breakers," said the pilot. "We must be near the shore."

"I cannot tell," said Ralph the Rover; "but I think we are not far from the Inchcape Rock. I wish we could hear the good abbot's bell."

The next moment there was a great crash. "It is the Inchcape Rock!" the sailors cried, as the ship gave a lurch to one side, and began to sink.

"Oh, what a wretch am I!" cried Ralph the Rover. "This is what comes of the joke that I played on the good abbot!"

What was it that he heard as the waves rushed over him? Was it the abbot's bell, ringing for him far down at the bottom of the sea?

Day 132

1. Read the first three little chapters.
2. A **venture** is what they called the goods people bought and sent on a ship to be sold wherever it went. You could earn money, or it might get lost at sea. It was a risk, a kind of ad**venture**.
3. How much did he buy the cat for? (Answers)
4. What was the boy's venture? (Answers)

WHITTINGTON AND HIS CAT

I. THE CITY

There was once a little boy whose name was Richard Whit-ting-ton; but everybody called him Dick. His father and mother had died when he was only a babe, and the people who had the care of him were very poor. Dick was not old enough to work, and so he had a hard time of it indeed. Sometimes he had no break-fast, and sometimes he had no dinner; and he was glad at any time to get a crust of bread or a drop of milk.

Now, in the town where Dick lived, the people liked to talk about London. None of them had ever been to the great city, but they seemed to know all about the wonderful things which were to be seen there. They said that all the folks who lived in London were fine gen-tle-men and ladies; that there was singing and music there all day long; that nobody was ever hungry there, and nobody had to work; and that the streets were all paved with gold.

Dick listened to these stories, and wished that he could go to London.

One day a big wagon drawn by eight horses, all with bells on their heads, drove into the little town. Dick saw the wagon standing by the inn, and he thought that it must be going to the fine city of London.

When the driver came out and was ready to start, the lad ran up and asked him if he might walk by the side of the wagon. The driver asked him some questions; and when he learned how poor Dick was, and that he had neither father nor mother, he told him that he might do as he liked.

It was a long walk for the little lad; but by and by he came to the city of London. He was in such a hurry to see the wonderful sights, that he forgot to thank the driver of the wagon. He ran as fast as he could, from one street to another, trying to find those that were paved with gold. He had once seen a piece of money that was gold, and he knew that it would buy a great, great many things; and now he thought that if he could get only a little bit of the pave-ment, he would have everything that he wanted.

Poor Dick ran till he was so tired that he could run no farther. It was growing dark, and in every street there was only dirt instead of gold. He sat down in a dark corner, and cried himself to sleep.

When he woke up the next morning, he was very hungry; but there was not even a crust of bread for him to eat. He forgot all about the golden pavements, and thought only of food. He walked about from one street to another, and at last grew so hungry that he began to ask those whom he met to give him a penny to buy something to eat.

"Go to work, you idle fellow," said some of them; and the rest passed him by without even looking at him.

"I wish I could go to work!" said Dick.

II. THE KITCHEN

By and by Dick grew so faint and tired that he could go no farther. He sat down by the door of a fine house, and wished that he was back again in the little town where he was born. The cook-maid, who was just getting dinner, saw him, and called out,—

"What are you doing there, you little beggar? If you don't get away quick, I'll throw a panful of hot dish-water over you. Then I guess you will jump."

Just at that time the master of the house, whose name was Mr. Fitz-war-ren, came home to dinner. When he saw the ragged little fellow at his door, he said,—

"My lad, what are you doing here? I am afraid you are a lazy fellow, and that you want to live without work."

"No, indeed!" said Dick. "I would like to work, if I could find anything to do. But I do not know anybody in this town, and I have not had anything to eat for a long time."

"Poor little fellow!" said Mr. Fitz-war-ren. "Come in, and I will see what I can do for you." And he ordered the cook to give the lad a good dinner, and then to find some light work for him to do.

Little Dick would have been very happy in the new home which he had thus found, if it had not been for the cross cook. She would often say,—

"You are my boy now, and so you must do as I tell you. Look sharp there! Make the fires, carry out the ashes, wash these dishes, sweep the floor, bring in the wood! Oh, what a lazy fellow you are!" And then she would box his ears, or beat him with the broom-stick.

At last, little Alice, his master's daughter, saw how he was treated, and she told the cook she would be turned off if she was not kinder to the lad. After that, Dick had an eas-i-er time of it; but his troubles were not over yet, by any means.

His bed was in a garret at the top of the house, far away from the rooms where the other people slept. There were many holes in the floor and walls, and every night a great number of rats and mice came in. They tor-ment-ed Dick so much, that he did not know what to do.

One day a gentleman gave him a penny for cleaning his shoes, and he made up his mind that he would buy a cat with it. The very next morning he met a girl who was car-ry-ing a cat in her arms.

"I will give you a penny for that cat," he said.

"All right," the girl said. "You may have her, and you will find that she is a good mouser too."

Dick hid his cat in the garret, and every day he carried a part of his dinner to her. It was not long before she had driven all the rats and mice away; and then Dick could sleep soundly every night.

III. THE VENTURE

Some time after that, a ship that belonged to Mr. Fitzwarren was about to start on a voyage across the sea. It was loaded with goods which were to be sold in lands far away. Mr. Fitzwarren wanted to give his servants a chance for good fortune too, and so he called all of them into the parlor, and asked if they had anything they would like to send out in the ship for trade.

Every one had something to send,—every one but Dick; and as he had neither money nor goods, he staid in the kitchen, and did not come in with the rest. Little Alice guessed why he did not come, and so she said to her papa,—

"Poor Dick ought to have a chance too. Here is some money out of my own purse that you may put in for him."

"No, no, my child!" said Mr. Fitzwarren. "He must risk something of his own." And then he called very loud, "Here, Dick! What are you going to send out on the ship?"

Dick heard him, and came into the room.

"I have nothing in the world," he said, "but a cat which I bought some time ago for a penny."

"Fetch your cat, then, my lad," said Mr. Fitzwarren, "and let her go out. Who knows but that she will bring you some profit?"

Dick, with tears in his eyes, carried poor puss down to the ship, and gave her to the captain. Everybody laughed at his queer venture; but little Alice felt sorry for him,

After that, the cook was worse than before. She made fun of him for sending his cat to sea. "Do you think," she would say, "that puss will sell for enough money to buy a stick to beat you?"

At last Dick could not stand her abuse any longer, and he made up his mind to go back to his old home in the little country town. So, very early in the morning on All-hal-lows Day, he started. He walked as far as the place called Hol-lo-way, and there he sat down on a stone, which to this day is called "Whit-ting-ton's Stone."

As he sat there very sad, and wondering which way he should go, he heard the bells on Bow Church, far away, ringing out a merry chime. He listened. They seemed to say to him,—

"Turn again, Whittington, Thrice Lord Mayor of London."

"Well, well!" he said to himself. "I would put up with almost anything, to be Lord Mayor of London when I am a man, and to ride in a fine coach! I think I will go back and let the old cook cuff and scold as much as she pleases."

Dick did go back, and he was lucky enough to get into the kitchen, and set about his work, before the cook came down-stairs to get break-fast.

Day 133

1. Finish reading the story.
2. Who bought the cat? (Answers)

IV. THE CAT

Mr. Fitzwarren's ship made a long voyage, and at last reached a strange land on the other side of the sea. The people had never seen any white men before, and they came in great crowds to buy the fine things with which the ship was loaded. The captain wanted very much to trade with the king of the country; and it was not long before the king sent word for him to come to the palace and see him.

The captain did so. He was shown into a beautiful room, and given a seat on a rich carpet all flow-ered with silver and gold. The king and queen were seated not far away; and soon a number of dishes were brought in for dinner.

They had hardly begun to eat when an army of rats and mice rushed in, and de-voured all the meat before any one could hinder them. The captain wondered at this, and asked if it was not very un-pleas-ant to have so many rats and mice about.

"Oh, yes!" was the answer. "It is indeed un-pleas-ant; and the king would give half his treas-ure if he could get rid of them."

The captain jumped for joy. He remembered the cat which little Whittington had sent out; and he told the king that he had a little creature on board his ship which would make short work of the pests.

Then it was the king's turn to jump for joy; and he jumped so high, that his yellow cap, or turban, dropped off his head.

"Bring the creature to me," he said. "If she will do what you say, I will load your ship with gold."

The captain made believe that he would be very sorry to part with the cat; but at last he went down to the ship to get her, while the king and queen made haste to have another dinner made ready.

The captain, with puss under his arm, reached the palace just in time to see the table crowded with rats. The cat leaped out upon them, and oh! what havoc she did make among the trou-ble-some creatures! Most of them were soon stretched dead upon the floor, while the rest scam-pered away to their holes, and did not dare to come out again.

The king had never been so glad in his life; and the queen asked that the creature which had done such wonders should be brought to her. The captain called, "Pussy, pussy, pussy!" and the cat came up and rubbed against his legs. He picked her up, and offered her to the queen; but at first the queen was afraid to touch her.

However, the captain stroked the cat, and called, "Pussy, pussy, pussy!" and then the queen ventured to touch her. She could only say, "Putty, putty, putty!" for she had not learned to talk English. The captain then put the cat down on the queen's lap, where she purred and purred until she went to sleep.

The king would not have missed getting the cat now for the world. He at once made a bargain with the captain for all the goods on board the ship; and then he gave him ten times as much for the cat as all the rest came to.

The captain was very glad. He bade the king and queen good-by, and the very next day set sail for England.

V. THE FORTUNE

One morning Mr. Fitzwarren was sitting at his desk in his office. He heard some one tap softly at his door, and he said,—

"Who's there?"

"A friend," was the answer. "I have come to bring you news of your ship 'U-ni-corn.'"

Mr. Fitzwarren jumped up quickly, and opened the door. Whom should he see waiting there but the captain, with a bill of lading in one hand and a box of jewels in the other? He was so full of joy that he lifted up his eyes, and thanked Heaven for sending him such good fortune.

The captain soon told the story of the cat; and then he showed the rich present which the king and queen had sent to poor Dick in payment for her. As soon as the good gentleman heard this, he called out to his servants,—

"Go send him in, and tell him of his fame; Pray call him Mr. Whittington by name."

Some of the men who stood by said that so great a present ought not to be given to a mere boy; but Mr. Fitzwarren frowned upon them.

"It is his own," he said, "and I will not hold back one penny from him."

Dick was scouring the pots when word was brought to him that he should go to the office.

"Oh, I am so dirty!" he said, "and my shoes are full of hob-nails." But he was told to make haste.

Mr. Fitzwarren ordered a chair to be set for him, and then the lad began to think that they were making fun of him.

"I beg that you won't play tricks with a poor boy like me," he said. "Please let me go back to my work."

"Mr. Whittington," said Mr. Fitzwarren, "this is no joke at all. The captain has sold your cat, and has brought you, in return for her, more riches than I have in the whole world."

Then he opened the box of jewels, and showed Dick his treasures.

The poor boy did not know what to do. He begged his master to take a part of it; but Mr. Fitzwarren said, "No, it is all your own; and I feel sure that you will make good use of it."

Dick then offered some of his jewels to his mistress and little Alice. They thanked him, and told him that they felt great joy at his good luck, but wished him to keep his riches for himself.

Day 134

1. Read *Antonio Canova.*
2. What did he make the sculpture out of? (Answers)

ANTONIO CANOVA

A good many years ago there lived in Italy a little boy whose name was An-to-ni-o Ca-no-va. He lived with his grand-fa-ther, for his own father was dead. His grand-fa-ther was a stone-cut-ter, and he was very poor.

An-to-ni-o was a puny lad, and not strong enough to work. He did not care to play with the other boys of the town. But he liked to go with his grandfather to the stone-yard. While the old man was busy, cutting and trimming the great blocks of stone, the lad would play among the chips. Sometimes he would make a little statue of soft clay; sometimes he would take hammer and chisel, and try to cut a statue from a piece of rock. He showed so much skill that his grandfather was de-light-ed.

"The boy will be a sculp-tor some day," he said.

Then when they went home in the evening, the grand-moth-er would say, "What have you been doing to-day, my little sculp-tor?"

And she would take him upon her lap and sing to him, or tell him stories that filled his mind with pictures of wonderful and beautiful things. And the next day, when he went back to the stone-yard, he would try to make some of those pictures in stone or clay.

There lived in the same town a rich man who was called the Count. Sometimes the Count would have a grand dinner, and his rich friends from other towns would come to visit him. Then Antonio's grandfather would go up to the Count's house to help with the work in the kitchen; for he was a fine cook as well as a good stone-cut-ter.

It happened one day that Antonio went with his grandfather to the Count's great house. Some people from the city were coming, and there was to be a grand feast. The boy could not cook, and he was not old enough to wait on the table; but he could wash the pans and kettles, and as he was smart and quick, he could help in many other ways.

All went well until it was time to spread the table for dinner. Then there was a crash in the dining room, and a man rushed into the kitchen with some pieces of marble in his hands. He was pale, and trembling with fright.

"What shall I do? What shall I do?" he cried. "I have broken the statue that was to stand at the center of the table. I cannot make the table look pretty without the statue. What will the Count say?"

And now all the other servants were in trouble. Was the dinner to be a failure after all? For everything de-pend-ed on having the table nicely arranged. The Count would be very angry.

"Ah, what shall we do?" they all asked.

Then little Antonio Ca-no-va left his pans and kettles, and went up to the man who had caused the trouble.

"If you had another statue, could you arrange the table?" he asked.

"Cer-tain-ly," said the man; "that is, if the statue were of the right length and height."

"Will you let me try to make one?" asked Anto-nio "Perhaps I can make something that will do."

The man laughed.

"Non-sense!" he cried. "Who are you, that you talk of making statues on an hour's notice?"

"I am Antonio Canova," said the lad.

"Let the boy try what he can do," said the servants, who knew him.

And so, since nothing else could be done, the man allowed him to try.

On the kitchen table there was a large square lump of yellow butter. Two hundred pounds the lump weighed, and it had just come in, fresh and clean, from the dairy on the mountain. With a kitchen knife in his hand, Antonio began to cut and carve this butter. In a few minutes he had molded it into the shape of a crouching lion; and all the servants crowded around to see it.

"How beautiful!" they cried. "It is a great deal pret-ti-er than the statue that was broken."

When it was finished, the man carried it to its place.

"The table will be hand-som-er by half than I ever hoped to make it," he said.

When the Count and his friends came in to dinner, the first thing they saw was the yellow lion.

"What a beautiful work of art!" they cried. "None but a very great artist could ever carve such a figure; and how odd that he should choose to make it of butter!" And then they asked the Count to tell them the name of the artist.

"Truly, my friends," he said, "this is as much of a surprise to me as to you." And then he called to his head servant, and asked him where he had found so wonderful a statue.

"It was carved only an hour ago by a little boy in the kitchen," said the servant.

This made the Count's friends wonder still more; and the Count bade the servant call the boy into the room.

"My lad," he said, "you have done a piece of work of which the greatest artists would be proud. What is your name, and who is your teacher?"

"My name is Antonio Canova," said the boy, "and I have had no teacher but my grandfather the stonecutter."

By this time all the guests had crowded around Antonio. There were famous artists among them, and they knew that the lad was a genius. They could not say enough in praise of his work; and when at last they sat down at the table, nothing would please them but that Antonio should have a seat with them; and the dinner was made a feast in his honor.

The very next day the Count sent for Antonio to come and live with him. The best artists in the land were em-ployed to teach him the art in which he had shown so much skill; but now, instead of carving butter, he chis-eled marble. In a few years, Antonio Canova became known as one of the greatest sculptors in the world.

Day 135

1. Read *Picciola.*
2. Who decided that Charney should be set free? (Answers)

PICCIOLA

Many years ago there was a poor gentleman shut up in one of the great prisons of France. His name was Char-ney, and he was very sad and un-hap-py. He had been put into prison wrong-ful-ly, and it seemed to him as though there was no one in the world who cared for him.

He could not read, for there were no books in the prison. He was not allowed to have pens or paper, and so he could not write. The time dragged slowly by. There was nothing that he could do to make the days seem shorter. His only pastime was walking back and forth in the paved prison yard. There was no work to be done, no one to talk with.

One fine morning in spring, Char-ney was taking his walk in the yard. He was counting the paving stones, as he had done a thousand times before. All at once he stopped. What had made that little mound of earth between two of the stones?

He stooped down to see. A seed of some kind had fallen between the stones. It had sprouted; and now a tiny green leaf was pushing its way up out of the ground. Charney was about to crush it with his foot, when he saw that there was a kind of soft coating over the leaf.

"Ah!" said he. "This coating is to keep it safe. I must not harm it." And he went on with his walk.

The next day he almost stepped upon the plant before he thought of it. He stooped to look at it. There were two leaves now, and the plant was much stronger and greener than it was the day before. He staid by it a long time, looking at all its parts.

Every morning after that, Charney went at once to his little plant. He wanted to see if it had been chilled by the cold, or scorched by the sun. He wanted to see how much it had grown.

One day as he was looking from his window, he saw the jailer go across the yard. The man brushed so close to the little plant, that it seemed as though he would crush it. Charney trembled from head to foot.

"O my Pic-cio-la!" he cried.

When the jailer came to bring his food, he begged the grim fellow to spare his little plant. He expected that the man would laugh at him; but al-though a jailer, he had a kind heart.

"Do you think that I would hurt your little plant?" he said. "No, indeed! It would have been dead long ago, if I had not seen that you thought so much of it."

"That is very good of you, indeed," said Char-ney. He felt half ashamed at having thought the jailer unkind.

Every day he watched Pic-cio-la, as he had named the plant. Every day it grew larger and more beautiful. But once it was almost broken by the huge feet of the jailer's dog. Charney's heart sank within him.

"Picciola must have a house," he said. "I will see if I can make one."

So, though the nights were chilly, he took, day by day, some part of the firewood that was allowed him, and with this he built a little house around the plant.

The plant had a thousand pretty ways which he noticed. He saw how it always bent a little toward the sun; he saw how the flowers folded their petals before a storm.

He had never thought of such things before, and yet he had often seen whole gardens of flowers in bloom.

One day, with soot and water he made some ink; he spread out his hand-ker-chief for paper; he used a sharp-ened stick for a pen—and all for what? He felt that he must write down the doings of his little pet. He spent all his time with the plant.

"See my lord and my lady!" the jailer would say when he saw them.

As the summer passed by, Picciola grew more lovely every day. There were no fewer than thirty blossoms on its stem.

But one sad morning it began to droop. Charney did not know what to do. He gave it water, but still it drooped. The leaves were with-er-ing. The stones of the prison yard would not let the plant live.

Charney knew that there was but one way to save his treasure. Alas! how could he hope that it might be done? The stones must be taken up at once.

But this was a thing which the jailer dared not do. The rules of the prison were strict, and no stone must be moved. Only the highest officers in the land could have such a thing done.

Poor Charney could not sleep. Picciola must die. Already the flowers had with-ered; the leaves would soon fall from the stem.

Then a new thought came to Charney. He would ask the great Napoleon, the em-per-or himself, to save his plant.

It was a hard thing for Charney to do,—to ask a favor of the man whom he hated, the man who had shut him up in this very prison. But for the sake of Picciola he would do it.

He wrote his little story on his hand-ker-chief. Then he gave it into the care of a young girl, who promised to carry it to Napoleon. Ah! if the poor plant would only live a few days longer!

What a long journey that was for the young girl! What a long, dreary waiting it was for Charney and Picciola!

But at last news came to the prison. The stones were to be taken up. Picciola was saved!

The em-per-or's kind wife had heard the story of Charney's care for the plant. She saw the handkerchief on which he had written of its pretty ways.

"Surely," she said, "it can do us no good to keep such a man in prison."

And so, at last, Charney was set free. Of course he was no longer sad and un-lov-ing. He saw how God had cared for him and the little plant, and how kind and true are the hearts of even rough men. And he cher-ished Picciola as a dear, loved friend whom he could never forget.

Day 136

1. You are going to start reading a new book, *The Bobbsey Twins at Snow Lodge.* You've been reading lots of short stories. Let's read a whole, big book together. Today read the first part of chapter 1.
2. Bobbsey is the last name of the twins' family. What are the names of the twins? (Answers)
3. Who are older and who are younger? (Answers)
4. Who is Snap? (Answers)

Chapter 1 The Runaways (first half)

"Will Snap pull us, do you think, Freddie?" asked little Flossie Bobbsey, as she anxiously looked at her small brother, who was fastening a big, shaggy dog to his sled by means of a home-made harness. "Do you think he'll give us a good ride?"

"Sure he will, Flossie," answered Freddie with an air of wisdom. "I explained it all to him, and I've tried him a little bit. He pulled fine, and you won't be much heavier. I'll have the harness all fixed in a minute, and then we'll have a grand ride."

"Do you think Snap will be strong enough to pull both of us?" asked the little girl.

"Of course he will!" exclaimed Freddie firmly. "He's as good as an Esquimo dog, and we saw some pictures of them pulling sleds bigger than ours."

"That's so," admitted Flossie. "Well, hurry up, please, Freddie 'cause I'm cold standing here, and I want to get under the blankets on the sled and have a nice ride."

"I'll hurry all right, Flossie. You go up there by Snap's head and pat him. Then he'll stand stiller, and I can fix the harness on him quicker."

Flossie, with a shake of her light curls, and a stamp of her little feet to rid them of the snow from the drift in which she had been standing, went closer to the fine-looking and intelligent dog, who did not seem to mind being all tied up with ropes and leather straps to Freddie's sled.

"Good old Snap!" exclaimed Flossie, patting his head. "You're going to give Freddie and me a fine ride; aren't you, old fellow?"

Snap barked and wagged his tail violently.

"Hey! Stop that!" cried Freddie. "He's flopping his tail right in my face!" the little boy added. "I can't see to fasten this strap. Hold his tail, Flossie."

Snap, hearing the voice of his young master--one of his two masters by the way--wagged his tail harder than ever. Freddie made a grab for it, but missed. Flossie, seeing this, laughed and Snap, thinking it was a great joke, leaped about and barked with delight. He sprang out of the harness, which was only partly fastened on, and began leaping about in the snow. Finally he stood up on his hind legs and marched about, for Snap was a trick dog, and had once belonged to a circus.

"There now! Look at that!" cried Freddie. "He's spoiled everything! We'll never get him hitched up now."

"It--it wasn't my fault," said Flossie, a tear or two coming into her eyes.

"I know it wasn't, Flossie," replied Freddie, speaking more quietly. "It's always just that way with Snap when he gets excited. Come here!" he called to the dog, "and let me harness you. Come here Snap!"

The dog was well enough trained so that he knew when the time for fun was over and when he had to settle down. Still wagging his tail joyously, however, Snap came up to Freddie, who started over again the work of harnessing the animal to the sled.

"I guess you'd better stand at his tail instead of at his head," said Freddie. "So when he wags it you can grab it, Flossie, and hold it still. Then it won't slap me in the face, and I can see what I'm doing. Hold his tail, Flossie."

"Then he can't wag it," objected the little girl.

"I know he can't. I don't want him to."

"But it may make him angry."

"Snap never gets mad; do you, Snap?" asked Freddie, and the dog's bark seemed to say "No, never!"

So Flossie held the dog's tail, while Freddie put on the harness again. This time he succeeded in getting it all arranged to suit him, and the frisky Snap was soon made fast to the sled.

"Now get on, Flossie," called her brother, "and we'll see how fast Snap can pull us."

"But don't make him go too fast, Freddie," begged the little girl. "For it's hard pulling in the snow."

"No, I'll let him go slow," promised Freddie. "But it won't be hard work pulling us. My sled goes awfully easy, anyhow."

Freddie tucked Flossie in amid the robes and rugs which the children had taken from the house, near which they had started to harness the dog. Then Freddie took his place in front of his sister, holding to two reins that were fastened to the dog's head. Freddie had made no bit, such as is used for horses and goats, but he thought by making straps fast to a sort of muzzle by which he could guide Snap, by pulling his head to one side or the other.

"All ready, Flossie?" called Freddie, when he himself was comfortable on the sled.

"All ready," she answered.

"Giddap, Snap!" cried Freddie, and, with a bark, off the dog started, pulling the sled and the two children after him.

"Oh, he's going! He's giving us a ride! It's as real as anything!" cried Flossie in delight, holding fast to the sled. "Oh, Freddie!"

"Of course it's real!" said Freddie. "Bert and Nan said Snap wouldn't pull us, but I knew he would. I just wish they could see us now."

As if in answer to this wish a little later, when the two smaller twins had turned a corner, they saw coming toward them their brother and sister Nan and Bert, also twins, but four years older.

"Look, look!" cried Flossie to Nan. "See what a nice ride we're having."

"Oh, look, Bert!" exclaimed Nan, "Snap really is pulling them," and she grasped her brother's arm. Bert was pulling his own sled and that of his twin sister.

"Yes, he'll pull them a little way," admitted Bert, as if he knew all about it, "and then, the first thing they know, Snap will turn around short and tip them into a snowdrift. He hasn't been trained to pull a sled, no matter how many other tricks he can do."

"I trained him myself!" declared Freddie, as he pulled on the lines to bring the dog to a stop. But Snap, seeing Nan and Bert, was eager to reach them to be patted and made much of, so he did not obey the command given by the reins, but kept on.

"Whoa there!" cried Freddie, holding back with all his little strength.

"See, I told you he wouldn't mind," said Bert, with a laugh.

"Oh, but isn't it cute!" exclaimed Nan, flapping her hands. "I didn't think they'd get any ride at all."

"We'll show you! We'll have a fine ride!" panted Freddie, vainly trying to make Snap halt.

Then just what Bert said would happen seemed about to take place. The dog leaped around, and turned short to get nearer to the older Bobbsey twins.

"Look out!" cried Bert, but his warning came too late.

Over went the sled, and Flossie and Freddie were pitched from it into a big, fluffy bank of snow, falling into it deeply, but with no more harm to them than if they had landed on a bed of feathers.

"Oh dear!" cried Flossie, as she felt herself shooting toward the snow.

Day 137

1. Remember what had just happened at the end of your reading from Day 136?
2. Finish the chapter.
3. Who are "The Runaways?" (Answers)
4. Who is Danny Rugg? What is he like? (Answers)
5. Who is in danger at the end of the chapter? (Answers)
6. What do you think will happen? (Answers)

Chapter 1 (second half)

"Whoa there! Whoa! Don't you run away, Snap!" shouted Freddie. Then his mouth was filled with snow and he could say nothing more.

"Oh, Bert! They'll be smothered!" cried Nan. "Help me get them out!"

Bert was laughing, and trying to defend himself against the jumping up of Snap, who seemed to want to hug the boy with his paws.

"Stop laughing! Help me!" ordered Nan, who was already trying to lift Flossie from her snowy bed.

"I can't help laughing--Freddie looked so funny when he went over," said Bert.

"There's no danger of smothering, though. That snow is as dry as sand. Here you go, Freddie. Give me your hand and I'll pull you out."

In a few seconds the smaller Bobbsey twins stood beside their larger brother and sister, while Snap capered about them, barking loudly and wagging his tail.

"Oh, he's got loose, and the harness is all broken," said Freddie, and tears of disappointment stood in his blue eyes.

"Never mind," said Bert. "I'll help you make a better harness to- morrow, Freddie. That one wasn't strong enough for Snap, anyhow. I'll fix it differently."

"Oh, but we were going to have such a fine ride!" said Flossie, who was also ready to cry. The smaller twins were only about five years old, so it might have been expected.

"Well, come on and go coasting with Bert and me," said Nan, as she patted her little sister's head. "We're going over on the long hill. It's fine there, and you'll have just as much fun as if you had Snap to pull you."

"Shall we go, Freddie?" asked Flossie, who generally depended on him to start their amusements.

"I guess so," he answered. "This harness is all busted, anyhow."

Sadly he looked at the tangled strings and straps fast to the sled, where Snap had broken away from them. The harness Freddie had made with such care was all broken now.

"Never mind," said Bert again. "I'll make you a better one to-morrow, Freddie. Come along now, and we'll have some fun. And when we get through coasting I'll buy everybody a hot chocolate soda."

"Really?" asked Flossie, her sorrow forgotten now.

"Sure thing," promised Bert.

"Come on, then, Freddie," said his little sister. "We can harness Snap up to-morrow."

The useless harness was taken to the Bobbsey home, not far away, and then the four twins--the two sets of them, as it were--started for the coasting hill, Flossie and Freddie having one sled between them, and Nan and Bert each having one of their own.

On the way to the hill they met many of their friends, also bound for the same place. School was just out and the boys and girls were eager to have a good time in the snow.

"There's Charley Mason!" exclaimed Bert, seeing a boy he knew. "Hello, Charley!" he called. "Going coasting?"

"Sure. Where's the big bob?" For some time before this Bert and Charley had made, in partnership, a large bob sled.

"Oh, I didn't know you'd be out, or I'd have brought it," replied Bert. "Anyhow, I promised Nan I'd coast with her."

"Oh, that's all right. I guess the hill will be too crowded for a bob, anyhow. Danny Rugg was taking his over, though, for I saw him and some of his crowd hauling it from his barn a little while ago."

"Well, let 'em. We can get ours later. Got a new sled?" and Bert looked admiringly at the one Charley was pulling.

"No, it's only my old one painted over. But it makes it look like new."

"We had Snap hitched up, but he broke loose," said Freddie. "But we're going to have a stronger harness to-morrow."

"That's good," said Charley, with a broad smile.

Soon the children were on the hill. There was a large crowd of coasters there, and fun was at its height. There was merry shouting and laughter, and several spills and upsets. As Bert had said, the hill was very much crowded.

"I thought it would be no good for a bob," he remarked.

"There goes Danny Rugg now!" exclaimed Charley. "He's giving orders to everyone."

"He'd better not give any to me," said Bert, in a quiet voice, but with determination in his tones.

"Oh, Bert!" exclaimed Nan. "Please don't have any fuss; will you?"

"Not on my part," said Bert "But if Danny Rugg thinks he can boss me he is mistaken."

It was evident that Danny liked to play master. He could be heard giving orders to this one and the other one to get out of the way, to pull his bob around in place, and then to shove it off with its load of boys and girls.

Now, though Danny was a bully, some of the children were friendly with him for the sake of getting a ride on his sled, which was a large and expensive one.

Bert and Nan, and Flossie and Freddie, soon were coasting with their friends, having a good time on the hill. The two smaller twins went down together.

As Freddie came up the long slope, pulling his sled in readiness for another trip, Danny Rugg with his bob reached the head of the slope at the same time.

"Say, Danny, give me a ride this trip; won't you?" begged a small boy, who had no sled, but who often did errands for the bully, and played mean tricks for him that, Danny was too lazy to play himself. "Let me go on your bob?"

"Not this time, Sim," said Danny. "The bob is going to be filled. But here, you can take Freddie Bobbsey's sled. He doesn't want it," and without giving Freddie time to say whether he did or not Danny snatched the sled rope from him and held it out to Sim Watson.

For a moment Freddie was too surprised to utter a protest and then, as he realized what had happened, he cried out:

"Here, Danny Rugg, you let my sled alone! I do want it! Give it back to me!"

"Aw, go on!" said Danny. "You've had rides enough. Let Sim take your sled, or I'll punch you!" and Danny gave Freddie a shove, and held out the rope of the sled to Sim.

"Stop it!" cried Freddie. "I'll tell Bert on you."

"Pooh! Think I'm afraid of your brother. I can handle him with one hand tied behind my back."

"Then it's time you started in!" exclaimed a voice just back of Danny, and the bully turned suddenly to see Bert standing near him, Danny's face flushed, and then grew pale. Before he could make a move Bert grabbed away from him the rope of Freddie's sled, which Sim had not yet taken, and passed it back to his small brother.

"Don't you try that again," warned Bert.

"I will if I want to," said Danny, meanly, "I'm not afraid of you."

"Maybe not," said Bert, quietly, "and I'm not afraid of you, either. But if you take my brother's sled for some of your friends you'll have to settle with me. You leave Freddie alone; do you hear?"

"I don't have to mind you!"

"We'll see about that. Go ahead, Freddie. You and Flossie coast as much as you like, and if Danny bothers you any more let me know."

Danny, with an uneasy laugh, turned aside. Some of his particular chums gathered about him, and one murmured:

"Why don't you fight him?"

For a moment it looked as though there might be trouble, but an instant later all thoughts of it passed, for a series of girls' screams came from midway down the long hill.

All eyes were turned in that direction, and those at the top of the slope saw a team of runaway horses, attached to a heavy bobsled, plunging madly up the hill.

And, right in the path of the frightened animals was Nan Bobbsey, and one or two other girls, on their sleds, coasting straight for the runaways.

A cry of fear came from Bert Bobbsey as he noticed his sister's danger.

Day 138

1. Read the first part of chapter 2.
2. What were the children out doing? (Answers)

Chapter 2 Old Mr. Carford (first half)

"Stop the horses!"

"Yes, grab them, somebody, or they'll run into the girls!"

"Look out, everybody, they're coming right this way!"

"I'm going to get my bob to a safe place!"

It was Danny Rugg who called out this last, and the other boys had shouted the previous expressions, as they watched the oncoming, runaway horses.

Bert Bobbsey had thrown himself on his sled and was coasting toward the group of girls, of whom his sister Nan was one. They were on their sleds in the very path of the team. It seemed that nothing could save them. But Bert had a plan in his mind.

And, while he was preparing to carry it out, I will take just a moment to tell my new readers something about the characters of this story, and the books that have gone before in the series.

Bert and Nan, Freddie and Flossie Bobbsey were the twin children of Mr. and Mrs. Richard Bobbsey, who lived in an Eastern city called Lakeport, at the head of Lake Metoka. Mr. Bobbsey was a prosperous lumber merchant. Other members of the household were Dinah and Sam Johnson. Dinah was the cook, fat and good-natured. Sam was her husband, slim and also good-natured. He did all sorts of work about the place, from making garden to shoveling snow.

Then there was Downy, a pet duck; Snoop, a pet black cat, and, of late, Snap, the fine trick dog, who had come into the possession of the Bobbseys in a peculiar manner.

In the first book of this series, entitled "The Bobbsey Twins," I told of the good times the four children had in their home. How they played in the snow, went coasting, helped to discover what they thought was a "ghost," and did many other things. Bert even went for a sail in an ice boat he and Charley Mason had made, though it was almost more than the boys could manage at times.

The second volume, called "The Bobbsey Twins in the Country," told of the good times the four had when they went to the farm of Uncle Daniel Bobbsey and his wife, Aunt Sarah, who lived at Meadow Brook.

Such fun as there was!

There was a country picnic, sport in the woods, and a great Fourth of July celebration. A circus gave a chance to have other good times, and though once there was a midnight scare, it all turned out happily.

But though the twins had much happiness in the country they were destined to have still more fun when they went to the ocean shore, and in the third book, called "The Bobbsey Twins at the Seashore," I related all that happened to them there.

They went on a visit to their uncle, William Minturn, who lived at Ocean Cliff, and their cousin Dorothy showed them many strange scenes and sights. They had most delightful times, and toward the close of their visit there was a great storm at sea, and a shipwreck. The life savers were on hand, however, and did such good work that no one was drowned. And if you want to learn how a certain little girl was made very happy, when she found that her father was among those saved, you must read the book.

Then, after the storm ceased, there were more happy days at the shore. The time for the Bobbseys to leave came all too soon. School was about to open, and even the smaller twins must now settle down to regular lessons.

In the fourth book of the series, called "The Bobbsey Twins at School," there is told of the start for home.

But many things happened before the family arrived. There was the wreck of the circus train, the escape of the animals, the meeting with the very fat lady, and the loss of Snoop, the pet cat. Then, too, a valuable cup the smaller Bobbsey twins had been drinking from, seemed to be lost, and they were very sorry about it.

On the way home something else occurred. They were followed in the dark by some strange animal. At first they feared it was some wild beast from the circus but it proved to be only a friendly dog.

How Flossie and Freddie insisted on keeping the dog, now that their pet cat Snoop was gone, how they named him Snap, and how it was discovered that he could do tricks, are all part of the story.

There were many more happenings after the twins started in at school. Mr. Bobbsey's boathouse caught fire in a mysterious manner. Snap was found to be a circus dog, and it was pretty certain that the fat lady in the train had also belonged to the show, and that it was she who had the valuable silver cup.

In time all was straightened out, and how Snoop came back from the circus in far-off Cuba, how Snap was allowed to stay with the Bobbseys, and how even the cup was finally recovered--all this you will find set down in the fourth book of this series.

And now winter had come in earnest, though even before this story opens the Bobbsey twins had had a taste of snow and ice. The accident on the coasting hill now occupied the attention of all.

"Oh, Nan! Nan will be killed!" cried Flossie, as she stood with Freddie gazing down the slope.

"No, she won't!" exclaimed Freddie, "Bert is going to save her--you'll see!"

"Oh, if he only can!" murmured Nellie Parks, one of Nan's friends.

"I think he will! See, he is coming nearer to them," added Grace Lavine, another friend.

Day 139

1. Finish chapter 2. Remember what was happening when you stopped reading?
2. What were the boys throwing at the horses to try and help? (Answers)

Chapter 2 (second half)

Danny Rugg, mean as he was, was not quite so mean as to discourage this hope. Some of the girls on the sleds that were coming nearer to the rushing horses seemed about to roll off, rather than take chances of steering out of the way of the steeds.

"What can Bert be going to do?" asked Grace. "How can he save them?"

"I don't know," answered Nellie. "Let's watch him. Maybe he's going to stop the horses."

"He'd never dare!" murmured Grace.

"Oh, Bert is brave," was the answer.

But Bert had no intention of leaping for the horses' heads just now. His first idea was to get his sister and the other girls to a place of safety. As he came near to them, his sled going much faster than theirs, he called out:

"Steer to the right! Go to the right! I'll see if I can't make the horses go over to one side."

"All right!" cried Nan, who understood what her brother meant. "Keep to the right, girls," she called to her frightened chums, "and don't any of you fall off!"

Those who had been about to roll from their sleds now held on with firmer clasps. They were close to the runaway team now. Bert was near to them also, and, while wondering to whom they belonged, and whether they had injured their driver or anyone else in their mad rush, he caught up a handful of snow as his sled glided onward.

It was hard work to throw the snow ball at the horses, going down hill as he was, but Bert managed to do it. He had the good luck to hit one of the animals with the wad of snow, and this sent the horse over to one side, its mate following. This was just what Bert wanted, as it gave Nan and the others more room to coast past them.

And this is just what the girls did. Their sleds whizzed past the runaways, one sled, on which Hattie Jenson rode, almost grazing a hoof.

"Now you're safe!" cried Bert. "Keep on to the foot of the hill! You're all right!"

He gathered up another handful of snow, and threw it at the steeds, making them swerve more than ever towards the side of the hill. Then one of the animals slipped and stumbled. This caused them both to slow up, and Bert, seeing this, left his sled, rolling off, and letting it go down without him.

Hardly thinking of what he was doing, he ran for the heads of the horses. Perhaps it was not just wise, for Bert was not very tall, but he was brave. However, he was not to stop the runaways all alone, for just then some of the larger boys, who had been rushing down the hill, came up, and before the horses could start off again several lads had grasped them by the bridles and were quieting them.

"That was a good idea of yours, Bert Bobbsey," said Frank Miller. "A fine idea, lo throw snowballs at them. It made them go to one side all right, and slowed them up."

"I wanted to save the girls," said Bert, who was panting from his little run.

"Whose team is it?" asked another boy.

"I don't know," answered Bert. "I can't say that I ever saw them before. There's no one in the sled, anyhow, though it is pretty well loaded with stuff."

He and the other boys looked into the vehicle. It contained a number of boxes and bags. Then the boys looked down the hill and saw that the girls who had been in danger were now safe. Nan and the others were walking up, dragging their sleds.

The boys then noticed a man half running up the slope. He was waving his arms in an excited fashion.

"I guess that's the man who owns the horses," said Charley Mason.

There was no doubt of it a few minutes later, when the man came close enough to make himself heard.

"Are they all right, boys?" he asked. "Are my horses hurt?"

"They don't seem to be," answered Frank.

"That's good. Are my things all right?"

"Everything seems to be here," said Charley Mason, who was standing beside Bert. "I know who he is now," went on Charley in a low tone to his chum. "He's Mr. James Carford, of Newton."

"He's lame," observed Bert, for the man limped slightly.

"Yes, he was in the war," went on Charley. "He's real rich, too, but peculiar, they say."

By this time aged Mr. Carford was looking over the team and the sled and its contents. He seemed weary and out of breath.

"Yes, everything is all right," he said slowly. "I hope no one was hurt by my runaways, I never knew 'em to do that before. I left 'em outside the store a minute while I went in to get something, and they must have taken fright. I hope no one was hurt."

"No, everyone got out of the way in time," said Bert.

"That's good. Who stopped the horses?" the old man asked.

"Bert Bobbsey," answered Frank Miller. "He warned his sister and the other girls to steer to one side, and then he threw snow at the horses and made them fall down. Then they slowed up so we could grab 'em."

"Ha! Bert Bobbsey did that, eh?" exclaimed aged Mr. Carford. "So this is the second time a Bobbsey has mixed up in my family affairs. The second time," and Mr. Carford looked at Bert in a peculiar manner.

"Did you fall out of the sled, Mr. Carford?" asked another boy, coming up just then.

"No, they started off when I was in the store. Funny, too, that they should. Well, I'm glad there's no one hurt and no damage done. I couldn't walk home to Newton. I'm much obliged to you boys. And to you too, Bert Bobbsey.

"Are you Richard Bobbsey's son?" he suddenly asked, peering at Bert from beneath his shaggy eyebrows.

"Yes, sir."

"Ha! I thought so. You look like him. You do things like him, too, without stopping to be asked. Yes, this is the second time a Bobbsey has meddled with my family affairs. Trying to do me a good turn, I suppose. Well, well!" and he seemed lost in thought.

"What is it? What is the matter?" asked Nan, in a low voice of her brother, as she came to stand beside him. "Is he finding fault because you helped stop his runaway horses?"

"No, Nan. I don't exactly understand what he does mean," answered Bert. "There seems to be some mystery about it."

Day 140

1. Read chapter 3. While you read, picture in your mind what is happening. Make a movie of the book in your mind. It will help you remember what is happening.
2. What's the big snowball? (Answers)
3. Who do you think made the enormous snowball?

Chapter 3 The Big Snowball

For a time Mr. Carford seemed more worried about the possible injury to his team, and the loss of some of his goods in the sled, than he was concerned about thanking the boys who had stopped the runaways. Then, as he found by looking them over, that the horses were all right, and that nothing was missing, he approached Bert and the others, saying:

"Well, boys, I'm much obliged to you. I can't tell you how much. No telling what damage the horses might have done if you hadn't stopped 'em. And I'm glad no one was hurt.

"Now I reckon you boys aren't much different than I was, when I was a youngster, and I guess you like sweets about the same. Here are a couple of dollars, Bert Bobbsey. I wish you'd treat all your friends to hot chocolate soda or candy or whatever you like best. It isn't exactly pay for what you did, but it just shows I'm not forgetful."

"Oh, we didn't stop the horses for money!" cried Bert, drawing back.

"I know you didn't," answered Mr. Carford, with a smile, "and I'm not paying you either. You stopped the horses, or you tried to stop them, Bert, to save your sister and the other girls. I understand that all right. But the horses were stopped just the same, and please take this as a little thank offering, if nothing else. Please do."

He held out the two-dollar bill, and Bert did not feel like refusing. He accepted the money with murmured thanks, and as Mr. Carford climbed into the sled, limping more than ever after his run up the hill, the aged man muttered:

"The second time a Bobbsey has been mixed up in my affairs. I wonder what will happen when the third time comes?"

Calling good-byes to the boys and girls, and again thanking them for what they had done, Mr. Carford drove off amid a jingle of bells.

"What do you s'pose he meant by saying this was the second time a Bobbsey had been mixed up in his family affairs?" asked Charley Mason of Bert.

"I haven't the least idea. I never knew Mr. Carford before this. I'll ask my father."

"Is that bill real?" asked one boy, referring to the money.

"It sure is," answered Bert, looking at it. "Come on to the drugstore and well spend it. That's what it's for."

"Going to treat Danny Rugg, and his crowd, too?" asked Frank Miller.

"Well, I guess Mr. Carford wanted this money to be spent on everyone on the hill, so it includes Danny," answered Bert slowly.

But Danny and his particular friends held back from Bert, and did not share in the treat. Probably Danny did not want to come to too close quarters with Bert after the attempt made to get Freddie's sled.

The excitement caused by the runaway was over now. Bert got back his sled and, as interest in coasting had waned at the prospect of hot chocolate sodas, the crowd of boys and girls trooped from the hill and started toward town, where there was a favorite drug store.

Standing about the soda counter the boys and girls discussed the recent happening.

"What did you think, Nan, when you saw the team coming?" asked Grace Lavine.

"I really don't know what I did think," answered Nan.

"Weren't you awfully frightened?" inquired Nellie Parks.

"Oh, I suppose I was. But I hoped I could steer out of the way, and I remember hoping that Flossie and Freddie were in a safe place."

"Oh,--we were all right," said Freddie quickly. "Flossie and I were watching the horses. This chocolate is awful good!" he added with a sigh. "Is there any money left, Bert?"

"Yes, a little," answered his brother "But you have had your share."

"Oh, if there is any left let him and Flossie have it," suggested Grace. "They're the smallest ones here."

"Yes, do," urged Nellie, and as several others agreed that this was the thing to do, the two little Bobbsey twins each had another cup of chocolate.

"Though Freddie has almost as much outside his mouth as inside it," said Nan, with a laugh.

Then the merry party of boys and girls trooped homeward, Bert and Nan thinking on the way of the strange words of Mr. Carford and wondering what he meant by them.

Several of the older boys, who knew the old gentleman, told something of him. He was a strange character, living in a fine old homestead. He was said to be queer on certain matters, but kind and good, and quite charitable, especially at Christmas time, to the poor of that country neighborhood.

"We'll ask papa about him when we get home," said Bert. "Maybe he can explain it."

But when the Bobbsey twins reached their house they found that their father had suddenly been called away on a business trip to last for some days, and so they did not see him.

"I haven't the least idea what Mr. Carford meant," said Mrs. Bobbsey, when they had asked her. "I did not even know that your father knew him. I am sorry you children were in danger on the hill."

"Oh, it wasn't much, mother," said Bert quickly, for he feared if his parent grew too worried she might put a stop to the winter fun.

Supper was soon ready and then came a happy period before bedtime-- that is happy after lessons had been learned. Snoop the black cat, and Snap, the smart circus dog, were allowed in the living room, to do some of their tricks, Snoop having been taught a number while with the fat lady in the circus.

Bert fell asleep vainly wondering about the queer words of Mr. Carford, and he dreamed that he was sliding down hill on the back of a horse who turned somersaults, every now and then, into a bag of popcorn.

Coasting came to an end the next day, for there was a big snow storm, and the hill would not be in good condition until the white flakes were packed hard on the slope. But there were other forms of sport-- snowballing, the making of forts, snow houses and snow men, so that the Bobbseys and their friends were kept busy.

Then came a little thaw, and the snow was just soft enough to roll into big balls.

"It's just right for making a large fort!" exclaimed Danny Rugg one day, after school was out. "We'll roll up a lot of big balls, put them in lines on four sides and make a square fort. Then, we'll choose sides and have a snow fight."

The other boys agreed to this, and soon Bert and the others, including Danny and his friends, were busily engaged. For the time being the hard feeling between Danny and Bert was forgotten.

The fort was finished, and there was a spirited snow battle about it, one side trying to capture it and the other trying to stop them. Bert's side managed to get into the fort, driving the others out.

"Oh, we'll beat you tomorrow!" taunted Danny, when the battle was over.

The next morning, when the children assembled at school, they saw a strange sight. On the front steps of the building was a great snowball, so large that it almost hid the door from sight. And working at it, trying to cut it away so that the entrance could be used, was the janitor. He was having hard work it seemed.

"Who did it?"

"Who put it there?"

"Say, it's frozen fast, too!"

"Somebody will get into trouble about this."

These were only a few of the things said when the children saw the big snowball on the school steps.

"It's frozen fast all right enough," said the janitor, grimly. "Whoever put it there poured water over it, and it's frozen so fast that I'll have to chop it away piece by piece. All day it will take me, too, and me with all the paths to clean!"

When the classes were assembled for the morning exercises Mr. Tetlow, the school principal, stepped to the edge of the platform, and said:

"I presume you have all seen the big snow ball on the front steps. Whoever put it there did a very wrong thing. I know several boys must have had a hand in it, for one could not do it alone. I will now give those who did it a chance to confess. If they will admit it, and apologize, I will let the matter drop. If not I will punish them severely. Now are you ready to tell, boys? I may say that I have a clue to at least one boy who had a hand in the trick."

Mr. Tetlow paused. There was silence in the room, and the boys looked one at the other. Who was guilty?

Day 141

1. Read chapter 4.
2. Who is accused of playing the trick? (Answers)
3. Do you think he did it? Why or why not? (Answers)
4. Anytime you are reading something long and start to forget what's happening and feel confused, you need to STOP. Go back to what you remember and start from there.

Chapter 4 The Accusation

For what seemed a long time Mr. Tetlow stood looking over the room full of pupils. One could have heard a pin drop, so quiet was it. The hard breathing of the boys and girls could be heard. From over in a corner where Danny Rugg sat, came a sound of whispering.

"Quiet!" commanded the principal sharply. "There must be no talking. I will wait one minute more for the guilty ones to acknowledge that they rolled the big snowball on the steps. Then, if they do not speak, I shall have something else to say."

The minute ticked slowly off on the big clock. No one spoke. Bert glanced from side to side as he sat in his seat, wondering what would come next. Many others had the same thought.

"I see no one wishes to take advantage of my offer," said Mr. Tetlow slowly. "Very well. You may all go to your class-rooms, with the exception of Bert Bobbsey. I wish to see him in my office at once. Do you hear, Bert?"

There was a gasp of astonishment, and all eyes were turned on Bert. He grew red in the face, and then pale. He could see Nan looking at him curiously, as did other girls. Bert was glad Flossie and Freddie were not in the room, for the kindergarten children did not assemble for morning exercises with the larger boys and girls. Flossie and Freddie might have been frightened at the solemn talk.

For a moment Bert could hardly believe what he had heard. He was wanted in Mr. Tetlow's office! It did not seem possible. And there was but one explanation of it. It must be in connection with the big snowball. And Bert knew he had had no hand in putting it on the school steps.

There was a buzz of talk, many whisperings, and some one spoke aloud. It sounded like Danny Rugg, but poor Bert was so confused at his own plight that he could not be sure.

"Silence!" commanded Mr. Tetlow, as the boys and girls marched to their various rooms. "Bert, you will wait for me in my office," he added. Poor Bert looked all around. He met many glances that were kind, and others, from Danny Rugg's friends, that were not. Nan waved her hand at her brother as she passed him, and Bert smiled at her. He made up his mind to be brave. Bert went to the principal's office, and sat in a chair. There was another boy there, who looked at Bert in a questioning manner.

"Are you here to get some writing paper, Bert?" asked the other boy. "Miss Kennedy sent me for some."

"No," answered Bert. "I only wish I was. I guess Mr. Tetlow thinks I had something to do with the big snowball."

"Did you?"

"I did not!" exclaimed Bert quickly.

The principal entered a little later, gave to the other boy the package of writing paper Miss Kennedy had sent for, and then sat down beside Bert.

"I am sorry to have to do this, Bert," he said, "but this is a serious matter and I must treat it seriously. Now again, I ask if you have anything to say to me? Perhaps you were too worried to stand up before the whole school."

"No, sir," answered Bert, "I don't know that I have anything to say, if you mean about the big snowball."

"Then you deny that you had anything to do with it?"

"Yes, sir. I never helped roll it on the steps."

"Do you know who did?"

"No, sir. I haven't the least idea."

"And you were not anywhere near it?"

"No, sir."

"Ahem! Let me ask you, have you a knife, Bert?"

Without thinking Bert's hand went to his pocket, and then, as he recalled something, his face turned red, and he said:

"I have one, but I haven't got it now."

"Is this it?" asked Mr. Tetlow, suddenly holding out one.

Bert did not need to give more than a single glance at it to know that it was his knife. It had his name on the handle and had been given him by his father at Christmas.

"Yes, that's mine," he said slowly.

"So I thought. And do you know where it was found, Bert?"

"No, Mr. Tetlow, I haven't any idea."

"Suppose I told you the janitor picked it up on the steps almost under the big snowball? If I tell you that what have you to say?"

"Well, Mr. Tetlow, I'll have to say that I don't know anything about it. I didn't drop my knife there, I'm sure."

"Then someone else must have done it. Be careful now, Bert. I don't want to be hasty, but it looks to me very much as though you were one of the boys who had played this trick--a trick that has made considerable trouble. I am sure there must have been others concerned with you, and I am almost positive that you had a hand in it.

"Now I am not going to ask you to tell tales against your companions. I don't believe in that sort of thing. But I am very sorry that you did not admit at first that you had a share in rolling the big ball. Very sorry, Bert."

"But, Mr. Tetlow, I didn't do it!" cried poor Bert, the tears coming into his eyes. "I don't know how my knife got there, but I do know I didn't help roll that ball. Please believe me; won't you?"

For a moment the principal was silent. Then he said slowly:

"Bert, I would very much like to believe you, for I have always found you a good, manly and upright boy. But the evidence is strong against you I am sorry to say. And this trick was one I can not easily overlook. Rolling the snowball on the steps was bad enough, but when water was poured over it, to freeze, and become ice, making it so much harder to clean off, it made matters so much worse.

"Besides making a lot of work for the janitor, there was danger that some of the teachers might slip on the icy path and be injured. If your knife had only been found lying on top of the ice I might think you had come up merely to look at the big ball, and had dropped your property there. But the knife was found frozen fast, showing that it must have been dropped during the time the water was poured on the steps. So you see whoever left it there must have been on hand when the trick was played."

"That may be true, Mr. Tetlow!" cried Bert, "but I did not leave my knife there. I remember now--I can explain it! I couldn't think, at first, but I see it now."

"Very well," said Mr. Tetlow quietly, "I'll hear what you have to say, Bert."

Day 142

1. Read chapter 5. If you come to a word you don't know, sound it out and say it out loud. Read the sentence again with the word in it and then keep going. Usually it will explain or you can figure out what it is. You can also look for clues like how the characters are feeling. Are they happy or upset about what's happening?
2. Who played the trick? (Answers)

Chapter 5 Holidays at Hand

Bert Bobbsey was thinking rapidly. Something that he had nearly forgotten came suddenly to his mind, and he hoped it would clear him of the accusation.

And what he had seen, that brought back to his mind something that he had nearly forgotten, was the sight of an elderly gentleman driving past the school in a sled. It was aged Mr. Carford, whose runaway team Bert had helped stop that day on the hill.

"Will you let me call in Mr. Carford?" asked Bert of the principal.

"Call in Mr. Carford?" repeated Mr. Tetlow in some surprise. "What for?"

"Because, sir," said Bert eagerly, "he saw me lend my knife to Jimmie Belton last night, and he can tell you that I went on home, leaving my knife with Jimmie."

"Ha! Do you mean to say that Jimmie dropped it in the ice on the school steps?"

"No, Mr. Tetlow, I don't mean to say that. But I can prove by Mr. Carford that I went home last night without my knife. Please call him in."

Bert thought of the strange old man, who had made such an odd remark concerning the Bobbsey family. And Bert was determined to find out what it meant, but, as yet, he had had no chance, as his father was still away on a business trip.

"Very well, we shall see what Mr. Carford has to say," spoke the principal. "And I will have Jimmie Belton in also."

Mr. Tetlow pressed a bell button that called the janitor, and the latter, who was still chopping away at the frozen steps, came to see what was wanted.

"Just call to that old gentleman going past in the bob sled to come in here," said Mr. Tetlow. "He is Mr. Carford."

"Tell him Bert Bobbsey wants to see him," added the boy, amazed at his own boldness.

"Yes, you may do that," said Mr. Tetlow, as the janitor looked toward him. Somehow the principal was beginning to doubt Bert's guilt now.

From the office window Bert watched the janitor hail the aged man, who paused for a minute, and then, tying his team, came on toward the school. Bert's heart was lighter now. He was sure the old gentleman would bear out what he had said, and Bert felt he would be glad to do him a good turn in part payment for what Bert and his chums had done in catching the runaways.

"Mr. Carford," began Mr. Tetlow, who knew the aged man slightly, "there has been trouble here, and Bert Bobbsey thinks perhaps you can help clear it up. So I have asked you to step in for a moment." Then he told about the big snowball, and mentioned how he had come to suspect Bert.

"But Bert tells me," went on Mr. Tetlow, "that you saw him lending his knife to Jimmie Belton last night. May I ask you, is that so?"

"Why, yes, it is," said the aged man slowly. "I'll tell you how it was." He nodded at Bert in a friendly way, and there was a twinkle in his deep-set eyes.

"It was just toward dusk last evening," went on Mr. Carford, "and I was on my way home to Newton. I'd been in town buying some supplies, and near the cross roads I met Bert and another boy."

"That was Jimmie," said Bert eagerly.

"Well, I heard you call him Jimmie--that's all I know," said Mr. Carford. "Bert was cutting a branch from a tree, and when I came up to them I offered them a ride as far as I was going. They got in, and Bert here was whittling away with his knife as he sat beside me. Yes, that's the knife," said Mr. Carford, as the principal showed it to him.

"I was making a ramrod for a toy spring gun I have," explained Bert. "It shoots long sticks, like arrows, and I had lost one of my best ones, so on the way home I cut another. Then just before Mr. Carford gave us the ride, Jimmie came along and asked me to lend him my knife. I said I would as soon as I had finished making my arrow. I did finish it in the sled and I gave him my knife just before we got out."

Mr. Tetlow looked inquiringly at Mr. Carford, who nodded in answer.

"Yes," said the aged man, "that was the way of it. Bert did lend that other boy--Jimmie he called him--his knife. I saw the two boys separate and Jimmie carried off Bert's knife. But that's all I do know. The snowball business I have nothing to do with."

"No, I suppose not," said the principal slowly. "I am sorry now that I said what I did, Bert. But there still remains the question of how your knife got on the steps. Do you think Jimmie had a hand in putting the snowball there?"

"I don't know, Mr. Tetlow. I wouldn't like to say."

"No, of course not. I'll have Jimmie here." The principal called a messenger and sent him for Jimmie, who came to the office wondering what it was all about.

Without telling him what was wanted Mr. Tetlow asked Jimmie this question quickly: "What did you do with Bert's knife fie lent it to you last night?"

For a moment Jimmie was confused. A strange look came over his face. He clapped his hand to his pocket and exclaimed:

"I--I lent it to Danny Rugg."

"Danny Rugg!" cried Bert.

"No, I didn't exactly lend it to Danny," explained Jimmie, "for I knew, Bert, that you and he weren't very friendly. But after you let me take it last night, to start making that sailboat I was telling you about, I forgot all about promising you that I'd bring it back after supper. Then Danny came over, and he helped me with the boat. When he saw I had your knife, and when he heard me say I must take it back, he offered to leave it for you when he came past your house the next time."

"And did you give it to him?" asked the principal.

"Yes, I did," answered Jimmie. "I thought he would do as he said. He took the knife when he went home from my house."

"But he never gave it to me!" said Bert quickly.

"I am beginning to believe he did not," said the principal. "I think we will have Danny in here."

The bully came in rather defiant, and stared boldly around at those in the office. Mr. Tetlow resolved on a surprising plan.

"Danny," he said suddenly, "why did you put Bert's knife on the step, and let it freeze there to make it look as though Bert had helped place the snowball in front of the door? Why did you?"

"I--I--" stammered Danny, "I didn't--"

"Be careful now," warned the principal. "We have heard the whole story. Jimmie has told how you promised to leave the knife with Bert, but you did not."

Danny swallowed a lump in his throat. He was much confused, and finally he broke down and admitted that he had been present and had helped roll the snowball on the steps.

"But I wasn't the only one!" he exclaimed. "There was--"

"Tut Tut!" exclaimed the principal. "I want no tale-bearing. I think those who did the trick will confess now, after I tell them what has happened. Danny, it was very wrong of you to play such a joke, but it was much worse to try to throw the blame on Bert by leaving his knife there."

"I--I didn't do it on purpose," said Danny. "The knife must have slipped out of my pocket." But no one believed that, for Danny was known to have a grudge against Bert, and that was reason enough for trying to throw the blame on our little hero.

But Bert was soon cleared, for, a little later, when Mr. Tetlow called the school together, saying that he had been mistaken in regard to Bert, and relating what had come out about the knife, several of the boys who, with Danny had placed the big ball on the steps, admitted their part in it.

They were all punished, but Danny most of all, for his mean act in trying to make it look as though Bert had done it.

"Well," said Mr. Carford, as he took his leave, having helped to prove Bert's innocence "this time I have had a chance to do a Bobbsey a favor, in return for one you did me, Bert."

"Yes, sir," answered Bert, not knowing what else to say. He was puzzling over what strange connection there might be between his family and Mr. Carford.

"Come up and see me sometime," said the aged man. "And bring your brother and sisters, Bert. I'll be glad to see them at my place. I'm going to stay home all this winter. I'm getting too old to go to Snow Lodge anymore."

Bert wondered what Snow Lodge was, but he did not like to ask.

Thus was cleared up the mystery of the big snowball, and Bert's many friends were as glad as he was himself that he had been found innocent.

There came more snow storms, followed by freezing weather after a thaw, and the boys and girls had much fun on the ice, a number of skating races having been arranged among the school pupils.

The end of the mid-winter term was approaching, and the Christmas holidays would soon be at hand. Then would come a three week's vacation, and the Bobbsey twins were talking about how they could spend it.

"It's too cold to go to the seashore," said Nan with a shiver, as she looked out of the window over the snowy yard.

"And the country would be about the same," added Bert.

"Oh, it's lovely in the country during the winter, I think," said Nan.

"We could get up a circus in the barn, with Snoop and Snap," said Flossie, who was busy over a picture book.

"Then I'm going to be the ring-master and crack a big whip and wear big boots!" cried Freddie.

"I do hope papa will be home for Christmas," sighed Nan, for Mr. Bobbsey's business trip, in relation to lumber matters, had kept him away from home longer than expected.

"I have good news for you, children," said Mrs. Bobbsey, coming into the room just then with a letter. "Your father is coming home to- morrow."

"Oh, how nice!" cried Nan.

"I hope he brings us something," said Freddie.

"I'll have a chance to ask him about Mr. Carford," thought Bert. "I wonder what that old man meant by his strange words?"

Day 143

1. Begin reading chapter 6.
2. Their cook has a big accent. Read what she says out loud to help you figure out what she is saying.
3. What is happening in this chapter?

Chapter 6 A Visit to Mr. Carford

"Freddie, what in the world are you doing?"

"Flossie! Oh dear! You children! You have the place all upset!"

Mrs. Bobbsey, who had come into the big living room, to see the two younger twins engaged in some strange proceedings, paused at the doorway to look on. Indeed the place was upset, for the chairs had been dragged out from against the walls and from corners to be placed in a row before a large sofa. From one corner of this to a side wall was stretched a sheet, and in another corner, in a pen made of chairs, could be seen the wagging tail of Snap, the trick dog.

"What in the world are you doing?" asked Mrs. Bobbsey. "Oh, dear, how I do dread a rainy day!" for it was pouring outside, and the older, as well as the younger twins had to stay in doors.

"We're playing circus," explained Freddie gravely, as he peered between the "bars" of the cage made of chairs. "Snap is a lion," went on the little fellow. "Growl, Snap!"

And Snap, always ready to have fun, growled and barked to satisfy the most exacting circus lover.

"Oh dear!" cried Mrs. Bobbsey. "I'll never get this room straightened out again."

"Oh, we'll fix it, mamma, after the circus," said Flossie sweetly. "Sit down and see the show. I'll make Snoop do some of the tricks the fat circus lady taught her," and Flossie lifting up one corner of the sheet, showed the black cat curled up on a cushion, while back of her, tied by one leg, was Downy the pet duck.

"This was going to be the happy family cage," explained Flossie, "only when we had Snap in here he kept playing with Downy, and Downy quacked and that made Snoop nervous so we couldn't do it very well."

"So we made Snap the lion, and part of the time he's going to be the tiger," said Freddie. "Dinah is going to give us some blueing that she uses on the clothes, and I'm going to paint stripes on Snap."

"Don't you dare do it," said Mrs. Bobbsey, "The idea of painting blue stripes on poor Snap! Whoever heard of a blue-striped tiger?" and she tried hard not to laugh.

"Well, this is a new kind," said Freddie. "Sit down, mamma, and we'll make Snoop do a trick for you. Make her chase her tail, Flossie."

"No, I'll make her walk a tight rope," said the little girl. "That's more of a trick."

Flossie got her jumping rope, which she had little use for now, and tied it from the back of one chair to the back of another, placed some distance away. Then she pulled the rope tight between them, and, taking Snoop up in her arms, placed the cat carefully on the stretched rope.

Snoop stood still for a minute, meowing a little and waving her tail back and forth. Poor Snoop! The black cat did not like to do tricks as well as did Snap. No cats do. But Snap, when he saw what was going on, was eager to show off what he could do.

He leaped about in his chair "cage," barking loudly, much to the delight of Freddie who liked to hear the "lion" roar.

"Go on, Snoop!" called the twins, and gave the cat a gentle shove. Then Snoop did really walk across the rope, for it was almost as easy as walking the back fence, which Snoop had often done. Only the rope was not as steady as the fence. But the fat circus lady had trained the black cat well, and Snoop performed the trick to the delight of the children.

"That is very good," said Mrs. Bobbsey. "Oh, see! Snap is turning a somersault in his cage. Poor dog, let him out, Freddie; won't you?"

"He isn't a dog--he's a lion," insisted the little boy. "I dassen't let out a lion, or he might bite you."

But Snap had no idea of playing the lion all the while. Suddenly Downy, the duck, with a loud quack, got her leg loose from the string and flew out across the room. This so surprised Snoop, who had started back over the tight rope, that he fell off with a cry of alarm.

This was too much for Snap, who evidently did not think he was having his share of the fun. With a loud bark and a rush he burst from his cage of chairs, intent on playing with Snoop, for he and the cat were great friends.

Just at that moment fat Dinah, the colored cook, came into the room to ask Mrs. Bobbsey something. Snoop, seeing the open door, and being tired of doing tricks for the children, made a dash to get out, darting under Dinah's skirts.

Snap, thinking this was part of the game, rushed after his friend the cat, but when he tried to dive underneath Dinah's dress there was an accident.

He knocked the feet from under the fat cook, and she sat down on the floor with a force that jarred the whole house, just missing sitting on Snap.

"Fo' de lub ob goodness what am de mattah?" cried Dinah. "Am it an earfquake Mrs. Bobbsey?"

"I don't know, Dinah!" exclaimed Mrs. Bobbsey, wanting to laugh, and yet not wishing to hurt Dinah's feelings. "The children said it was a circus, I believe. Here, Snap!" she called, as the dog rushed on after Snoop.

Just then Downy, the duck, sailed back across the room, and lighted squarely on Dinah's black and kinky head, where the fowl perched "honking" loudly,

"Good land ob massy!" murmured Dinah over and over again. "Mo' trouble!"

Flossie and Freddie were so surprised at the sudden ending of their circus that they did not know what to do. Then they both raced to capture the duck.

"One of the dining-room windows is open!" called Freddie. "If Downy flies out he'll freeze. Grab him, Dinah!"

"Chile!" cried the colored cook slowly, "I ain't got bref enough lef to ketch eben a mosquito. But yo'-all don't need to worry none about dish yeah duck gittin loose. His feet am all tangled up in mah wool, an' I guess you'l hab t' help git 'em loose, chilluns!"

It was indeed so. Downy's webbed feet were fast in Dinah's kinky hair, and it took some time to disentangle them. Then the cook could get up, which she did with many a sigh and groan.

"Are you hurt, Dinah?" asked Flossie. "If you are you can come to our circus for nothing; can't she, Freddie?"

"Yes," he answered, "only we haven't got a circus now. It's all gone except Downy."

"Well, I think you have played enough circus for today," said Mrs. Bobbsey "Straighten up the room now, and have some other kind of fun."

Day 144

1. Finish reading chapter 6. Do you remember what had just happened at the end of your reading on Day 143?
2. Who is going to tell the children about Snow Lodge? (Answers)
3. Why does he "almost wish" Snow Lodge had burned down? (Answers)
4. What do you think might have been Mr. Carford's trouble? (Answers)

Chapter 6 (second half)

The dog and cat, satisfied to get out of their cages, had gone to the kitchen, where they could generally find something good to eat. Then Flossie and Freddie were kept busy putting back the chairs, and setting the room in order.

It was a day or so after the return of Mr. Bobbsey from his business trip, and though Bert had asked his father about Mr. Carford, the lumber dealer had not yet had time to give any explanation.

"It is quite a little story," he said. "I'll tell you about it some time, Bert. But now I have a lot of back work to catch up with, on account of being away so long, and I'll have to go to the office early, and I'll be late getting home."

So the little incident had not yet been explained. The Christmas holidays were drawing nearer, and there were busy times in the Bobbsey household. Flossie and Freddie were expecting a visit from Santa Claus, and they wrote many letters to the dear old saint, telling what they wished to receive.

"But have you thought of what you are going to give?" asked Mrs. Bobbsey one day, a short time before Christmas. "It is more fun to give things than it is to get them, you know."

"Is it?" asked Flossie, who had never heard of it in that way before.

"Indeed it is," said Mrs. Bobbsey. "You just try it. If you have any toys you don't care for any more, or even some that you do, and wish to give away, or books or other playthings, and if you will gather them up, I'll see that they are given to some poor children who may not have a very good Christmas."

The smaller twins thought this would be very nice, and they were soon busy over their possessions. Bert and Nan heard what was going on, and they insisted on giving their share also, so that quite a box full of really good toys were collected.

A day or so later, when the weather had cleared, Bert came in from coasting, and said,

"Mother, couldn't Nan and I take a ride over to Mr. Carford's house? He is out in front in his sled, and he says he'll bring us back before dark. May we go?"

"Why, I guess so," said Mrs. Bobbsey, slowly. "I don't believe your father would object. But wrap up well, for it is chilly."

"And can't we go, too?" begged Flossie

"Yes, we want to," added Freddie. "Please, Mamma!"

"Well, I guess so," agreed Mrs. Bobbsey, "Will you look after them, Bert and Nan?"

"Oh, yes," promised the two older twins, while Bert explained that he had met Mr. Carford, who was on his way home from the store, and had been given a ride. The invitation had followed.

"I'll take good care of them, Mrs. Bobbsey," said the elderly gentleman, as Mrs. Bobbsey went out to tuck in Flossie and Freddie "I've got to run into Newton and back again this afternoon, so I thought they'd like the ride."

"Indeed it is very kind of you," said the children's mother. "I hope they will be no trouble."

"Of course they won't. Remember me to Mr. Bobbsey when he comes home. Ask him to come and see me when he has time. I want to talk to him about a certain matter."

"All right," said Mrs. Bobbsey, and Bert wondered if it had to do with the secret.

The drive out to Newton, which was a few miles from Lakeport, was much enjoyed by the Bobbsey twins. The speedy horses pulled the sled over the white snow, the jingle of the strings of bells around them mingling with other musical chimes on sleds that they met, or passed.

They saw Danny Rugg out driving with his mother in a stylish cutter, and Danny rather "turned up his nose" at the old bob sled in which the Bobbseys were riding. But Bert and his sisters and brother did not mind that. They were having a good time.

"Here we are!" called Mr. Carford after a fine ride. "Come in and get warm. I guess my sister has a few cookies left," for a maiden sister kept house for the old gentleman.

Into the big old-fashioned farmhouse the children tramped, to be met by a motherly-looking woman, who helped them brush the snow from their feet. Then she bustled about, and brought in a big pitcher of milk, a plateful of molasses cookies, and some glasses. The children's eyes sparkled at the sight of this fine lunch.

"There you are!" cried Mr. Carford heartily, as he passed around the good things. "Eat as much as is good for you. I've got to go out to the barn for a while. Emma," he asked his sister, "have you got any more packages made up?"

"James Carford, are you going to give away more stuff?" demanded his sister. "Why, you'll be in the poorhouse first thing you know."

"Oh, I guess not," he said with a laugh, "We can afford it, and there's many who can't. It's going to be a hard winter on the poor. Put up a few more packages, and I'll tie up some bags of potatoes!"

"I never saw such a man--never in all my born days!" exclaimed Miss Carford, shaking her head. "He'd give away the roof over us if I didn't watch him."

"What is he doing?" asked Bert.

"Oh, the same as he does every Christmas," said the sister- housekeeper. "He makes up packages, bundles, baskets and bags of things to eat, and gives them to all the poor families he can hear of. He was poor once himself, you know, and he never can forget it."

"He is very kind," said Nan, in a low voice.

"Yes, he is that," agreed Miss Carford, "and I suppose I oughtn't to find fault. But he does give away an awful lot."

She went out to look after matters in the kitchen, leaving the children to eat their lunch of milk and cookies alone for a few minutes. Presently Mr. Carford came back, stamping the snow from his boots.

"Ha!" he cried, as he went close to the stove to warm his hands. "This reminds me of the winters I used to spend at Snow Lodge on Lake Metoka. Were you ever up there?" and he looked at Bert.

"No, sir."

"Ha! I thought not. It's a fine place. But I don't go there any more-- never any more," and he shook his head sadly.

"Did it burn down?" asked Freddie, who was always interested in fires and firemen. "Couldn't they put it out?"

"No, Freddie, it didn't burn down," said Mr. Carford. "Sometimes I almost wish it had-- before my trouble happened," he added slowly. "Yes, I almost wish it had. But Snow Lodge still stands, though I haven't been near it for some years. I couldn't go. No, I couldn't go," and he shook his head sadly. "I just couldn't go."

The Bobbsey children did not know what to think. Mr. Carford seemed very sad. Suddenly he turned away from the fire that blazed on the hearth, and asked:

"Did I ever tell you about Snow Lodge?"

"No," said Bert, softly.

"Then I will," went on the aged man. "I don't tell many, but I will you. And maybe you could make some use of the place now that the holidays are here. I used to spend all my Christmas holidays there, but I don't any more. Never any more. But I'll tell you about it," and he settled himself more comfortably in the big chair.

Day 145

1. Read chapter 7.

2. Who owned Snow Lodge? (Answers)
3. Who is Henry Burdoch? (Answers)
4. When did Mr. Carford leave Snow Lodge? (Answers)
5. Draw a picture of Snow Lodge. There's a description of it in this chapter.

Chapter 7 The Story of Snow Lodge

"When I was a boy," began Mr. Carford after a pause, during which he looked into the blazing fire, "I lived on a farm, and I had to work very hard."

"We were on a farm once, weren't we, Flossie?" interrupted Freddie.

"Hush, dear," said Nan in a low voice "Listen to Mr. Carford's story."

"That isn't a story," insisted Flossie. "He didn't begin it right. He must say: 'Once upon a time, a good many years ago--!'"

Mr. Carford laughed.

"So I should, my dear!" he exclaimed. "It's been so long since I've told a story to little folks that I've forgotten how, I guess.

"So I'll begin over again. Once upon a time, a good many years ago, I was a little boy, and I lived on a farm. I guess it must have been the same sort of a farm you and Flossie went to, Freddie, for we had cows and horses and pigs and chickens and sheep. There was lots of work, and, as my father was not rich, I had to help as soon as I got old enough.

"But, for all that, I had good times. I thought so then and, though I'm an old man now, I still think so. But the good times did not last long enough. I wish I could go back to them.

"But I stayed on the farm a good many years, with my brothers and sisters, and finally when I grew up, and thought I was big enough to start to work for myself, I ran away."

"Did you--did you get lost?" asked Flossie, with her eyes wide open, staring at Mr. Carford.

"No, my dear, I didn't exactly get lost. But I thought there was easier work than living on a farm, so, instead of staying and helping my father, as I think now I should have done, I ran away to a big city. I wanted to be dressed up, and wear a white collar instead of overalls and a jumper.

"But I found that life in the city, instead of being easier than on the farm, was harder, especially as I didn't know much about it. Many a time I wished I was back with my father, but I was too proud to admit that I had made a mistake. So I kept on working in the city, and finally I began to forget all about the farm.

"I won't make this story too long, for you might get tired of it," said Mr. Carford, as he got up to put a log on the fire.

"Oh, we like stories; don't we, Freddie?" said Flossie.

"Yes," said Freddie softly.

"I know, my dear," said the old man kindly, "but I am afraid you wouldn't like my kind. Anyhow I kept on working in the city--in one city after another--until I became successful and then, in time, I got rich."

"Rich!" cried Freddie. "Very rich?" and his big eyes opened wide.

"Freddie!" cautioned Nan, with a sharp look.

"Oh, I don't mind!" laughed Mr. Carford "Yes, I got quite rich, and then I thought it was time to go back to the old farm, and see my father. My mother had died before I went away. Maybe if she had lived I wouldn't have gone. And then I began to find out that life wasn't all happiness just because you had money.

"My father had died too, and the old farm had been sold. My brother and sisters had gone--some were married and some had died. I found I was a lonesome old man, with few friends, and hardly any relatives, left. I had been too busy getting rich, you see, to take time to make friends.

"Well, I didn't know what to do. All the while, you understand, I had been counting on going back to the farm, with a lot of money, and saying to my father: 'Now, daddy, you've worked hard enough. You can stop now, and have happiness the rest of your life.' But you see my father wasn't there. I was too late.

"So I made up my mind the best thing I could do was to buy back the old farm, and spend the rest of my days there, for the sake of old times. Well, I did buy the place, and I named it 'Snow Lodge,' for there used to be lots of snow there in the winter time. I fixed the old house all over new, put in a furnace, and other things to make it comfortable, and I lived there for some time.

"I heard from some of my brothers and sisters who had also gone away from the farm, and one of my sisters, who had married a man named Burdock, had become very poor. Her husband had died, and she was very sick. I brought her to Snow Lodge to live with me, and her son, Harry, a fine lad, came along.

"My poor sister did not live very long, and when she died I took Henry Burdock to live with me. I felt toward him as toward a son, and for years we stayed in Snow Lodge together.

"Then I bought this place, and we used to spend part of the year here and part of it at Snow Lodge. It was a fine place winter or summer, Snow Lodge was."

Mr. Carford became silent and looked again into the glowing logs on the hearth.

"Don't you go to Snow Lodge any more?" asked Nan in a low voice.

"No," replied the old man. "Never any more. Not--not since Henry went away," and he seemed to be in pain. "I have never gone there since Henry went away," he added, "though the place is well kept up, and it is ready to live in this minute."

"Did your nephew Henry run away, as you did?" asked Bert.

"No--not exactly," was the reply. "I don't like to talk about that part of it. I like to think of Snow Lodge on the shore of the lake as a place where I lived when I was a boy.

"Oh, it's just fine there!" went on Mr. Carford. "In summer the grass is so green, and you can sit on the porch and look down at the lake. In the winter, when the lake is frozen over, there is skating and ice boating on it, and you can fish through the ice. And such hills as there are to coast down! and such valleys filled with snow! Sometimes it seems as if the whole house would be covered with the white flakes.

"But you can always keep warm in Snow Lodge, for there are big fireplaces, as well as the furnace, and there is plenty of wood. Many times I've had a notion to go back there, but somehow I couldn't, since--since Henry went away. So I came here to live with my other sister, and here I guess I'll stay the rest of my life. Snow Lodge is shut up, and I guess it always will be."

Mr. Carford sighed, and kept looking at the fire. Nan thought what a pity it was that Snow Lodge could not be used, while Bert wondered what had happened between Henry Burdock and his uncle, Mr. Carford, that caused Henry to go away. Also Bert wondered if Mr. Carford would explain his strange remark, made at the time the runaway horses were caught. But the aged man seemed to have forgotten it.

"Yes, Snow Lodge is closed up," said Mr. Carford. "I don't suppose it will ever be used again. But I've told you the story of it, and I'm afraid I've tired you."

"No you haven't," said Nan. "We enjoyed it very much."

"That's right!" exclaimed Bert.

"Did--did you ever see any bears there?" asked Freddie, "any real big bears?"

"Or tigers--or--or elephants?" asked Flossie, not to let her brother get ahead of her in asking questions.

"Huh! Elephants don't grow here--only bears," said Freddie.

"No, I never saw anything bigger than foxes," said Mr. Carford with a laugh. "Snow Lodge isn't very far from here, you know, so you have the same kind of animals there that you have here. Only there are more woods at Snow Lodge.

"But I must be getting back with you youngsters. It is getting late and your folks may worry about you. I'll bring the sled around, and my sister Emma can tuck you in. Then I'll get you home, and see to my Christmas packages. It's going to be a hard winter on the poor."

"We give the poor people something," said Freddie. "At school we all brought something just before vacation, and Mr. Tetlow is going to give it to all the poor people."

"That was at Thanksgiving, dear," said Nan.

"Well, maybe they've got some left for Christmas," said Freddie, as the others laughed.

"That's right--try and make other people happy, little man," said Mr. Carford, patting Freddie's head.

The big sled with the horses and their jingling bells was soon at the door. Miss Carford had warmed some bricks to put down in the straw, to keep the children's feet warm, and soon, cozily wrapped up, they were on their way home.

Day 146

1. Read chapter 8.
2. What does Mr. Carford give the Bobbsey twins at the very, very end of the chapter? (Answers)

Chapter 8 A Kind Offer

"Nan!" called Freddie from under a big fur robe, as he sat in the warm straw of Mr. Carford's sled next to his sister.

"Yes, what is it?" asked Nan, bending over him to look at his face in the gathering dusk of the winter afternoon. "Are you warm enough, Freddie?"

"Yes, I'm as warm as the toast Dinah makes for breakfast. But say, I want to ask you--do you think we'll meet Santa Claus before we get home?"

"No, Freddie. The idea! What makes you think that?"

"Well, it's near Christmas, and we're out in a sled, and he goes out in a sled, only with reindeers of course, and--"

Freddie's voice trailed off sleepily. In fact he had aroused himself from almost a nap to ask Nan the question. Flossie, warmly wrapped up, was already slumbering in Bert's arms.

"No, I don't believe we'll meet Santa Claus this trip," said Nan. "He is only supposed to travel at night, you know, Freddie."

"That's so. Well, if we do meet him, and I'm asleep, you wake me up: will you?"

"Yes, Freddie," promised his sister, and she looked across at Bert and smiled. The two younger twins were soon both soundly slumbering, for being out in the cold air and wind does seem to make one sleepy when, later on, one gets warm and comfortable.

Mr. Carford sat up on the seat in front driving the sturdy horses, while the string of bells around them jingled at every step.

"Wasn't that a queer story of Snow Lodge?" asked Nan of Bert, in a low voice.

"It surely was," he replied. "It seems too bad to have the place all shut up, with no one to use it this winter. It would be just great, I think, if we could go up there for the Christmas holidays. We could go up right after Christmas, and not come back until the middle of January, for school doesn't open again until then. Wouldn't it be great!"

"Fine!" agreed Nan. "But I don't s'pose we could. Mr. Carford doesn't want Snow Lodge used, I guess. But he gave us a good time at his house."

"Indeed he did," agreed Bert.

On glided the sled, the bells making merry music. A light snowfall began, and Mr. Carford urged the horses to faster speed, for he wanted to get back home before the storm broke.

"Wake up, Freddie!"

"Wake up, Flossie!"

Nan and Bert gently shook their little brother and sister to arouse them. The sled had stopped in front of the Bobbsey home.

"Is it--is it morning?" asked Flossie, as she rubbed her eyes.

"Did Santa Claus come?" demanded Freddie, trying to wiggle out of Bert's arms.

"Not yet," laughed Mr. Carford. "But I think he soon will be here. Can you manage them, Nan--Bert?" he asked.

"Oh, yes, we often carry them," replied Nan. "They'll soon be wide awake again, and they won't want to go to sleep until late to-night, on account of the nap they've had."

Mrs. Bobbsey was at the door waiting for the children Flossie and Freddie soon roused up enough to walk in.

"Won't you come in?" asked Mrs. Bobbsey of Mr. Carford. "I can give you a cup of tea. Mr. Bobbsey just came home. Perhaps you'd like to say 'how-d'ye-do.'"

"Thanks, I'll come in for just a minute," was the answer. "Then I must be getting back before the storm breaks. And I'll tie my horses, too. I can't risk another runaway," Mr. Carford said with a smile at Bert.

Mr. Bobbsey greeted the caller cordially, and the children were soon telling their parents of the nice visit they had had.

"And Miss Carford can make almost as good cookies as Dinah!" cried Freddie.

"Ha! Ha!" laughed Mr. Carford. "I'll have to tell my sister that. She'll be real proud."

Bert, looking from his father to Mr. Carford, wondered what could have once taken place between the two men. That there was some sort of secret he felt sure, and up to now there had been no explanation of the strange words used by the aged man at the time Bert and the others caught the runaways.

"I haven't seen you in some time, Mr. Bobbsey," said Mr. Carford, after they had talked about the weather.

"No, I've been very busy, and I suppose you have also. Have you been at Snow Lodge lately?"

"No, and I don't expect to set foot in the place again. I guess you know why. And I want to say now, that though I was rather cross with you when you tried to get me to change my mind about that matter, some time ago, I want to say that I'm sorry for it. I realize that you did it for the best."

"Yes," said Mr. Bobbsey, "I did, but I know how you felt about it. I believed then, and I believe now, that you made a mistake about your nephew Henry."

"No, I don't think I did," was the slow reply. "I am afraid Henry is a bad young man. I don't want to see him again, nor Snow Lodge either. But I'm glad you tried to help me. However,

I have come about a different matter now. How would you and your family like to spend the winter there? How would a vacation at Snow Lodge suit you?"

No one spoke for a few seconds. All were surprised at the kind offer made by Mr. Carford.

"A vacation at Snow Lodge!" said Mr. Bobbsey slowly.

"Do you mean it, Mr. Carford?" asked Mrs. Bobbsey.

"I certainly do," was the answer. "I have told your youngsters something about Snow Lodge, and they seemed to like the place. I heard them talking among themselves, on the way back here, how they'd like to go there.

"Oh, that's all right--no harm done!" exclaimed Mr. Carford, as he looked at the blushing faces of Nan and Bert. "I'm glad I did overhear what you were saying. It is a shame to keep that place locked up, and I'm just beginning to realize it.

"I don't want to go there myself, but that's no reason why others shouldn't. So, Mr. Bobbsey, if you like, you can take your whole family up there to Snow Lodge, near the lake, and in the woods, and stay as long as you like. Here are the keys!" and Mr. Carford tossed a jingling bunch on the table.

Day 147

1. Read chapter 9.
2. What is Mr. Bobbsey's story?

Chapter 9 Mr. Bobbsey's Story

"Snow Lodge! Oh, Papa, could we go there?" cried Flossie, now wide awake.

"What fun we could have!" exclaimed Freddie, whose eyes were now as wide open as ever they had been.

Bert and Nan said little, but there was a look of pleased anticipation on their faces. They, too, realized what fun they could have in a big, old-fashioned farmhouse in winter, particularly when the building was refitted with a furnace, and had big fireplaces in it.

And Bert was wondering, more than ever, what strange reason Mr. Carford could have for not wanting to go back to lovely Snow Lodge.

"Say we can go, Daddy!" pleaded the two smaller twins, as they tried to get into their father's lap.

"Well," said Mr. Bobbsey slowly, "this is certainly very kind of, you, Mr. Carford, but I am not sure I can accept it. I am very much obliged to you, however--"

"Accept! Of course you can accept!" exclaimed the aged man. "There's no reason why you and your family shouldn't have a holiday vacation at Snow Lodge. The place has been closed up a long time, but a day or so, with a good fire in it, would make it as warm as toast. I know, for I've been there on the coldest winter days. Now you just plan to go up there with the wife and children, and have a good time. It might as well be used as to stand idle and vacant, as it is."

"What do you say, Mother?" and Mr. Bobbsey looked at his wife. "Shall we go to Snow Lodge?"

"The children would like it," said Mrs. Bobbsey slowly.

"Like it! I should say we would!" cried Nan. "I can take some pictures of the birds with my new camera--the one I am going to get for Christmas," she added with a smile.

"Oh ho! So you are going to have a camera for Christmas; are you?" laughed her father.

"I--I hope so," she replied.

"And I can build a snowhouse and live in it like the Esquimos," added Bert.

"Then I'm going to live with you!" cried Freddie. "Please go to Snow Lodge, Mamma!"

"Yes, take the youngsters up," urged Mr. Carford. "At least don't decide against it now. I'll leave the keys with you, and you can go any time you like. I don't suppose it will be until after Christmas, though, for Santa Claus might not be able to get up there," and he pinched Freddie's fat cheek.

"No, don't go until after Santa Claus has been here," urged Flossie seriously, and her mother laughed.

"Well, I must be going, anyhow," said Mr. Carford, after a pause. "It will be dark before I get back, and the storm seems to be coming up quickly. Emma will worry, I'm afraid. Now you just think it over about Snow Lodge," he concluded, "and I guess you will go, Mr. Bobbsey. You know my reasons for not wanting to set foot in the place, so I don't need to tell you.

"Now, good-bye. Go to Snow Lodge, and have a good time, and when you come back, children, tell me all about it. If I can't go there at least I like to hear about the place."

Mr. Carford went out to his team, through the now driving snow. He little realized what a joyful story the Bobbsey twins were to bring back to him from Snow Lodge, nor how it was to change his feeling in regard for his boyhood home.

"Papa," said Bert soberly, after the visitor had gone, leaving the keys of Snow Lodge behind him, "what is the secret about Mr. Carford and that winter place? And you're mixed up in it, I'm sure."

"What makes you sure, Bert?"

"Well, I've been thinking so ever since that day I helped to catch his runaway horses, and he said this was the second time a Bobbsey had tried to do him a favor.'"

"Had your favor anything to do with Snow Lodge, Papa?" asked Nan, as she put her arms about his neck.

"Well, yes, daughter, in a way. And, since Mr. Carford has told you part of the story, I may as well tell you the other half, I suppose."

"Oh, another story!" cried Flossie, in delight.

"Yes, we must be quiet and listen," said Freddie, as he drew up a stool close to his father.

"It isn't a very nice sort of story," went on Mr. Bobbsey. "In fact it is rather sad. But I'll tell it to you, anyhow. Did Mr. Carford tell you about when he was a boy?"

"Yes, and how he went away, and came back rich, and found all his folks gone and the farm sold," said Nan.

"Yes. Well, I guess he told you then, how he took his nephew, Henry Burdock, to live with him. He loved Henry almost as if he were his own son, and did everything for him. In fact he planned to leave him all his money. Then came a quarrel."

"What about?" asked Bert softly.

"Over some money. Henry was a young man who liked to spend considerable, and though he was not bad he was different from the country boys. Mr. Carford gave him plenty of spending money, however, and did not ask him what became of it.

"Then, one day, a large sum of money was missing from Snow Lodge. Mr. Carford accused Henry of taking it, and Henry said he had seen nothing of it. Then came a quarrel, and Mr. Carford, in a fit of temper, drove Henry away from Snow Lodge. There were bitter words on both sides, and after that Mr. Carford closed up the place, and has not been near it since. That is the part of the story Mr. Carford did not tell you."

"But where do you come in, Daddy?" asked Nan. "Did you find the missing money?"

"No, Nan, though I wish I had. But I was sure Henry had not taken it, and I tried to make Mr. Carford believe so. That is what he meant by me trying to do him a favor. But he would not have it so, and, for a time, he had some feeling against me. But it passed away, for he realized that I was trying to help him.

"But since then Mr. Carford and his nephew, Henry Burdock, have not spoken. As I said, Mr. Carford drove the young man away from Snow Lodge. It was in a raging storm and Henry might have frozen, only I found him and took him to a hotel. I helped look after him until he could get a start. It was a very sad affair, and it has spoiled Mr. Carford's life, for he loved Henry very much."

"And did Henry really take the money?" asked Freddie. "That was wicked, I think."

"You must not say so, Freddie," spoke Mr. Bobbsey. "We do not know that Henry did take it. No one knows. It is a mystery. I, myself feel sure that Henry did not, but I can not prove that he did not take it. His uncle believes that he did. At any rate the money disappeared."

"And where was it when Mr. Carford last saw it?" asked Nan.

"Mr. Carford left it on the mantlepiece in the big living room of Snow Lodge," said Mr. Bobbsey. "Henry was the only other person, beside himself, who was in the room, and in some way the money was taken. I even went so far as to have a man from the police station look all over the house, hoping he could find the roll of bills somewhere, but it did not come to light. And so, ever since, there has been a bad feeling between Henry and his uncle."

"What does Henry Burdock do now?" asked Bert.

"He roams about the woods, as a sort of guide and hunter. Sometimes, I am told, he comes close to Snow Lodge and looks down on it from a distant hill, thinking of the happy days he spent there."

"Maybe we'll see him when we go up," said Freddie. "If I do I'll give him all the money in my bank so he can be friends with his uncle again."

"No, Freddie," said Mrs. Bobbsey solemnly. "You must not speak of what you have just heard. It is a sad story, and is best forgotten. Both Mr. Carford and Henry feel badly enough about it, so it will be best not to mention it. Just forget all about it if we go to Snow Lodge."

"But we are going; aren't we, Papa?" asked Bert. "The trip to the woods would do us all good."

"Well, I think we might take advantage of Mr. Carford's kind offer," said Mr. Bobbsey. "Yes, we'll plan to go to Snow Lodge!"

"Hurrah!" cried Nan and Bert, grasping each other by the hands and swinging around in a sort of waltz.

"Can we take our sleds," asked Flossie.

"I'm going to take my skates--maybe I'll skate all the way there--I could--on the lake!" exclaimed Freddie, and he wondered why the others laughed.

"Well, we'll make our plans later," said Mrs. Bobbsey. "Now, children, we'll have an early supper and then you must all get to bed. Christmas will come so much earlier if you go to sleep now."

"Oh, jolly Christmas!" cried Nan. "I can hardly wait!"

Day 148

1. Read the beginning of chapter 10.

Chapter 10 Unwelcome News (first half)

"Merry Christmas!"

"Merry Christmas to everybody!"

"Oh, Christmas is here! I wonder what I got?"

"I'm going to get up and see!"

The Bobbsey twins were calling to one another from their rooms, and papa and mamma Bobbsey were replying to their children's happy greetings. It was Flossie who had made the exclamation about wondering what Santa Claus had brought her, and it was Freddie who declared he was going to get up to see.

Soon the patter of bare feet announced that the two younger twins were scampering downstairs.

"You must put on your dressing gowns and slippers, my dears!" called Mrs. Bobbsey. "You'll take cold. Nan, look after them; will you?"

"Yes, mother, in just a minute. As soon as I can find my own things," and Nan got out of bed. She and Bert were not in so much of a hurry as Flossie and Freddie for they were getting older, and though Christmas was still a source of great joy to them they were not so anxious to see what gifts they had. Still Nan was eager to know if her camera had come.

From the parlor below came cries, shouts and peals of delighted and surprised laughter as Flossie and Freddie discovered their different gifts.

"Look at my book!" cried Flossie. "And a doll--a doll that you can wind up, and she walks and says 'mamma.' Look, Freddie!" and the little girl started the doll off across the room.

"Pooh! Look at what I got!" cried Freddie. "It's a fire engine, and it squirts real water. I'm going to put some in it, and play fire."

He started for the kitchen with his toy, but Nan caught him.

"Not just yet, little fat fireman," she said with a laugh, as she took him up in her arms. "You can't splash in the cold water until you have more clothes on. Get dressed and then you may play with your toys."

"All right!" answered Freddie. "Oh, look, I've got a wind-up steamboat, too. Oh! let me down so I can look at it, Nan! Now please do!"

Nan saw a pile of her own gifts, so she set Freddie down for a moment, intending to carry him up stairs a little later. She had wrapped a robe about Flossie, who was contentedly playing with her newest doll, and looking at her other presents. Santa Claus had been kind to the Bobbsey twins that Christmas.

Bert, big boy though he thought himself getting to be, could no longer resist the temptation to come down in his bath robe to see what he had received, and a little later fat Dinah, roused earlier than usual by the joyous shouts of the children, came lumbering in.

"Oh, Dinah! Dinah! Look what you got!" cried Flossie. "Your things are all here on this chair," and the little girl led the fat cook over toward it.

"Things fo' me? What yo'-all talkin' 'bout chile? Ole Dinah don't git no Christmas!" protested the jolly colored woman, laughing so that she shook all over.

"Yes, you do get a Christmas, Dinah. Look here!" and Flossie showed where there were some useful presents for the cook,--large aprons, warm shoes, an umbrella, and a bright shawl that Dinah had been wanting for a long time.

"What? All dem fo' me?" asked the surprised cook. "Good land a' massy! I guess ole Santa Claus done gone an' made a beef-steak this time, suah!"

"No, there's no mistake! See, they've got your name on!" insisted Flossie. "See, Dinah!" and she led the cook over to the chair where the presents were piled. There was no doubt of it, they were for Dinah, and near them was another chair containing gifts for her husband, Sam. He would not be in until later, however. But Dinah saw a pair of rubber boots that would be very useful in the deep snow, and there were other fine presents for Sam.

Bert and Nan were now looking at their things, and Mr. and Mrs. Bobbsey could be heard moving around upstairs, having decided that it was useless to lie abed longer now that the children were up.

"Come, come, Flossie and Freddie!" called Mrs. Bobbsey. "You must get dressed and then you can play as much as you like. I don't want you to get cold. If you do you can't go to Snow Lodge, remember!"

This was enough to cause the small Bobbseys to scamper upstairs. Flossie carried her doll with her, and Freddie took along his fire engine, for that was the gift he had most wanted, and for which he had begged and pleaded for weeks before Christmas.

Feeling that a little liberty might be allowed on this day, Mrs. Bobbsey did not insist on the younger children dressing completely until after breakfast, so in their warm robes and slippers Flossie and Freddie were soon again examining their toys, discovering new delights every few minutes.

Nan was busy inspecting her camera, while Bert was looking at a new postage stamp album he had long wanted, when from the kitchen where Dinah was getting breakfast came a series of excited cries, mingled with laughter and shouts of:

"Fire! Fire! Fire!"

"Mercy! What's that?" screamed Mrs. Bobbsey, turning pale.

Mr. Bobbsey made a rush for the kitchen. Nan and Bert, with Flossie, gathered about their mother. Then they heard Dinah calling:

"Stop it, Freddie! Stop it I done tell you! Does yo'-all want me t' git soaked? An' yo'-all will suah spoil them pancakes! Oh, now yo' hab done it! Yo' squirted right in mah mouf! Oh mah goodness sakes alive!"

Mrs. Bobbsey looked relieved.

"Freddie must be up to some prank," she said.

"Freddie, stop it!" commanded Mr. Bobbsey, and then he was heard to laugh. The others all went out to the kitchen and there they saw a curious sight.

Day 149

1. Finish chapter 10. They all just went to the kitchen where they find a curious sight.
2. Who is going to be their neighbor at Snow Lodge? (Answers)

Chapter 10 (second half)

Freddie, with his new toy fire engine, was pumping water on fat Dinah, who was laughing so heartily that she could do nothing to stop him. Mr. Bobbsey, too, was shouting with mirth, for the hose from the toy engine was rather small, and threw only a thin, fine spray.

"I'm a fireman!" cried Freddie, "and I'm pretending Dinah is on fire. See her red apron-- that's the fire!" and the little fellow turned the crank of his engine harder than ever, throwing the tiny stream of water all over the kitchen.

"That's enough, Freddie," said Mr. Bobbsey, when he could stop laughing. Dinah was still shaking with mirth, and Freddie, looking in the tank of the engine, said:

"There's only a little more water left. Can't I squirt that?"

Without waiting for permission Freddie made the water spurt from the nozzle of the hose. At that moment the door of the kitchen opened, to let in Sam. With him came Snap, the trick dog, and the tiny stream of water caught Sam full in the face.

"Hello! What am dat?" he demanded in surprise. "Am de house leakin'?"

"It's my new fire engine!" cried Freddie. "I didn't mean to wet you, Sam, but I was playing Dinah was on fire!"

"Well, yo'-all didn't wet me so very much," replied Sam, with a grin that showed his white teeth. "Dat suah am a fine fire engine!"

Snap sprang about, barking and wagging his tail, and, there being no more water in Freddie's engine, he had to stop pumping, for which every one was glad.

"You must not do that again," said Mrs. Bobbsey, when the excitement was over, and laughing Dinah had dried her face, and put on another apron. "You frightened us all, Freddie, and that is not nice, you know."

"I won't, Mamma, but I did want to try my fire engine."

"Then you must do it in the bath room where the water will do no harm. But come now, children, get your breakfast and then you will have the whole day to look at your toys."

Breakfast was rather a hurried affair, and every now and then Flossie and Freddie would leave the table to see some of their gifts. But finally the meal was over and then came more joyous times. Sam received his presents, and Mr. and Mrs. Bobbsey had time to look at theirs, for Santa Claus had not forgotten them.

"And there's something for Snap, and for Snoop, too!" exclaimed Freddie. "Snoop has a new ribbon with a silver bell, and Snap a new collar, with his name on," and soon the cat and dog, newly adorned, were being put through some of their tricks.

If I tried to tell you all that went on in the Bobbsey house that Christmas this book would contain nothing else. So I will only say that the holiday was one of the most delightful the twins ever remembered.

"And then to think, with all this, that we are to go to Snow Lodge! It's great!" cried Bert.

"I hope I can get some good pictures up there with my camera," said Nan. "Will you show me how it works, Bert?"

"Yes, and we'll go out to-day and try it. I want to see how my new skates go, too. The lake is frozen and we'll have some fun."

The day was cold and clear. There had been a little fall of snow during the night, but not enough to spoil the skating, and soon Bert and Nan were on their way to the lake, while Flossie and Freddie, after inspecting all their presents over again, had gone out to play on their sleds.

This gave Dinah and Mrs. Bobbsey time to get ready the big Christmas dinner, with the roast turkey, for Mr. Bobbsey had brought home one of the largest he could find.

While Flossie and Freddie were playing on the hill, a small one near their home, they heard a voice calling to them:

"Want a ride, youngsters?"

Looking up they saw Mr. Carford in his big sled. It was filled with baskets and packages, and the Bobbsey twins guessed rightly that the generous old man was taking around his Christmas contributions to the poor families.

"Yes, we'll go!" cried Freddie. "What shall we do with our sleds?" asked Flossie.

"Oh, Harry Stone will look after them; won't you Harry?" asked Freddie, "He can use mine, and his sister Jessie can use yours until we come back, Flossie," and Freddie turned the coasters over to a poor boy and girl who lived near the Bobbsey home. Harry and his sister were delighted, and promised to take good care of the sleds.

"I won't take you far--only just around town," said Mr. Carford, as the twins got in his sled. "When are you going up to my Snow Lodge?"

"We're going soon, I guess," answered Flossie. "I heard mamma and papa talking about it yesterday."

"And we're ever so much obliged to you for letting us have your place," said Flossie. "Will you come up and see us while we're there? I've got a doll that can talk."

"And I'm going to take my fire engine along, so if the place gets on fire I can help put it out," exclaimed Freddie. "Will you come up?"

Mr. Carford started. He looked at the children in a strange sort of way, and then stared at the horses.

"No--no--I guess I won't go to Snow Lodge any more," he said slowly, and Flossie and Freddie were sorry they had asked him, for they remembered the story their father had told them about the sorrow that had come to the aged man.

But the children soon forgot this in the joy of helping in the distribution of the good things in the sled, and the happiness brought to many poor families seemed to make up, in a way, for what Mr. Carford had suffered in the trouble over his nephew.

When all the gifts had been given out from the sled, Mr. Carford drove the two younger Bobbsey twins back to the hill where they again had fun coasting.

Meanwhile Nan and Bert were having a good time on the ice. Nan's camera was used to take a number of pictures, which the children hoped would turn out well.

While Bert was taking a picture of Nan, Charley Mason came skating up, and Bert, whose best chum he was, insisted that Charley get in the picture also.

"My!" exclaimed Charley, as he saw Nan's camera, "that's a fine one!"

"I just got it to-day," said Nan, with a pleased smile. "I'm going to take a lot of pictures up at Snow Lodge."

"Snow Lodge," repeated Charley. "You mean that place Mr. Carford owns?"

"Yes," replied Bert. "He is going to let us all go up there for three weeks or so."

"Say, that's funny," spoke Charley. "You'll have some other Lakeport folks near you."

"Who else is going up to Snow Lodge?" asked Nan.

"Well, they're not exactly going to Snow Lodge," replied Charley, "but I heard a while ago that Danny Rugg and his folks were going up to a winter camp near there. Mr. Rugg has bought a lumber tract in the woods, and he's going to see about having some of the trees cut. Danny is going, too. So you'll have him for a neighbor."

"Oh, dear!" exclaimed Nan, in dismay. "That spoils everything!"

"Well, if Danny tries any of his tricks I'll get after him!" exclaimed Bert, firmly. But he looked anxious over the unwelcome news Charley had brought.

Day 150

1. Read chapter 11.
2. What plans do they have to make?

Chapter 11 Making Plans

"Are you sure this is so--is Danny Rugg really going up to the woods near Snow Lodge?" asked Bert of Charley, after a pause.

"That's what Frank Smith told me," replied Charley, "and you know Frank and Danny are great chums."

"That's so. Well, if Danny doesn't bother us we won't make any trouble for him," said Bert. "Still, I'd rather he would go somewhere else."

"If Mr. Rugg is going up to see about having lumber cut," said Nan, "I guess there won't be much fun for Danny. Maybe he won't bother us at all."

"He will if he gets a chance," declared her brother. "Danny's just that kind. But we'll wait and see."

Bert, Nan and Charley talked for some time longer about the trip to Snow Lodge, and then, as it was getting nearly time for dinner, they skated down the lake toward their homes.

"How are you folks going up to the lodge?" asked Charley, before parting from Bert and Nan.

"Oh, I guess father will take one of his big lumber sleds and drive us all up," replied Bert. "We'll have to take along lots of things to eat, for it's a good ways to the store, and we might get snowed in."

"That's right," said Charley. "But say, why don't you and Freddie go up in our iceboat, the Ice Bird? It isn't much of a run to Snow Lodge, on the lake, and it's good going now."

"I never thought of that!" exclaimed Bert. "I wonder if father would let us?"

"You can ask him," said Nan. "I'd like to skate up, if it wasn't so far. But I don't believe it would be safe to take Freddie on the ice- boat, Bert. He's so little, and so easily excited that he might tumble out."

"That's right. And yet it will be no fun to sail it alone. I wish you could go with me, Charley."

"I wish I could, but I don't see how I can. My folks are going to my grandmother's for a couple of weeks. Otherwise I'd be glad to go."

"Well, maybe my father will sail in the ice-boat with me," spoke Bert. "I guess I'll ask him."

Bert and Nan had much to talk about as they skated on, having bidden Charley goodbye, and their conversation was mostly about the new idea of getting to Snow Lodge on the ice.

"I don't want to skate alone, any more than you want to go in the ice- boat alone," said Nan. "But maybe mamma and papa will let us invite some of our friends to spend a week or so at Snow Lodge with us. Then it would be all right."

"It surely would," said Bert.

The Christmas dinner at the Bobbsey home was a jolly affair, and while it was being eaten Bert spoke to his father about the ice-boat.

"Do you think it will carry you to the upper end of the lake?" asked Mr. Bobbsey with a smile, for Bert and Charley had made the boat themselves, with a little help. Though it was a home-made affair, Bert was as proud of it as though a large sum had been spent for it.

"Of course it will carry us to Snow Lodge," he said. "There would be room for four or five on it, if the wind was strong enough to carry us to the head of the lake. But I don't want to go alone, Father. Could you come?"

"I'm afraid not," laughed Mr. Bobbsey. "I'll have to go in the big sled with your mother, and the provisions. We're going to take Dinah and Sam along, you know. Can't you ask some of your boy friends? I guess there's room enough at the Lodge."

"That's just what I'll do!" exclaimed Bert "I'll see who of the boys can go."

"And may I ask Grace Lavine or Nellie Parks?" inquired Nan. "We could skate up, or go part way in the ice-boat with the boys."

"I think so," said Mrs. Bobbsey.

"I know who you could take on the iceboat," said Freddie, passing his plate for more turkey.

"Who?" asked Bert.

"Dinah!" cried the little fellow. "She would be so heavy that she couldn't roll off, and if the ice-boat started to blow away she'd be as good as an anchor."

"That's right!" cried Nan. "Dinah, did you hear what Freddie is planning for you?" she asked as the fat cook came in with the plum pudding.

"I 'clar t' goodness I neber knows what dat ar' chile will be up to next!" exclaimed Dinah with a laugh. "But if he am plannin' to squirt any mo' fire injun water on me I's gwine t' run away, dat's what I is!"

They all laughed at this, Dinah joining in, and then Freddie explained what he had said.

"No, sah! Yo' don't cotch me on no ice-cream boat!" declared Dinah. "I'll go in a sled, but I ain't gwine t' fall down no hole in de ice and be bit by a fish! No, sah!"

There was more laughter, and then the plum pudding was served. Freddie begged that Snoop and Snap be given an extra good dinner, on account of it being Christmas, and Dinah promised to see to this.

Mr. and Mrs. Bobbsey discussed the plans for going to Snow Lodge. They agreed that Bert and Nan, if they wished, might each ask a friend, for the old farmhouse in the woods on the edge of the lake contained many rooms. It was completely furnished, all that was needed being food.

"So if you young folks want to skate or ice-boat up the lake I see no objection," said Mr. Bobbsey. "The rest of us will go in a big sled."

"Couldn't I go in the ice-boat?" asked Freddie. "I'm getting big. I'm almost in the first reader book."

"We're going so fast your fire engine might be lost overboard," said Bert with a smile, and that was enough for his little brother. He didn't want that to happen for the world, so he gave up the plan of going on the Ice Bird.

"I don't like the idea of that Danny Rugg going to be near us," said Mrs. Bobbsey to her husband, when Bert had told this news. "He's sure to make trouble."

"Perhaps not," said Mr. Bobbsey. "Bert generally manages to hold his own when Danny bothers him."

"Yes, I know. But it always makes hard feelings. I do wish Danny wasn't going up there."

"Well, the woods are open, and we can't stop him," said Mr. Bobbsey, with a smile. The children had gone out to play, and the house was quiet once more.

"There is a great deal to do to get ready," went on Mrs. Bobbsey. "But I think the trip will do us all good. I only hope none of us take cold."

"Don't worry," advised her husband. "I'll see Mr. Carford, and have the fires made up a couple of days before we arrive. That will make the house good and warm, and dry it out."

They talked over the various things they had to do in order to make their stay at Snow Lodge pleasant, and then went out to call on some friends.

That afternoon Bert and Nan extended the invitation to Snow Lodge to a number of their boy and girl friends, explaining how they were going to make the trip on skates or on the ice-boat.

But one after another declined. Either their parents had made other plans for spending the Christmas holidays, or they did not think it wise to let their children go off in the woods.

Bert asked a number of boys he knew, but none of them could go, and Grace Lavine, Nellie Parks, and many other girls to whom Nan spoke, made excuses.

"I guess we'll have to give up the ice-boat plan," said Bert, regretfully that night to Nan. "No one seems able to go. Will you risk it with me, Nan?"

"I wouldn't be afraid," she answered. "If mamma and papa will let me I'll sail in the Ice Bird with you."

"Then we'll go that way!" cried Bert. But the next day something occurred that made a change in the plans of the Bobbsey twins.

Day 151

1. Read chapter 12.
2. Who is coming to Snow Lodge with the twins? (Answers)

Chapter 12 The Letters

The day after Christmas, when Bert and Nan came home from having been to see a number of their friends, but not having succeeded in getting any of them to promise to make the trip to Snow Lodge, the two older Bobbsey twins were quite discouraged.

"I'll need another fellow to help me sail the ice-boat," spoke Bert. "Of course I know you'll do all you can, Nan, but we can't tell what might happen. I don't see what's the matter with all the fellows, anyhow, that they can't go."

"And the girls, too," added Nan. "I couldn't get one of them to promise. And I don't know whether mamma and papa will let you and me go in the ice-boat by ourselves."

And, when they heard of this plan, both Mr. and Mrs. Bobbsey objected to it.

"It would be too risky," decided Mr. Bobbsey. "Your ice-boat is a small one. I know, Bert, but in a stiff wind it might capsize if you did not have some other boy along to help you manage it. I guess you and Nan had better come with us in the big sled."

"I think so, too," added Mrs. Bobbsey.

There seemed to be no other way out of it, and Nan and Bert felt quite badly. Not even the tricks of Snap and Snoop, when Freddie and Flossie put the dog and cat through them before going to bed, would cause their older brother and sister to look happy.

"Never mind," said Mamma Bobbsey, "when we get to Snow Lodge you'll have such a good time that you won't mind not having made the trip on skates or on the ice-boat. And you can skate all you like when you get up there."

The next day Freddie was playing quite a game. He had a little toy village, made of pasteboard houses, and this he had set up in the playroom. He was pretending that a fire had broken out in one of the dwellings and he was going to put it out with his toy engine. Of course there was not even a match on fire, for Mrs. Bobbsey was very careful about this, but Freddie pretended to his heart's content. He was allowed to have real water, but Dinah had spread on the floor an old rubber coat so that the spray would do no harm.

With a great shout Freddie came running out of the "engine house," which was a chair turned on its side. He was pulling his toy after him, racing to the make-believe blaze.

Just then Flossie came into the room with her new walking doll, and, not seeing her, Freddie ran into and knocked her over.

Flossie sat down quite hard, and for a moment was too surprised to cry. But a moment later, when she saw Freddie's fire engine run over her new doll, which cried out "Mamma!" as if in pain, the tears came into Flossie's eyes.

"Oh, you bad boy!" she exclaimed, forgetting her own pain, at the sight of her doll, "you've run right over her!"

"I--I couldn't help it!" said Freddie, stopping in his rush to the fire to pick up his sister's toy. "You got right in my way."

"I did not--Freddie Bobbsey!"

"Yes, you did, too, and I'm going to squirt water on you, and put you out. You're on fire! Your cheeks are all red!"

This was true enough. Flossie did get very red cheeks when she was excited.

"Don't you put any water on me!" she cried. "I'll tell mamma on you! And you've broke my best doll, too! Oh, dear!" and Flossie burst into tears, so there was no need for Freddie to use his toy engine to wet her flaming cheeks.

This frightened Freddie. He seldom made his twin sister cry, and he was very much alarmed.

"I--I didn't mean to, Flossie," he said, putting his arms around her. "I guess I was running pretty fast. Don't cry, and you can squirt my engine. Maybe if you squirted some water on your doll she'd be all right," and Freddie picked up the talking toy.

"Don't you dare put any water on her!" screamed Flossie. "You'll make her catch cold, and then she won't talk at all, Oh, dear! I wish you didn't have that old engine."

Mrs. Bobbsey came into the room just then, or there is no telling what might have happened. She knew what to do, and soon she had straightened out matters. It was not very often that Flossie and Freddie had trouble of this kind, but they were only human children, just like any others, and they had their little disputes now and then.

"Oh, dear! This will never do!" said Mrs. Bobbsey. "Freddie, you must not rush about the house so fast."

"But, mamma, firemens is always fast. They have to be fast, and I was going to a fire," the fat little fellow said.

"I know, dear, but you should look where you are going. And, Flossie, dear, you must watch out before you rush into a room, you know."

"Yes, mamma, but, you see, I was pretending my doll was sick, and I was running to the doctor's with her."

"Oh, dear!" cried Mamma Bobbsey. "You were both in too much of a hurry, I think. Never mind. Let's see if the doll is hurt, much."

It seemed that she was, for though she would walk across the room when wound up, she would not cry out "Mamma!" But Mrs. Bobbsey was used to mending broken toys, and after poking about in the wheels and springs with a hairpin she soon had the doll so it would talk again. Then Flossie was happy, and her tears were forgotten.

Freddie said he was sorry he had been in such a hurry, so all was forgiven, and he went on playing fireman. He was in the midst of putting out a make-believe blaze in the village church when the doorbell rang, and the postman's whistle was heard.

"Will you get the mail, dear?" asked Mrs. Bobbsey of Freddie. "Dinah is busy, I'm sure. Let me see how mamma's little fat fireman can get the letters. But don't run!" she exclaimed, "or you might fall downstairs."

"I won't, mamma," said Freddie.

He came back with several letters, and he was again playing he was a fireman, and Flossie was making believe she was a doctor for her sick doll, when Mrs. Bobbsey exclaimed:

"Oh, this will be good news for Bert," and she looked up from a letter she was reading.

"What is it, mamma?" asked Flossie. "Is someone sending him more Christmas presents?"

"No, dear, but Harry, your cousin from the country, you know, is coming to visit us. Bert will have someone to play with. Won't that be nice?"

"And can I play with him, too?" asked Freddie.

"I guess so, sometimes," said Mrs. Bobbsey. "But you must remember that Harry is about ten years old, and he won't always want to be with little boys."

"I'm a big boy!" declared Freddie. "I'm 'most as big as Bert."

"Well, I guess you can have some fun," said Mrs. Bobbsey. "Bert will be glad to hear this. Now, who can this other letter be from?" and she tore open the envelope.

"Why!" she cried, as she quickly read it "It's from Uncle William Minturn, at the seashore, and he says his daughter Dorothy is coming to pay us a visit. Well, did you ever! Our two cousins--one from the country and the other from the seashore--both coming at the same time! Oh, this will please Bert and Nan!"

"And can't we have a good time, too?" asked Flossie.

"Of course," said Mrs. Bobbsey. "Let me see now; how will I arrange the rooms for them? Oh, I forgot, we're going to Snow Lodge soon. I wonder what I can do? Both Dorothy and Harry will be here before I can tell them not to come. I must telephone to papa!"

Bert and Nan came in just then, in time to hear this last.

"Telephone to papa!" exclaimed Bert "What's the matter, mother? Has anything happened?"

"Nothing, only your cousins, Dorothy and Harry, are coming to visit you. And I don't know what to do about it, as we are going to Snow Lodge!"

"Do about it?" cried Bert. "Why, we won't do anything about it, except to let them come. Say, this is the best news yet! Harry can go with me on the ice-boat. Hurray! Hurray!"

"Yes, and Dorothy and I can skate on the lake!" said Nan. "Oh, how glad I am!"

"We'll take them both to Snow Lodge!" cried Bert. "Now we won't have to look for any other boys or girls. Well have our own cousins! Whoop!" and he threw his arms around his mother, while Nan tried to kiss her. Flossie and Freddie looked on in pleased surprise. The letters had come just in time. Now there would be a jolly party at Snow Lodge.

Day 152

1. Read the beginning of chapter 13.
2. Tell someone about what's happening.

Chapter 13 In a Hard Blow (first part)

"Are you girls warm enough?" asked Bert Bobbsey, as he and his cousin Harry started toward the frozen lake one afternoon, the day before they were all to start for Snow Lodge.

"If we aren't we will never be," answered Dorothy Minturn, who was Nan's "seashore cousin" as she called the visitor. "I've got on so many things that it would be easier to roll along instead of walking," went on Dorothy with a laugh.

"Well, it's a good thing to be warm, for it will be cold on the ice- boat; won't it, Bert?" asked Harry.

"That's what it will. There's a good wind blowing, too. It's stronger than I thought it was," and Bert bent to the blast as he walked along with the others.

"Will there be any danger?" asked Dorothy, who was not used to the activities of the Bobbseys.

"Oh, don't worry!" cried Harry. "We'll look after you girls."

"They think they will," murmured Nan looking at her cousin, "I guess I know almost as much about the Ice Bird as Bert does."

"Where is your ice-boat?" asked Harry of Bert, as they kept on along the path that led to the lake.

"Over in the next cove. I had her out the other day, and the wind died out, leaving me there. Since then we've been so busy getting ready to go to Snow Lodge that I haven't had time to bring her back to the dock."

"Will she be safe over there?"

"I guess so--hardly anybody goes there in winter."

The two cousins--Harry from the country and Dorothy from the seashore,--in each of which places the Bobbseys had spent part of the preceding summer,--had followed soon after their letters, and had been warmly welcomed by Nan, Bert, Flossie and Freddie. The visitors were rather surprised to learn that the Bobbsey family was preparing to go away for a winter vacation in the woods, but they were only too glad to accept an invitation to go along.

So it was arranged, and in another day the start to Mr. Carford's former home would be made. Mr. Bobbsey had a big sled gotten ready, there were boxes, barrels and packages of provisions, Snow Lodge had been opened by a farmer living near there, who remained in it all night, keeping up the fires so that the long-deserted house would not be chilly, and all was in readiness.

The plans of Nan and Bert to go to Snow Lodge by means of skates and on the ice-boat had been agreed to.

Dorothy and Nan thought they would rather skate than go all the way on the ice-boat, but Bert and Harry decided to keep to the ice craft all the way.

"And when you girls get tired of skating just wave your handkerchiefs, and we'll wait for you," said Bert.

Now they were going to take a little trial sail on the *Ice Bird* before starting off on the longer cruise.

As the four walked around a point of land, and came within sight of the ice-boat, tied to a stake in the ice of the cove, Harry uttered a cry.

"Look!" he exclaimed to Bert, "someone is at your boat!"

"That's right!" cried Bert, starting to run. Just then a figure skated away from the craft, and Bert breathed a sigh of relief.

"I guess it was only someone taking a look at her," he said "There aren't many on the lake."

"We can't go very far," said Nan, as they neared the boat, "for mamma said to be back early. We've got a great deal of packing to do yet."

"We'll just take a little spin," replied Bert.

They were soon on the ice-boat, gliding up and down the lake, which was frozen to a glassy smoothness.

"If it's like this to-morrow it will be grand for skating!" exclaimed Nan.

"Yes, and fine for ice-boating, too," replied her brother. "We'll beat you to Snow Lodge."

"Well, you ought to," said Dorothy, "but we'll be warmer skating than you will be on the ice-boat."

"Not when we take along all the fur robes I've got out for the trip," replied Bert. "I didn't bring 'em this time, as it was too far to carry. But to-morrow Harry and I will be regular Eskimos."

Back and forth on the lake sailed the Ice Bird with the merry- hearted boys and girls. Bert did not go very far, as he noticed that the wind was growing much stronger and his boat, though sturdy and well-built, was not intended to weather a gale.

"Well, I think we'd better start for home now," said Nan after about an hour's sailing. "Mamma will be expecting us."

"All right," assented Bert. "Do you want to steer her, Harry?"

"I'm afraid I don't know how," replied the country lad.

"Oh, you'll soon learn. I'll be right beside you here, and tell you what to do."

"Don't upset, please, whatever you do," urged Dorothy.

"I'll try not to," promised Harry.

When they got out of the sheltered cove they felt the full force of the wind, and for a moment even Nan, who had been on the boat many times, felt a bit timid. The Ice Bird tilted to one side, the left hand runner raising high in the air.

"Oh!" screamed Dorothy. "We're going over!"

"No, we're not! Sit still!" cried Bert, grasping the tiller, which Harry was not holding just right. By turning the ice-boat to one side the wind did not strike it so hard, and the craft settled down on the level again.

"There! That's better!" exclaimed Dorothy, who had grabbed hold of Nan.

"Oh, that's nothing," said Nan. "Bert and I are used to that."

But as the ice-boat proceeded it was evident that those on her were not going to have an easy time to get to the Bobbsey dock. The wind blew harder and harder, and the sail seemed ready to rip apart. It took both Bert and Harry to hold the rudder steady, and even then the tiller was almost torn from their grasp.

Even Nan began to look a little frightened, and she did not laugh when Dorothy stretched out flat and held on to the side of the boat with all her strength.

"I don't want to be blown away if I can help it," said Dorothy.

Harder and harder blew the wind, sending the ice-boat along at great speed. In a few minutes more it would be at the dock, where Bert kept it tied.

"If it blows this way to-morrow we won't be long getting to Snow Lodge," cried Bert in Harry's ear. He had to shout to be heard above the howling of the wind.

"That's right," agreed the country boy. "The girls can never skate along as fast as this."

"We'll have to use less sail," went on Bert, "and then we won't go so fast."

Day 153

1. You are going to finish chapter 13 and then begin reading chapter 14.
2. Tell someone about what's happening.
3. What do you think is going to happen?

Chapter 13 (second part)

He and Harry shifted the rudder to steer closer to shore. Suddenly the wind came in a fierce gust. The ice-boat seemed about to turn completely over. The two girls screamed, even Nan being frightened now.

"Oh, what is it? What is it?" cried Dorothy.

Then came a sharp crack. There was a sound as though a hundred pop- guns were being fired, and the boat slackened speed.

"Look!" cried Harry pointing ahead "Our sail has burst, Bert"

"No, it's the sheet rope--the main rope that holds the sail fast- that's broken," replied Bert. "Lucky it did, too, or we might have gone over. I was going to let go of it."

The ice-boat slid along a short distance, and then came to a stop. The sail, no longer held in place so as to catch the wind, was blowing and flapping, making snapping sounds like a line of clothes in a heavy wind.

"All right, girls, no danger now," called Bert, as he got out to make the flapping sail fast again. As he looked at the end of the broken rope he uttered a cry of surprise.

"Look here!" he called to Harry, "this rope has been cut!"

"Cut?"

"Yes. Someone hacked it partly through with a knife, and the wind did the rest."

There was no doubt of it. The main rope had been partly severed, and the strain of the hard blow had done the rest.

"That fellow we saw near the ice-boat!" began Harry. "It must have been him! Who was he?"

"Danny Rugg--if anybody," answered Bert. "I thought it looked like him. Probably he heard that we were going to use the boat to go to Snow Lodge, and he wanted to make trouble for us. He's going to camp up there near us, I hear."

"Gracious!" cried Dorothy. "I hope he doesn't play any tricks like that up there."

"If he does I guess Harry and I can attend to him," cried Bert. "But, in a way, it's a good thing the rope did break or we might have upset. Only Danny, if he did it, had no idea of doing us a good turn. He just wanted to make trouble."

"Can you fix it?" asked Nan of her brother.

"Oh, yes, it can be spliced and will be stronger than ever. But I won't do it now. We can walk the rest of the way to the dock. The wind is blowing harder than ever, and we don't want any accidents."

Indeed, the wind was blowing a gale now, and even with the sail down the ice-boat went along at such a speed that it was all Harry and Bert could do to hold it.

But finally it was gotten to the dock, and made fast, and while the girls went on to the Bobbsey home to finish with their packing, Bert and Harry mended the broken rope.

"I'll have to teach Danny Rugg a good lesson," said Bert to his cousin.

"Yes, and I'll help you," returned Harry.

Chapter 14 At Snow Lodge (first part)

"Are we all here?"

"Have we got everything?"

"Here, Snap! If you jump out again you can't go!"

"Dinah, you hold Snap, will you?"

"Good lan' chile! I'se got about all I kin do to hold mah own self!"

These were some of the cries and exclamations as the Bobbsey family prepared to start on the trip to Snow Lodge. With the exception of Nan and Bert, and Dorothy and Harry, they were all in a big sled, drawn by four horses that were prancing about in the snow, anxious to get started. At every step the bells jingled. Sam, the colored man, was driving. With him on the front seat sat fat Freddie.

"I'm going to drive, as soon as we get out on the country road!" cried Freddie.

"He is not; is he, Sam?" demanded Flossie, who was taking one of her dolls on the trip, and with the doll, and her big muff, little Flossie had about all she could manage.

"Yes, I am too," declared Freddie. "You said I could, Sam; you know you did!"

"Well I guess you kin drive, where the roads are easy," promised the colored man, with a scratch of his black, kinky head.

Mr. and Mrs. Bobbsey were now on their seat, with Flossie between them. Dinah was on the seat behind, while in back of her were piled the packages of food.

Snap, the trick dog, was to be taken along, but it had been decided to leave Downy the duck, and Snoop, the fat, black cat at home. A neighbor had promised to look after them and feed them.

"Well, I guess we're all ready," said Mr. Bobbsey, as he looked back at the well-loaded sled. "Now be careful," he called to Nan and Bert, who with their cousins were to go to Snow Lodge on the icy lake. The girls would skate part of the way and ride on the ice-boat the remainder of the distance.

"We'll be careful," said Bert.

The day was cold, and clouds overhead seemed to tell that it was going to snow. But the young folks hoped the storm would hold off until night, when they would be safe in the big, old-fashioned farmhouse.

Everyone was well wrapped up, and Flossie and Freddie were almost lost in big rugs that had been tucked around them, for their mother did not want them to get cold.

Piles of rugs and blankets had been put on the ice-boat so those aboard would be comfortable.

"Well, let's start!" called Mr. Bobbsey finally. "We'll see who will get there first, Bert, or us."

"All right--a race then!" cried Nan.

Down to the glittering, icy lake went the boys and girls, down to where the ice-boat awaited them. It had been put in good shape for the trip, but before starting Bert and Harry looked over all the ropes to make sure none were frayed, or had been cut. Nothing had been seen of Danny Rugg, and Charley Mason told Bert he thought the bully had gone to the wood camp with his father.

"Don't you girls want to come on the iceboat for a ways first?" asked Bert of his sister and Dorothy. "Then, when you get tired of riding, you can skate."

"Shall we?" inquired Nan.

"I guess so," answered Dorothy, and so they did. The wind was not as strong as it had been the day before, but it was enough of a breeze to send the Ice Bird along at a good speed. Well wrapped in the robes and blankets, the young people enjoyed the trip very much.

"I'm sure we'll be there before papa and mamma are," said Nan as they glided along. "See how fast we are going."

"Yes, but this wind may not keep up all the way," spoke her brother. "And it's a good ways to Snow Lodge."

"Oh, well, we'll have a good time, anyhow," said Dorothy.

"And we'll stop and build a fire and have lunch when we're hungry," added Harry, for they had brought some food with them, and could make chocolate over a little fire.

Day 154

1. Finish chapter 14.
2. Tell someone about the chapter.

Chapter 14 (second part)

Meanwhile the sled-load of the Bobbseys with their two colored servants, and Snap was proceeding along the snowy road. The path had been well broken, and the going was good, so they made fairly fast time. But every now and then Snap would insist on jumping out to run along the road, and every time he did this Flossie and Freddie would set up a howl, fearing he would get lost.

"Snap!" exclaimed Mr. Bobbsey, when this had happened four or five times, "if you don't stay here quietly I'll tie you fast. Lie down, sir!"

Snap barked, wagged his tail, and looked at Mr. Bobbsey with his head tilted to one side as much as to say:

"Very well sir. I'll be good now. But I did want a little run." Then Snap curled up at Dinah's feet and gave no more trouble.

"I 'clar t' goodness!" exclaimed the colored cook, with a laugh that made her shake all over, "dat ar' Snap am a good foot-warmer, so he be. I jest hopes he don't jump out no mo', so I does." And, for a time at least, the trick dog seemed content to lie quietly in the sled.

It was not a very exciting trip for those in the sled, as they went along through the streets of Lakeport and so out into the open country. Then they passed through village after village, with little occurring. The roads were good, and occasionally they met other teams.

Once they came to a narrow place between two big drifts, and as another sled was coming toward them it was rather a race to see which one would get to the opening first.

"You can't go through when he does, Sam," said Mr. Bobbsey, nodding toward the other driver.

"I knows I can't, sah. But I'll get there first."

Sam called to his horses and they sprang forward. A little later they had reached the opening between the drifts and the other sled had to wait until the Bobbseys got out of the narrow place.

All this time Bert and the others were making their way up the lake on the ice. After going a mile or two on the ice-boat the wind died down so that the craft did not go very fast.

"Come on, Dorothy," called Nan, "let's skate for a ways. And if you get too far ahead of us, please wait, Bert," she added, and her brother promised that he and Harry would.

For a time Dorothy and Nan enjoyed the skating very much, and it was a welcome change from sitting still on the ice-boat. Then the wind sprang up again, and Harry and Bert got so far ahead that the two girls thought they should never be able to skate to them.

"Oh, I wish they'd wait," said Dorothy. "I'm getting tired."

"I'll wave to them--maybe they'll see my handkerchief," said Nan.

Bert and Harry did see the girls, and, guessing what the white signal meant, they lowered the sail of the ice-boat and waited for the two to come up. And the girls were glad enough now to sit amid the comfortable robes and blankets.

"Skating such a long distance is harder than I thought it would be," confessed Nan, with a sigh.

"Yes, the ice-boat is good enough for me," agreed Dorothy. "But when we get to Snow Lodge we'll do some skating."

"That's what we will," said Nan.

Mile after mile was covered by the Ice Bird. They passed small towns and villages on the shore of the frozen lake. Many of the places were known to Nan and Bert, who had often visited them in the summer time, rowing to them in their boat, or sailing to them with the older folks.

"Isn't it almost time to eat?" asked Bert after a bit. "That sun looks as if it were noon, Nan."

"It's half-past eleven," spoke Harry, glancing at his watch. "There's a nice little cove where we can be out of the wind, and where we can build a fire," he went on, pointing ahead.

"That's what we'll do!" cried Bert, steering toward it. "Now you girls will have a chance to show what sort of cooks you are."

"Humph! There's nothing to cook but chocolate!" said Nan. "Any one could make that."

They had brought with them the chocolate all ready to heat in a pot, and soon it was set over a fire of sticks which the boys had made on shore, scraping away the snow from the ground. Nan and Dorothy got out the packages of sandwiches and cake, and soon a merry little party was seated on the ice-boat, eating the good things.

The meal was soon over and then the young people got ready to resume their trip. Nan and Dorothy wanted to skate a bit, but Bert looking up at the sky, said:

"I don't think it will be safe. It looks as though it were going to storm soon, and we don't want to be caught in it. It isn't far to Snow Lodge now, and once we are there let it snow as much as it likes. But if it comes down before we get there we'll have hard work to keep on in the ice-boat. Even a little snow on the ice will clog the runners."

So the skating idea was given up, and soon they were under way in the ice-boat again. The clouds grew darker, and there were a few scattering flakes of snow.

"I guess we're going to be in for it," said Bert. "If the wind would only blow harder we could go faster."

As if in answer to his wish the wind started up and the boat fairly flew over the ice. Then the storm suddenly broke and the snow was so thick that they could not see where they were going.

"What shall we do?" cried Dorothy, who was not used to being out in such a blow.

"Keep on--that's the only thing to do," answered Bert. "We will go as far as we can in the boat and then we'll walk."

"Walk to Snow Lodge!" cried Nan. "We could never do it!"

"Oh, it isn't so far now," said her brother.

The snow fell so fast that soon the ice-boat went slower and slower. Finally it stopped altogether, the runners clogged with snow. The wind blowing on the sail nearly turned the craft over.

"Cast off those ropes!" cried Bert to Harry. "We'll have to leave her here and walk on."

The sail was lowered, the blankets and robes were picked up to be carried, and the four girls and boys set out over the ice.

"We must keep near the shore," said Bert, "Snow Lodge is right on the shore of the lake, and we can't miss it."

"Oh, suppose we did, and had to stay out all night?" cried Dorothy.

"We won't worry until we have to," spoke Nan.

It snowed harder and harder, and grew quite dark. Even Bert was worried. He and Harry walked on ahead, to keep the wind and snow as much as possible out of the faces of the girls.

"Bert, I'm sure we're lost!" cried Nan a little later. "We can't see where we're going! Don't go on any farther."

"We can't stay here on the ice all night," objected Bert.

"Well, it is pretty dark," said Harry. "Are there any houses around here?"

They gazed at the fast-gathering blackness all about them. They were beginning to be very much afraid. The wind howled, and the snow came down harder than ever.

"There's a light!" suddenly called Dorothy.

"Where?" cried all the others eagerly.

"There," answered Dorothy, pointing toward where they had last seen the land. "Right over in those trees."

"Then let's go toward it," suggested Bert. "Maybe they can tell us where Snow Lodge is, and if it's too far we'll stay there all night, if they'll let us."

The welcome light shone out through the storm and darkness. The four young folks made their way toward it as best they could, and, as they came nearer they could see that it was a big house in the midst of trees. Bert rubbed his eyes. He looked again, and then he cried:

"Why, it's Snow Lodge! It's Snow Lodge! We've found it after all! We're all right now! We're at Snow Lodge!"

"Hurray!" cried Harry.

"Oh, how glad I am!" said Nan, with her arms around Dorothy.

A door opened and the light streamed out over the snow.

"Who is there?" called Mr. Bobbsey. "Is that you, Bert?"

"Yes, father. We're here at last."

"Oh, thank goodness!" said Mrs. Bobbsey. "We were just going out to search for you!"

Day 155

1. Read chapter 15.
2. Who do you think pushed the snowball over on them?

Chapter 15 The Snow Slide

How warm and cozy it was in Snow Lodge! How bright were the lights, and how the big fire blazed, crackled and roared up the chimney! And what a delightful smell came from the kitchen! It could easily be told that Dinah was out there.

"Where have you been?"

"What happened to you?"

"Was there an accident?"

"Did you get lost?"

"Did the ice-boat sink?"

It was Freddie and Flossie who asked the last two questions, and Mr. and Mrs. Bobbsey who asked the others as Bert, Nan, Harry and Dorothy came into the farmhouse. Oh, how good it seemed after their battle in the darkness with the storm!

"The ice-boat couldn't go on account of the snow," explained Bert, "so we had to leave it and walk."

"And we got lost," added Nan. "Oh, it was terrible out there on the frozen lake!"

"Indeed it was," agreed Dorothy. "I never had such a time in all my life."

"It was too bad," said Mrs. Bobbsey. "You children should have come in the sled with us."

"Oh, we didn't mind it much," spoke Harry. "We had a good lunch. We saw the light and thought it was some farmhouse. We didn't think it was Snow Lodge. But we're glad it is," he added with a laugh.

"We got here some time ago," said Mr. Bobbsey. "The farmer had the fires all going finely, and it was as warm as toast. We began getting things to rights, but when it got dark, and snowed, and you children weren't here, we all got worried."

"And we were going to look for you," added Mrs. Bobbsey. "Oh, I was so worried I didn't know what to do!"

The evening was spent in playing a few games, and in talking and telling stories. Everyone was too tired to stay up long, after the day's trip, and so "early to bed" was the rule, for the first night at least.

As Bert went up to his room with his cousin Harry he looked out of the window. It was too dark to see much, but the boy could get a glimpse of the snow blowing against the panes with great force.

"Poor Henry Burdock!" thought Bert. "If it wasn't for that missing money he and his uncle might be living here at Snow Lodge. I wonder where Henry is now? Maybe off somewhere in the woods, lost--as we nearly were!"

The thought made him feel sad. Surely it was a terrible night to be out in the forest, amid the storm and darkness.

"I wish I could help him," thought Bert, but he did not see how he could. Mr. Carford was a stern old man, and he believed his nephew had taken the money that was missing.

The storm raged all night, and part of the next day. Then it cleared off, leaving a great coating of white in the woods, and over the fields.

"No skating or ice-boating now," said Bert, "and not for some days. We'll have to wait for a thaw and another freeze."

"But we can take walks in the woods; can't we?" asked Nan. "Would you like that, Dorothy?"

"Indeed I would," was the answer.

"Can't we come?" asked Freddie. "Flossie and I have rubber boots."

"Yes, you may come for a little way," said Bert. "We won't go far. Say, Harry, we ought to have snowshoes for this sort of thing."

"That's right," agreed his cousin. "I saw a picture of some, but I don't believe I would know how to make them."

"I made some once, but they weren't much good," admitted Bert. "We'll get my father to show us how some day. It would be fun to take a trip on them over the snow."

Well wrapped up, the young folks set off through the woods, Snap trotting along with them, barking joyously. All about Snow Lodge, back from the lake, and on either side, were dense woods, and under the trees the snow was not as deep as in the open fields, for the branches kept part of it off. But it was deep enough to make walking hard.

"We can't go very far at this rate," said Nan, as she and Dorothy struggled on through the drifts.

"Let's go to that hill, and see what sort of view there is," suggested Harry.

"All right," agreed Bert.

"And we can stop there and eat our lunch," put in Freddie.

"Our lunch!" exclaimed Nan. "We didn't bring any lunch, dearie!"

"Flossie and I did!" cried "the little fat fireman," as his papa often called Freddie. "We thought we'd get hungry, so we had Dinah make us some sandwiches, and give us a piece of cake."

"I'm hungry now," said Flossie, and from under her cloak she drew out a bundle, which she opened, showing a rather crumpled sandwich and a piece of cake.

"I'm going to eat, too," decided Freddie, as he brought out his lunch.

"Well, I declare; you two are the greatest ever!" cried Bert. "But it was a good idea all the same!"

"Yes, I could eat something myself," admitted Harry. "I guess this air makes you hungry."

"We--we haven't got enough for all of us--I guess," said Freddie, looking wistfully at his package.

"Don't worry!" answered Harry with a laugh. "I won't take any, Freddie. I can wait until we get home."

Thereupon the two smaller twins proceeded to eat the lunch they had brought, doing this while trudging through the snow toward the little hill.

They reached the top, and stood for a time looking over the broad snow-covered expanse of lake and woods. Then they started down. But it was not easy work, especially for Flossie and Freddie, so the whole party stopped for a rest about half way.

They were sitting under a sheltering tree, looking at some flitting snow-birds, when from behind them came a curious sound. Bert looked back, and leaping to his feet, cried: "It's a snow slide! A snow slide! It's coming right toward us!"

Indeed a great drift of white snow was sliding down the side of the hill toward the children. A great white ball seemed to have started it, and as Harry looked up he gave a cry of surprise.

"I saw a boy up there!" he said. "He pushed that snowball on us!"

Day 156

1. Read the first part of chapter 16 and tell someone about what you read.

Chapter 16 Lost in the Woods (first part)

"Quick!" cried Bert, as he looked at the swiftly-sliding snow, "get close to the tree--on the downward side of it, and maybe the drift will go around us. Harry, you look after Freddie, and I'll take care of Flossie!"

As he spoke Bert grabbed up his little sister and hurried closer to the tree. It was a big pine, and they had been sitting under its branches, on some big rocks, as the slide started.

"What shall we do?" cried Nan. "Can't Dorothy and I help?"

"Take care of yourselves," answered Bert. "I guess it will split at the tree and not hurt us."

The snow slide had started at the top of the hill, whether from some snowball a boy had made, and rolled down, or from some other cause, Bert did not stop to consider. He was too anxious to get his little brother and sister to safety.

The snow was rather soft, and just right for the making of big balls, of the kind that had been put on the school steps. And, as it continued to slide down the hill, the mass of snow got larger and larger, until it was big enough to frighten even older persons than the Bobbsey twins and their cousins.

Harry had reached the tree with Freddie at the same time that Bert came to the protecting trunk with his little sister. Nan and Dorothy also were struggling toward it.

"Form in line!" called Bert. "In a long string down the hill, and every one stand right in line with the tree. The big trunk may split the snow slide in two."

He and Harry took their positions nearest the trunk, with Flossie and Freddie between them. Nan and Dorothy came next. Bert clasped the tree trunk with both arms, and told Harry to grasp him as tightly as he could.

"And you and Flossie hold on to Harry, Freddie," Bert directed. "Nan, you and Dorothy hold on to the little ones. Here she comes!"

By this time the snowslide had reached the tree, and the mass was now much larger than at first. Freddie and Flossie felt like crying, but they were brave and did not. It was an anxious moment.

Then just what Bert had hoped would happen came to pass. The snow slide was split in two by the tree trunk, and slid to either side, leaving the Bobbsey twins and their cousins safe.

"Oh!" gasped Nan.

"What was that you said about seeing someone up there on top of the hill?" asked Bert of Harry, a little later.

"I did see someone there just before the snow began to slide, and I'm almost sure I saw him roll that ball down that started the slide," answered Harry.

"Is that so? Could you see his face?"

"Not very well."

"Never mind. You don't know Danny Rugg, anyhow."

"Oh, Bert! Do you think Danny could have done such a thing as that?" asked Nan, in shocked tones.

"He might; not thinking how dangerous it would be," answered her brother. "I'm going up there and take a look."

"What for?" asked Dorothy.

"To see if I can find any marks in the snow. If someone was up there making a big snow ball to roll down on us there will be some marks of it. And if it was Danny Rugg I'll have something to say to him."

"He wouldn't be there now, probably," said Harry. "But do you think it would be safe to go up the side of the hill?"

"Yes, it would, by keeping right in the path of where the snow slide came down," answered Bert. "There's hardly any more snow to come down, now."

"Then I'll go with you," said Harry.

Leaving the two girls, with Flossie and Freddie, at the tree, Bert and Harry made their way up to the top of the slope. There they saw the signs of where, some one--a boy to judge by the marks of his shoes-- had tramped about, rolling a big snowball.

"That's what happened," decided Bert. "Danny Rugg, or some other mean chap, started that slide toward us. And I think it must have been Danny. He's up around here somewhere, and he's the only one who would have a grudge against me."

Several days went by at the Lodge, and they were very busy ones. As soon as breakfast was over the boys and girls would go for a walk, or would coast down hill on a slope not far away from the old farmhouse. Freddie and Flossie were not allowed to go very far away, as it was hard traveling. But they had good times around the house, and out in the old barn.

Bert and Harry made snowshoes out of barrel staves, fastening them to their feet with straps. They managed to walk fairly well on the crust.

The lake was still covered with a coating of snow, and there was no skating, nor could the ice-boat be used. Mr. Bobbsey, with Harry and Bert, took the team of horses one afternoon and went after the Ice Bird. They found it where Bert had left it the night of the storm. and hitching the horses to it, pulled the craft to the dock in front of Snow Lodge.

"It will be all ready for us when the snow is gone," said Bert.

The nights in Snow Lodge were filled with fun. Mr. Bobbsey had bought a barrel of apples, and when the family gathered about the fireplace there were put to roast in the heat of the glowing embers.

Corn was popped, and then it was eaten, with salt and butter on, or with melted sugar poured over it. Sometimes they would make candy, and once, when they did this, a funny thing happened.

Bert, Nan, Flossie and Freddie, with the two cousins, had been out in the kitchen making a panful of the sweets. I must say that Dinah did the most work, but the children always declared that they made the candy. Anyhow, Dinah always washed up the pans and dishes afterward.

"Now we'll set it out on the back steps to cool," said Nan, "and then we'll pull it into sticks."

The candy was soon in the condition for "pulling" and, putting butter on their fingers, so the sweet stuff would not stick to them, the children began their fun.

The more they pulled the candy the harder it got, and the lighter in color, Flossie and Freddie soon tired of the work, that was hard on their little arms, and Nan set their rolls of candy outside again to cool, ready for eating.

All at once a great howling was heard at the back stoop, and Flossie cried:

"Oh, someone is taking my candy!"

Bert laid the lump he was pulling down on the table, and rushed to the kitchen door. As he looked out he laughed.

"Oh, look!" he cried. "Snap tried to eat your candy, Freddie, and it's stuck to his jaws. He can't get his mouth open!"

This was just what had happened. Snap, playing around outside, had smelled the cooling candy. He was fond of sweets and in a moment had bitten on a big chunk. In an instant his jaws seemed glued together, and he set up a howl of pain and surprise.

Day 157

1. Finish reading chapter 16 and begin chapter 17.
2. Tell someone about what's happening.

Chapter 16 (second part)

"Oh, my lovely candy!" cried Freddie. "You bad Snap!"

"I guess Snap is punished enough," said Mrs. Bobbsey, coming to the kitchen to find out what the trouble was. And the poor dog was. He would not get his jaws open for some time, so sticky was the candy, and finally Bert had to put his pet's mouth in warm water, holding it there until the candy softened. Then Snap could open his jaws, and get rid of the rest of the sweet stuff in his mouth. He looked very much surprised at what had happened.

Freddie was given more candy to pull, and this time he set the pan in which he put it up high where no dog could get at it.

With the roasting of apples, making of popcorn and pulling of candy, many pleasant evenings were spent. Then came a thaw, and some rain that carried off most of the snow. A freeze followed, and the lake was frozen over solidly.

"Now for skates and our ice-boat!" cried Bert, and the fun started as soon as the lake was safe. The children had many good times, often going up to the nearest village in the ice-boat.

Sometimes Bert had races with other ice-boats, and occasionally he won even against larger craft that were bought, instead of being home-made. But almost as often the Ice Bird came in last. But Bert and the others did not care. They were having a good time.

Bert met Danny Rugg in the woods one day, and spoke to him about the snow slide. Danny said he had had nothing to do with it, but Bert did not believe the bully.

Then came a spell of fine, warm weather, and as there was no snow on the ground, Bert, Nan, Dorothy and Harry decided to take a long walk one afternoon. Nan wanted to get some views with her new camera.

So interested did they all become that they never noticed how late it was, nor how far they had come.

"Oh, we must turn back!" cried Nan, when she did realize that it would soon be dark. "We're a good way from Snow Lodge."

"Oh, we can easily get back," declared Bert. "I know the path."

But though Bert might know the path they had come by daylight, it was quite different to find it after dark. However, he led the way, certain that he was going right. But when they had gone on for some distance, and saw no familiar landmarks, Nan stopped and asked:

"Are you sure this is the right path, Bert? I don't remember passing any of these rocks," and she pointed to a group of them under some trees.

"I don't, either," said Dorothy.

"Well, maybe this path leads into the right one," suggested Harry. "Let's keep on a little farther."

There seemed to be nothing else to do, so forward they went. Then a few flakes of snow began to fall, and they rapidly increased until the air was white with them. It made the scene a little lighter, but it caused Bert and the others to worry a good deal.

"I hope this isn't going to be much of a storm," said Bert in a low voice to Harry.

"Why not? It would make good sleigh riding."

"Yes, but it's no fun to be in the woods when it storms; especially at night and when you're--lost."

"Lost!" cried Harry. "Are we lost?"

"I'm afraid so," answered Bert, solemnly. "I haven't seen anything that looked like the path we came over for a long time. I guess we're lost, all right."

"Oh! Oh!" cried Dorothy.

"Will we have to stay out in the woods all night?" Nan wanted to know.

Bert shook his head sadly.

"I'm afraid so," he said.

Chapter 17 Henry Burdock (first part)

With the wind blowing about them, whirling the snowflakes into their faces, and with night fast coming on, the four young folks stood close together, looking at one another. Bert's solemn words had filled the hearts of the others with fear. Then Harry, sturdy country boy that he was, exclaimed:

"Oh, don't let's give up so easily, Bert. Many a time I've been off in the woods, and thought I was lost, when a little later, I'd make a turn and be on the road home. Maybe we can do that now."

"Oh, I do hope so!" murmured Dorothy.

"Let's try!" exclaimed Nan, taking hold of her brother's arm.

"Wait a minute!" exclaimed Bert as Harry and Dorothy were about to start off. "Do you know where you're going?"

"We're going back that way," declared Harry, pointing off to the left.

"Why, that way?" asked Bert.

"I think that's the way to Snow Lodge," was the answer. "We've tried lots of other ways, and haven't struck the right one, so it can't do any harm to go a new way."

"Now just hold on," advised Bert. "I don't mean to say that I know more than you about it, Harry, but it does seem to me that it won't do any good to wander off that way, especially if you're not sure it's the right path. We'll only get more lost than we are, if that's possible."

"Well, maybe you're right," admitted Harry. "But we can't stay here all night, that's sure."

"Of course not," added Dorothy, looking around with a shiver. The snow seemed to be coming down harder than ever and the cold wind blew with greater force.

"We may have to stay here," said Bert. "But don't let that scare you," he said quickly, as he saw Dorothy and his sister clutch at each other and turn pale. "We can build a sort of shelter that will keep us warm, and there won't be any danger of freezing."

"No, but how about starving?" asked Harry. "I'm real hungry now."

"We had a good dinner," observed Dorothy. "If we don't get anything more to eat until morning I guess we can stand it. But I do hope we can find some sort of shelter."

"We'll have to make one, I guess," said Nan, looking about her.

"That's right," cried Bert. "It's the only way. If we go wandering about, looking for a shelter, we may get into trouble. We'll make one of our own. There's a good place, over by that clump of trees. We can cut down some branches, stand them up around the trees and make a sort of tent. Then, when the snow has covered it, we'll be real warm."

"Well, let's start building that snow tent," proposed Harry. "It will give us something to do, and moving about is warmer than standing still. I know that much, anyhow."

"Yes, it is," agreed Bert. "Come on, girls. Harry and I will cut the branches and you can stack them up."

Day 158

1. Finish chapter 17.
2. Tell someone what is happening in the story. What was this chapter about?

Chapter 17 (second part)

Bert led the way to where three trees grew close together in a sort of triangle. The trees had low branches and it would be an easy matter to stand other branches up against them, one end on the ground, and so make a fairly good shelter.

With their pocket-knives Bert and Harry began cutting branches from the evergreen trees that grew all about. As fast as they were cut the girls took them, and piled them up as best they could. All the while the wind blew the falling snow about, and it became darker.

"Oh, if we only had some sort of a fire!" exclaimed Nan.

"A fire?" said her brother.

"That's so," agreed Dorothy. "It would not be so lonesome then, and it--would scare away--the bears!" and she looked over her shoulder in some fear.

"Bears!" cried Bert "There aren't any within a hundred miles, unless they're tame ones. But we might as well have a fire. I never thought of that. I've got a box of matches. Harry, if you'll gather wood, and the fire, I'll keep on cutting branches. We've got almost enough, anyhow."

"Sure, I will!" said the other boy, and soon he had scraped away the snow from a spot on the ground, and had piled some sticks on it. He managed to find some dry twigs and leaves in a hollow stump, and these served to start a blaze. The wood was rather wet, and it smoked a good deal, but soon some of the fagots had caught and there was a cheerful fire reflecting redly on the white snow that was falling faster than ever.

"That's something like!" cried Bert, coming over to the blaze to warm his cold fingers. "We'll get a pile of wood and keep the fire going all night. Then, if any of our folks come looking for us, they can see it."

Harry, who had just come up with an armful of wood, plunged his hands into his pockets to warm them. The next moment he uttered a joyful cry, and drew out two small packages.

"Look!" he cried. "Here's our supper!"

"Supper?" asked Bert, slowly. "What do you mean?"

"It's chocolate candy," went on Harry. "I forgot I had it, but it's fine stuff when you're hungry. Lots of travelers use it when they can't get anything else to eat. Here, I'll divide it, and we'll imagine we're having a fine feast."

He was about to do this when Bert suddenly exclaimed:

"Wait a minute! I have a better plan than that if I can only find a tin can. Everybody look for one. There may have been picnickers here during the summer, and they may have left a lot of tin cans."

"But what do you want of one?" asked Nan.

"I'll tell you if I find one," said her brother. "If I told you now, and we didn't pick up one, you'd be disappointed."

But they were not to be, for a little later Harry, kicking about in the snow, turned up a rusty tin can.

"That's it!" cried Bert. "Now we'll put some snow in it, and melt it over the fire. That will give us water, and when it boils we'll be sure the can is clean. Then we'll melt snow and have hot chocolate. We'll dissolve the chocolate candy in the water, Harry, and drink it. That will be something hot for us, and better than if we ate the cold candy. I've got a folding drinking cup we can use."

"Say, that's a fine idea!" cried Dorothy. "Bert, you're wonderful."

"Oh, no, the idea just popped into my head," he replied.

The can, with some snow in it, was soon on the fire, and in a little while steam arising from it told that the water, formed from the melting snow, was boiling. They rinsed the can out carefully, made more hot water, and then put in the chocolate candy, saving half for another time.

Nan and Dorothy took turns stirring it with a clean stick until the mixture was foamy and hot. Then it was passed around in the single drinking cup.

"Oh, but I feel so much better now," sighed Nan, after taking her share. "So warm and comfortable!"

"So do I!" exclaimed Dorothy, and the boys admitted that the drink of chocolate was very good, even though it had no milk in it.

Then they finished making the shelter, brought up more wood for the night, and went in the little snow-tent. Though it was only partly covered with a coating of white flakes, it was already warm and cozy, and they knew that they were in no danger of freezing.

As much of the snow as possible was scraped away from the ground inside, and thick hemlock branches were laid down for a sort of carpet. Then, with the cheerful fire going outside, the four young people prepared to spend the night. That it would be lonesome they well knew, but they hoped Mr. Bobbsey would come and find them, perhaps with a searching party.

The warm chocolate, the warmth of the fire, the effect of the wind, weariness of the long walk, and the work of making a shelter, all combined to make the boys and girls sleepy in spite of their strange situation. First one and then the other would nod off, to awake with a start, until finally they were all asleep.

How long he had been slumbering thus, in little snow-tent, Bert did not know. He suddenly awoke with a start, and listened. Yes, he heard something! The sound of someone tramping through the woods. A heavy body forcing its way through the bushes!

At first Bert's heart beat rapidly, and he thought of wild animals. Then he realized that none was near Snow Lodge. He glanced about. The campfire was burning only dimly, and by the light of it, as it came in through the opening of the shelter, the boy could see the others sleeping, curled up on the soft branches.

The sound of someone approaching sounded louder. Bert looked about for some sort of weapon. There was none in the tent. Then he almost laughed at himself.

"How silly!" he exclaimed. "Of course it's Father, or someone looking for us. I'll give a call."

He crawled to the edge of the shelter, looked out, and raised his voice in a shout:

"Hello there! Here we are! Father, is that you?"

Those inside the little snow-covered tent awoke with a start. Bert tossed some light wood on the fire and it blazed up brightly. By its glow the boy saw, coming into the circle of light, a man dressed in thick, heavy garments, with a coonskin cap on his head. Over his shoulder was a gun, and he had some rabbits and birds slung at his back.

"Hello!" called the man to Bert, who was now outside the little tent. "Who are you?"

"Bert Bobbsey," was the answer. "My sister and cousins are here. We got lost and made this shelter. Were you looking for us?"

"Well, not exactly," said the hunter slowly, as he leaned on his gun, and looked at the fire, then at Bert and next on Nan, Dorothy and Harry, who by this time had come from the tent. "Not exactly, but maybe it's a good thing I found you. The storm is growing worse. What did you say your name was?"

"Bert Bobbsey."

The hunter started.

"Any relation to Mr. Richard Bobbsey?" he asked.

"He's my father."

"You don't say so! Well, I'm glad to hear that. It will give me a chance to do him a good turn. I'm Henry Burdock," the hunter went on.

It was the turn of Bert and Nan to be surprised.

"Henry Burdock!" repeated Bert. "Are you the nephew of Mr. Carford?"

"Yes," was the low reply. "Do you know him?"

"Why, we're stopping at his place--Snow Lodge," said Bert. "We got lost coming from there to take some pictures. Oh, Mr. Burdock, can you take us back there?"

"Snow Lodge--Snow Lodge," said the hunter slowly. His voice was sad, as though the place had bitter memories for him.

Day 159

1. Read chapter 18.
2. Who do you think was throwing snowballs at the end of the chapter?

Chapter 18 Snowballs

"Are we very far from Snow Lodge?" asked Nan, after a pause. "We didn't think we would have any trouble getting back to it."

"You're about three miles away, and the path is hard to find in the darkness and storm," said the young hunter slowly. "Let me think what is best to do."

He remained leaning on his gun, staring into the fire, which was now burning brightly. Then he spoke again.

"You youngsters certainly have made this a fine shelter. I couldn't have done it much better myself. It's just the thing to keep out the cold wind."

"We thought we'd have to stay here all night," said Bert. "We made some hot chocolate. We've got a little left. Will you take some?"

"No, thank you," replied Henry Burdock. "I generally carry a little to eat with me, and I just finished my night lunch. I had some cold coffee that I warmed up, too. I'm sorry, but if I had known I was going to meet you folks I'd have saved some."

"Oh, we're all right," declared Harry. "We can finish our chocolate, and then perhaps you can show us the way back to Snow Lodge."

"Yes," spoke Henry Burdock, slowly, "I could do that. I know the way well enough. But it's a hard path to travel in the storm, and after dark. I don't believe you girls could manage it," and he looked at Nan and Dorothy.

"Oh, yes, we could!" Nan exclaimed. "We've had a good rest, and papa and mamma will be so anxious about us!"

"I'd like first rate to take you all home," said the hunter, "but I think I have a better plan. My shack isn't far from here. I could take you all there, and you could stay until morning. Then I could go to Snow Lodge and tell them you were all right. When it was daylight they could come for you in the sled."

"Maybe that would be best," agreed Bert.

"But won't it be too much of a trip for you?" asked Nan.

"No, I'm used to roaming about the woods," said Mr. Carford's nephew, with a sad smile. "A few miles more or less won't make any difference, and I know every inch of this forest. I've had to," he added. "It's the only home I have now."

"Yes, we--we heard about you," said Nan quickly, and there was kindness in her voice. "It's too bad your uncle acted as he did, and sent you away."

"Well, he thought he was doing right," said Henry. "I don't know as I blame him. Your father, though, he stuck to me, and I'm glad I can do his children a favor."

"Indeed, it seems too much to ask," spoke Dorothy, for Nan had whispered to her and Harry the details of the story of the missing money which Henry Burdock was suspected of taking.

"I don't mind," said the hunter. "I didn't do much walking to-day. Game was not very plentiful, though I got some. Now I'll lead you to my shack. It's small, but it's warm, and you can be comfortable there until daylight. I was walking through the woods, when I saw the flicker of your fire, and came up to see what it was."

"And I couldn't imagine what it was I heard when I woke up," said Bert. "I was a bit frightened at first," he admitted, with a smile.

"I don't blame you," said Henry. "And, since we are talking about Snow Lodge, I want to say that I never took that money. It was on the mantel in the living room, just as my uncle says it was, for I saw it. I don't deny but what I would have been glad to have it, for I had been foolish, and I owed more than I could pay. But I never took that roll of bills."

"Have you any idea who did?" asked Bert.

"Not in the least. And as I was the only one in the house, besides my uncle, of course it made it look as if I had taken it, especially as the money totally disappeared. But I never laid a hand on it."

"It is too bad," said Bert. "Maybe some day the bills will be found and you will be cleared."

"I hope so," sighed Henry. "But it's been some years now, and my uncle has considered me a thief all that while. I've gotten so I don't much care any more. Living in the woods makes you sort of that way. You do a lot of thinking.

"But there!" exclaimed the young hunter, straightening up. "This isn't doing you children any good. I'd better be taking you to my place instead of staying here. Have you anything to carry?"

"My camera--that's all," said Nan. "I'll get it," and she darted into the shelter after it. Then, when the fire had been extinguished so there would be no danger of it spreading, the young folks set off after Henry Burdock, who led the way. He seemed to know it, even in the darkness, but of course the white snow on the ground made the path rather easy to pick out.

In a short time they came to a log cabin, which was the "shack" the hunter had mentioned. It was the work of but a few minutes to open it, and blow into flames the fire that was smouldering on the hearth. A lamp had been lighted and the place was warm and cozy enough for anyone.

"Oh, this is fine!" cried Nan. "If the folks knew we were here we would be all right, and not worry."

"They'll soon know it," said Mr. Burdock. "I'm going to set off at once for Snow Lodge. Will you be afraid to stay here?"

"Not a bit of it!" exclaimed Bert, and the others agreed with him.

Leaving the game he had shot, Henry Burdock started off again through the storm-swept woods, while Bert and the others made themselves at home in the cabin. Mr. Burdock had showed them where he kept his food, and the boys and girls enjoyed a midnight lunch, for it was now after twelve o'clock.

It was about three in the morning when the hunter came back, to find his young friends asleep. He let himself in quietly, and not until daylight, when they awoke, did he tell them of his trip.

He had reached Snow Lodge safely, there to find Mr. and Mrs. Bobbsey almost distracted over the absence of the children. Mr. Bobbsey and Sam had searched as well as they could, and they were just going off to arouse some nearby farmers and make a more thorough hunt when Mr. Burdock came in.

That his news was welcome need not be said, and Mrs. Bobbsey wept for joy when she knew that her children and the others were safe. They wanted the young hunter to remain until daylight, and go back with them in the sled, but he said he would rather go on to his cabin now. Perhaps he did not feel that he should remain in Snow Lodge, from where his uncle had driven him in anger years before.

Mr. Burdock gave Mr. Bobbsey directions how to find the cabin, and, as soon as the first streak of daylight showed, the lumber merchant and Sam set off in the big sled. Flossie and Freddie were not awake, or they might have been taken along.

And a little later Bert, Nan, Dorothy and Harry were safe in Snow Lodge once more.

For some days after this the weather was stormy, so that the young folks could not go far from Snow Lodge. But they managed to have good times indoors, or out in the big barn.

Then came another thaw, and a freeze followed some days later, making good skating. One afternoon Bert proposed to Harry that they go for a trip on the ice-boat.

"But not too far," cautioned his father. "We don't want you to get lost again."

"No, we'll only go a mile or so," said Bert. "Want to come, Nan and Dorothy?"

The girls did, and so, also, did Flossie and Freddie, but their mother would not allow this. So Freddie got out his engine and played fireman, while his little sister put her walking and talking doll through her performance. Snap, the trick dog, with many barks, raced off with Bert and the older children.

The Ice Bird sailed well that day, skimming over the frozen lake at a fast pace, and the children greatly enjoyed the sport. Snap sat on with the others, looking as though he liked it as well as anyone.

They sailed up the lake for some distance and then got out to look for a cave which Bert had heard was a short distance from shore. They did not find it at once, but while they were climbing up a little hill, thinking the cave might be somewhere near it, Harry was suddenly startled to receive a snowball on his ear.

"Ouch!" he cried. "Who threw that?"

They all stopped and looked around. No one was in sight.

"Maybe it fell off a tree," suggested Nan.

"It came too hard for that," declared Harry. "It was thrown."

They looked about again, but, seeing no one, went on. Then, suddenly there came another ball, and Dorothy cried:

"There, that came out of a tree, for I saw it. Right over there," and she pointed.

"Then if it came out of a tree someone is up the tree!" declared Bert, "and I'm going to see who it is."

As he rushed forward a snowball struck him full in the face.

Day 160

1. Read chapter 19.
2. Who's missing at the end of the chapter? (Answers)

Chapter 19

Dorothy screamed, and turned back toward Nan when she saw Bert struck with the snowball. But plucky Nan kept on.

"That must be Danny Rugg!" cried Bert's sister. "No one else around here would be as mean as that!"

Bert stopped a moment to brush the snow from his eyes, and then he rushed toward the tree.

"Who is it?" cried Harry.

"I don't know--but I'm going to find out," was Bert's answer. "Come along!"

The two boys hurried on, the girls lingering in the rear.

Again a snowball flew out of the tree, but it struck no one, though coming near to Nan.

By this time Bert was close to the tree. It was a hemlock, and the branches were quite thick, but Bert got a glimpse of someone hiding among them.

"Come down out of that!" Bert cried. "I see you!"

There was no answer.

"What do you mean by hitting us?" asked Harry angrily. "We didn't do anything to you."

Still there was no answer.

"I'm going to do some snowballing on my own account," spoke Bert. "Here goes!"

He quickly made a hard ball, and, circling around the tree to find an opening in the branches, he saw the figure of the boy more plainly.

"Danny Rugg!" cried Bert. "So it's you; is it? First you start a snowslide down on us and then you snowball us. This has got to stop. Take that!"

Bert threw, but though his aim was good, Danny, for it was the bully, managed to climb up higher in the tree, and the snowball broke into pieces against the branches.

"Ha! Ha!" laughed Danny.

"Oh, there's plenty more snow," said Harry, "and you can't have an awful lot up there."

His answer was another snowball, which struck him on the shoulder, doing no harm. Danny must have taken some snow-ammunition up the tree with him, and, in addition, there was a supply of the white flakes on the wide branches of the hemlock.

Bert and Harry both began throwing snowballs up into the tree, but they were at a disadvantage, for their missiles broke to pieces against the trunk or branches. On the other hand Danny could wait his chance and hit them when they came within sight.

"This won't do!" exclaimed Bert, after a bit. "We've got to get him out of that tree."

"How can we?" asked Harry. "Climb up it, and pull him down?"

"Oh, don't do that!" cried Nan. "You might get hurt."

"Yes, that would be risky," admitted Bert. "One of us might slip and fall. Hey you, Danny Rugg!" cried Bert. "Come on down, and we'll give you a fair show. Only one of us will tackle you at a time."

"Huh! Think I'm coming down?" asked Danny. "I'm not afraid of you, but I'm going to stay up here."

"Oh, are you?" asked Bert, as he thought of a new plan. "We'll see about that. Come here, Harry."

From the tree Danny looked down anxiously while Harry and Bert whispered together. The girls had walked off to one side.

"How are you going to get him down?" asked Harry.

"Cut the tree," answered Bert. "It's only a small one."

"But we can't even cut that down with our knives."

"I know. But on the ice-boat is that hatchet father gave me to take to be sharpened. I forgot about it on the way up the lake, and I was going to do it on the way back. There's a blacksmith shop in the big cove. But the hatchet is sharp enough to chop down this tree. We'll get it and give Danny a good scare."

"That's what we will. You stay here and I'll run down and get it."

Harry started off on a run, and Danny, still up the tree, wondered what plan was afoot. The bully had been out for a walk when he saw Bert and the others coming up the hill. He quickly climbed the tree in order to throw snowballs at them.

When Harry came back with the hatchet Bert once more called to Danny.

"Are you coming down and fight fair? I give you my promise that only one of us will tackle you at a time. You can have your choice."

"I'm not coming down!" cried Danny.

"Chop away, Harry!" called Bert. "I guess I can pepper him with a few snowballs if he tries to throw any at you."

The tree trunk was not very thick, and the hatchet was fairly sharp. In a little while the tree began swaying.

"I say now, stop that!" cried Danny, trying to get a better hold in the branches.

"Better come down before you fall," suggested Bert, who had a pile of snowballs ready.

The tree swayed more and more. Bert and Harry knew that even if Danny fell with it he could not get hurt in the soft drifts. So Harry kept on chopping.

The tree swayed more and more. There was a cracking sound. Then Danny cried:

"Don't chop any more--I'm coming down!"

"Get ready, Harry!" called Bert. "We'll give him some of the same kind of a thing he gave us!"

In another instant Danny jumped, and as the swaying tree sprang back, when relieved of his weight, Bert and Harry leaped forward to pelt the bully with snowballs.

Danny tried to fight back, but he was no match for the two of them, and soon he began to look like a snow image, so well was he plastered with white flakes.

"Give it to him!" cried Bert, whose face still stung where Danny had struck him with a snowball.

"That's what I will," agreed Harry, whose ear was quite sore.

For a time Danny said nothing, but tried to block off the rain of snowballs, throwing some of his own back. Then, as he was almost overwhelmed by the ones Harry and Bert threw, the bully cried:

"Stop! Stop! I've had enough! I won't bother you any more!"

Danny was soon out of sight, running off in the direction of his father's lumber tract, and soon Bert and the others went back to the ice-boat.

They stopped at the blacksmith shop to have the hatchet sharpened, and reached home after a little sail on the Ice Bird.

"Did anything happen this time?" asked Freddie, as he greeted them on the return to Snow Lodge.

"Not much," replied Bert. "We just had a snow fight; that's all."

The skating and ice-boating lasted for some time, and the girls and boys had lots of fun. Nights were spent in popping corn, telling stories, roasting apples, and once, in the big sled, they all went to an entertainment in a nearby school hall.

It was on returning from this, in the evening, that Dinah met them at the door, asking:

"Did yo' all take dat dog Snap wif yo?"

"Take Snap? No," said Mr. Bobbsey.

"Isn't he here?"

The children began to look alarmed.

"He was here," said Dinah, "but I can't find him now, nohow. He suah am missin'."

Day 161

1. Read the beginning of chapter 20.
2. Tell someone about what's happening.
3. Practice *The City Zoo* vocabulary either by using the link on the Review Games page on the Easy Peasy website or by going to Day 25.

Chapter 20 The Big Storm (first part)

For a moment they all looked at one another by turns. Flossie and Freddie showed the most alarm. Bert started for the outside door, as though intending to make a search for his pet. Mr. Bobbsey questioned Dinah.

"Are you sure," he asked, "that Snap isn't around?"

"I suah am suah," she replied. "I done called him to git suffin to eat, an' when Snap won't come fo' dat he ain't around."

"That's so," said Mrs. Bobbsey. "I wonder if he could have followed after us, and got lost? Did any of you see him trailing us?"

"He did come a little way, when we started," came from Dorothy.

"Yes, but Dinah called him back; didn't you?" asked Nan of the cook.

"Yes, missis, dat's what I did. An' Snap come. Den, t' make suah he wouldn't sneak off an' foller yo'-all, I shut him up in de kitchen an' gibe him a chicken bone. Arter a while I let him out. He run around, kinder disappointed like, an' come back. Den I didn't look fo' him until a little while ago, but he was gone, an' I thought maybe, arter all, he'd come wif yo'."

"No, he didn't," said Mr. Bobbsey, with a shake of his head. "But we'll have a look around."

With Bert and Harry he went outside. But neither calling nor whistling brought any bark from Snap. Nor did he come bounding joyfully up, as he usually did when summoned. The darkness about Snow Lodge was quiet. There was no sign of Snap.

"He's gone off in the woods and is lost," said Harry.

"Snap knows better than to get lost," declared Bert. "He could find his way home from almost anywhere. I think he must have followed someone away."

"Would he do that?" asked Harry.

"He might with someone he knew, if that person petted him," said Mr. Bobbsey.

"That hunter--Henry Burdock!" suddenly exclaimed Bert. "Snap made great friends with him when we met him out in the woods the other day, and Henry said he'd make a fine hunting dog."

"I don't believe Henry Burdock would entice our dog away," said Mr. Bobbsey, with a shake of his head.

"Oh, of course I didn't mean on purpose," said Bert. "But Snap may have been running about in the woods at dusk when he met Henry. Then he may have followed him, for Snap is part hunting dog, and he gets crazy when he sees a gun. Maybe he followed Henry, and wouldn't be driven back through the snow."

"Maybe that's so," agreed Mr. Bobbsey. "In that case Snap will be all right, and we can get him in the morning. So don't worry any more."

They went back in the Lodge, to find Freddie and Flossie almost in tears. But the little twins felt better when it was explained to them that Snap might, after all, be safe with the young hunter.

"And will you get him first thing in the morning?" asked Freddie.

The following day was so nice that Flossie and Freddie were allowed to go with Bert, Nan, Harry and Dorothy to the cabin of Henry Burdock to look for Snap. The small twins were put on two sleds, the older children taking turns pulling them.

They easily found Henry's cabin, having been there several times since the night they spent in it. The hunter was just about to start off on a trip.

"Where's Snap?" called Bert, eagerly.

"Snap? I haven't seen him since that day I met you with him in the woods," answered the hunter.

"What! Isn't he here?" asked Harry.

Then they told of the missing dog. But Henry Burdock had not seen him.

"Where can he be?" spoke Nan, wonderingly.

Flossie and Freddie began to cry.

"Oh, a bear has Snap!" wailed Flossie.

"No, he hasn't!" declared Bert. "We'll find him."

"But where can he be?" said Dorothy. "Is there anyone else around here who might take him?"

Bert and Nan thought of the same thing at the same time.

"Danny Rugg!" they exclaimed.

"What do you mean?" asked Henry Burdock.

"He's a mean boy who is camping with his father near us," explained Bert. "Harry and I pelted him good with snowballs the other day, after he bothered us. I think he has enticed Snap away."

"Would your dog go with him?"

"Yes, he's friendly with Danny, for sometimes Danny is fairly good, and comes to our house. If he offered Snap a nice bone our dog might go with him."

"Then I advise you to have a look over where Danny is camping," said the young hunter.

It was quite a trip back to Snow Lodge and then over to the Rugg lumber camp, and Mrs. Bobbsey thought it too far to take Flossie and Freddie, so they were left behind on the second trip, Nan and Dorothy going with Bert and Harry.

They saw Danny Rugg standing in front of a log cabin which was on the edge of a lumber camp. The bully seemed uneasy at the sight of Harry and Bert, and called out:

"If you're coming here to make any trouble I'll tell my father on you. He's right over there."

"We're not going to make any trouble, Danny Rugg, if you don't," said Bert slowly, "But we came for Snap, our dog."

"I don't know anything about your dog," answered Danny, in surly tones.

"I think you do," said Bert, quietly. Then raising his voice, he called:

"Snap! Snap! Where are you, old fellow? Snap!"

There was a moment of silence, and then, from a small cabin some distance away, came loud barks.

"There's Snap! That's our dog!" cried Nan, joyfully, and at the sound of her voice the barking grew louder. There could also be heard the rattling of a chain.

"You've got him tied, Danny Rugg!" cried Bert, angrily. "Let him go at once or I'll hit you!"

"Don't you dare touch me!" cried the bully. "And you get off our land!"

"Not until I get my dog," said Bert, firmly.

He started for the cabin where the dog was, but Danny stepped in front of him. Bert shoved Danny to one side, and just then Mr. Rugg came up.

"Here! What does this mean?" he asked. "Bert Bobbsey, you here?"

"Yes, sir. I came after my dog. Danny has him tied up!"

Day 162

1. Read the rest of chapter 20 and read chapter 21.
2. Tell someone about what's happening.

Chapter 20 (second part)

"Danny, is this so?" asked Mr. Rugg, who knew some of his son's mean ways, and had tried in vain to break him of them. "Have you Bert's dog?"

"Well, maybe it is his dog. It was dark when he followed me home last night, and I tied him in that shack."

"I guess he wouldn't have followed you if you hadn't coaxed him," said Bert.

"Well, I couldn't drive him back," went on Danny, but the Bobbseys believed that he had deliberately coaxed Snap off to make trouble.

"Let the dog out at once," said Mr. Rugg to his son, and Danny had to do so, though he was angry and sullen over it.

How Snap leaped about his master and mistress and their cousins! How delightedly he barked! And his tail wagged to and fro so fast that it looked like two tails, as Freddie said afterward.

"Poor Snap!" said Bert, as he patted his pet "And so you were tied up all night? It was a mean trick!" and his eyes flashed at Danny, who looked on sneeringly.

"I am sorry for this, Bert," said Mr. Rugg. "If I had known Danny enticed away your dog I would have made him bring it back. Now I am going to punish him. You go back home to-day, Danny. You can't stay in the lumber camp any longer."

Danny felt badly, of course, but it served him right.

The Bobbseys and their cousins lost no time for getting back to Snow Lodge with Snap, who was hugged so much by Flossie and Freddie that Dinah said:

"Good land a' massy! Dat dog must be mos' starved, an' yo'-all is lubbin him so dat he ain't time to eat a sandwich. Let him hab some breakfast, an' den hug him!"

"Oh, but we like him so!" cried Flossie.

So Snap was restored, and Danny was sent home out of the woods, so there was no more trouble from him.

In the days that followed, the Bobbsey twins at Snow Lodge had many more good times. They made snow forts, and had snow-battles, they made big snow men and threw snowballs at them, and went on sleigh rides, or skated and ice-boated and played around generally, to their hearts' content.

Occasionally the two older boys went on long tramps with Henry Burdock as he visited his traps. They invited him to come to Snow Lodge, but he said:

"No, I'm never coming there until I can prove to my uncle that I never touched his money. Then I'll come."

One day, when Bert and Harry had been in the woods with the young hunter, he said to them:

"Don't go far away from Snow Lodge tomorrow, boys."

"Why not?" asked Bert.

"Because I think we're in for a big storm, and you might easily get lost again. Unless I'm mistaken, it's going to snow hard before morning."

Henry Burdock proved a true weather prophet, for when the Bobbseys and the other got up the next morning the ground was covered with a mantle of newly-fallen snow, and more was sifting down from the clouds. The wind, too, was blowing fiercely.

"It's going to be a bad storm," said Mr. Bobbsey, looking out after breakfast. "Luckily we have plenty of wood and plenty to eat."

The wind howled around Snow Lodge while the white flakes came down thicker and faster.

"Maybe we'll be snowed in," said Nan.

"That would be fun!" cried Bert.

Chapter 21 The Falling Tree

How the wind did blow! How the snow swirled and drifted about the old farmhouse! But within it all were warm and comfortable. The fire on the open hearth was kept roaring up the chimney, Sam piling on log after log. In the cozy kitchen Dinah kept at her work over the range, singing old plantation melodies.

The blowing wind and the drifting snow kept up all day. Flossie and Freddie begged to be allowed to go out for a little while, but their mother would not think of it. Bert and Harry tried to go a little way beyond the barn but were driven back by the cold, wintry blasts. Dorothy and Nan managed to have a good time in the attic of the old house, dressing up in some clothes of a by-gone age, which they found in some trunks.

"My! I hope the chimneys don't blow off!" exclaimed Mrs. Bobbsey, as a particularly fierce blast shook the old house. "A fire now would be dreadful."

"I don't imagine there is much danger," said Mr. Bobbsey, with a laugh. "The way they built houses and chimneys when Snow Lodge was put up was different from nowadays. They were built to stay."

"Oh, but this is a terrible storm!"

"Yes, and it seems to be getting worse," agreed Mr. Bobbsey. "I hope no one is out in it. But, as I said, we have plenty to eat, and wood to keep us warm, and that is all we can ask."

The day slowly passed, but toward afternoon Flossie and Freddie grew fretful from having been kept in. They were used to going out of doors in almost any kind of weather.

"Come on up in the attic with us," suggested Nan, "and we'll have a sort of circus."

"And Snap can do tricks," cried Freddie, "and I'll give an exhibition with my fire engine."

"Of course!" exclaimed Dorothy, and the little Bobbsey twins forgot their fretfulness in a new series of games.

Harder blew the wind, and fiercer fell the snow. The path Mr. Bobbsey had shoveled was soon filled up again. Out at the back door was a drift that covered the rear stoop.

"If this keeps up we will be snowed in," said Mr. Bobbsey to his wife, as they prepared to lock up for the night.

They were gathered around the big open fire, popping corn and roasting apples, when a louder blast of wind than ever shook the house.

"Oh, what a night!" said Mrs. Bobbsey, with a shudder. "I wish we were in our home again!"

Hardly had she spoken than there came a fearful crash, and the whole house trembled. At the same time a blast of cold wind swept through it, scattering the fire on the hearth.

"Oh, what was that?" cried Mrs. Bobbsey.

"That old apple tree, at the corner of the house," said Mr. Bobbsey. "The storm has blown it over, and it has smashed a corner of the Lodge. Don't be afraid. We'll be all right," and he ran to close the door, to keep out the cold wind.

Day 163

1. Read chapter 22.
2. How does the book end?

Chapter 22 The Missing Money

"What happened?" asked Mrs. Bobbsey, when her husband had come back after going out to take a look around. "Is the house safe?"

"As safe as ever," he answered. "Just as I told you, the old apple tree blew over, and smashed the corner of the house near this living room. That's why we felt the crash so. But there is no great harm done. We can keep this door closed and not use that other part of the house at all. We have room enough without it. The wind and storm can't get at us here."

"I suah 'nuff thought de house was comin' down," said Dinah, who had run in from the kitchen at the sound of the crash.

"It was a hard blow," said Bert "Look, all the ashes are scattered," and he pointed to where the wind had blown them about the hearth.

Dinah soon swept them up, however, and more wood was put on the fire, and the Bobbseys were as comfortable as before. The part of the house which had been smashed by the tree was closed off from the rest.

Soon it was time to go to bed, but all night long the storm raged, making Snow Lodge tremble in the blast. Everyone was up early in the morning to see by daylight what damage had been done.

The sun rose clear, for the storm had passed. But oh? what a lot of snow there was! In big drifts it was scattered all over the place, and one side door was snowed in completely; and could not be opened. Sam had to shovel a lot of snow away from the kitchen steps before Dinah could go out.

"Let's go see where the tree fell," suggested Bert to Harry, when they were dressed, Nan and Dorothy joined them. They went to the corner of the house and there saw a strange sight. The old apple tree lay partly in the room into which it had crashed through the side of the house. And much snow had blown in also.

This room, however, was little used, except for storage, and there was nothing in it to be damaged save some old furniture. Bert and Harry made their way into the apartment, and the girls followed.

They were looking about at the odd sight, when something in a corner of the room, along the wall that was next to the living room, where the Bobbseys had spent the evening, caught Bert's eyes. He went toward it. He picked up a roll of what seemed to be green paper. It had been in a crack of the wall that had been made wider by the falling tree.

"Oh, look?" he cried. "What is this? Why, it's money!"

"A roll of bills!" added Harry, looking over his cousin's shoulder.

Slowly Bert unrolled them. There seemed to be considerable money there. One bill was for a hundred dollars.

"Where did it come from?" asked Nan.

"From a crack in the wall," spoke her brother. "It must have slipped down, and the falling tree made the crack wider, so I could see it."

"I wonder who could have put it there?" said Dorothy.

Bert and Nan looked at each other. The same thought came into their minds.

"The missing money!" cried Bert, "The roll of bills that Mr. Carford thought his nephew took! Can this be it?"

"Oh, if it only is!" murmured Nan. "Let's tell papa right away!"

Carrying the money so strangely found, the young folks went into the house where Mr. and Mrs. Bobbsey were. The roll of bills was shown, and Mr. Bobbsey was much surprised.

"Do you think this can be the money Mr. Carford lost?" asked Bert.

"I shouldn't be surprised," said Mr. Bobbsey, quickly. "I'll take a look. Mr. Carford said he left it on the mantel in the living room, and you found it in the room back of that. I'll look."

Quickly he examined the mantel. Then he said:

"Yes, that's how it happened. There is a crack up here, and the money must have slipped down into it. All these years it has been in between the walls, until the falling tree made a break and showed where it was. Mr. Carford was mistaken. His nephew did not take the money. I always said so. It fell into the crack, and remained hidden until the storm showed where it was."

"Oh, how glad I am!" cried Mrs. Bobbsey. "Now Henry's name can be cleared! Oh, if he were only here to know the good news!"

There seemed to be no doubt of it. Years before Mr. Carford had placed the money on the shelf of the living room. He probably did not know of the crack into which it slipped. The roll of bills had gone down between the walls, and only the breaking of them when the tree fell on the house brought the money to light.

"It is a strange thing," said Mr. Bobbsey. "The missing money is found after all these years, and in such a queer way! We must tell Henry as soon as possible, and Mr. Carford also."

Suddenly there came a knock on the door. Bert went to it and gave a cry of surprise. There stood the young hunter--Henry Burdock.

"I came over to see if you were all right," he said. "We have had a fearful storm. Part of my cabin was blown away, and I wondered how you fared at Snow Lodge. Are you all right?"

"Yes, Henry, we are," said Mr. Bobbsey, "And the storm was a good thing for you."

"I don't see how. My cabin is spoiled. I'll have to build it over again."

"You won't have to, Henry. You can come to live at Snow Lodge now."

"Never. Not until my name is cleared. I will never come to Snow Lodge until the missing money is found, and my uncle says I did not take it."

"Then you can come now, Henry," cried Mr. Bobbsey, holding out the roll of bills. "For the money is found and we can clear your name!"

"Is it possible!" exclaimed the young hunter, in great and joyful surprise. "Oh, how I have prayed for this! The money found! Where was it? How did you find it?"

Then the story was told, the children having their share in it.

"I can't tell you how thankful I am," said the young hunter. "This means a lot to me. Now my uncle will know I am not a thief. I must go and tell him at once."

"No, I'll go," said Mr. Bobbsey. "I want to prove to him that I was right, after all, in saying you were innocent. You stay here until I bring him."

Mr. Bobbsey went off in the big sled with Sam to drive the horses. It was a hard trip, on account of the drifts, but finally Newton was reached and Mr. Carford found. At first he could hardly believe that the money was found, but when he saw and counted it, finding it exactly the same as when he had put it on the shelf years before, he knew that he had done wrong in accusing Henry.

"And I'll tell him so, too," he said. "I'll beg his pardon, and he and I will live together again. Oh, how happy I am! Now I can go to Snow Lodge with a light heart."

Uncle and nephew met, and clasped hands while tears stood in their eyes. After years of suffering they were friends again. It was a happy, loving time for all.

"And I'll never be so hasty again," said Mr. Carford. "Oh, what a happy day this is, after the big storm! We must have a big celebration. I know what I'll do. I'll get up a party, and invite all the people in this part of the country. They all know that I accused Henry of taking that money. Now they must know that he did not. I will admit my mistake."

And that is what Mr. Carford did. He sent out many invitations to an old-fashioned party at Snow Lodge. The place where the tree had crashed through, to show the missing money, was boarded up, and the house made cozy again.

Then came the party, and the Bobbseys were the guests of honor-- particularly the twins and their cousins, for it was due to them, in a great measure, that the money had been found.

Mr. Carford stood up before everyone and admitted how wrong he had been in saying his nephew had taken the money.

"But all our troubles are ended now," he said, "and Henry and I will live in Snow Lodge together. And we will always be glad to see you here--all of you--and most especially--the Bobbseys."

"Three cheers for the Bobbsey twins!" someone called.

The children were pleased at this praise. They did not know that soon they would be helping some other people. You may read about this in "The Bobbsey Twins on a Houseboat."

Then followed a fine feast--a happy time for all, while Henry and his uncle received the good wishes of their friends and neighbors.

Snap raced about, barking and wagging his tail. Bert, Nan, Dorothy, Harry and Freddie and Flossie were here, there, everywhere, telling how the tree had blown down, and how they had found the money.

"Dear old Snow Lodge!" said Nan, when the party was over, and the guests gone. "We will have to leave it soon!"

"But perhaps we can come back some time," said Nan.

"I'd like to," agreed Bert. "Next winter I am going to build a bigger ice-boat, and sail all over the lake."

"And we'll make regular snowshoes, and go hunting in the woods," said Harry.

"But it will be summer before it is winter again," said Freddie. "I'm going to have a motor boat and ride in it. And I'll take my fire engine along, and pump water."

"Can I come, with my doll?" asked Flossie.

"Yes, you may all come!" exclaimed Mamma Bobbsey, as she hugged the two little twins.

"And don't forget," said Mr. Carford, "that Snow Lodge is open in the summer as well as in the winter. I expect you Bobbsey twins to visit me once in a while. I never can thank you enough for finding that missing money."

"Neither can I," said Henry.

And now that the story is all told, we will say good-bye to the Bobbsey twins and their friends.

Day 164

1. Write a report about this book. Write the title of the book, write the author's name. Tell who and what the book was about. Tell what you liked about the book.
2. Save this in your portfolio.

Day 165

1. Practice the vocabulary from *The Adventures of Old Mr. Toad.* You can go to Day 46 or to level 2 on the Review Games page on the Easy Peasy website.
2. We are going to read a few more short stories as we end the year.
3. Read the story of *Christopher Columbus and the Egg.*

CHRISTOPHER COLUMBUS discovered America on the 12th of October, 1492. He had spent eighteen years in planning for that wonderful first voyage which he made across the Atlantic Ocean. The thoughts and hopes of the best part of his life had been given to it. He had talked and argued with sailors and scholars and princes and kings, saying, "I know that, by sailing west across the great ocean, one may at last reach lands that have never been visited by Europeans." But he had been laughed at as a foolish dreamer, and few people had any faith in his projects.

At last, however, the king and queen of Spain gave him ships with which to make the trial voyage. He crossed the ocean and discovered strange lands, inhabited by a people unlike any that had been known before. He believed that these lands were a part of India.

When he returned home with the news of his discovery there was great rejoicing, and he was hailed as the hero who had given a new world to Spain. Crowds of people lined the streets through which he passed, and all were anxious to do him honor. The king and queen welcomed him to their palace and listened with pleasure to the story of his voyage. Never had so great respect been shown to any common man.

But there were some who were jealous of the discoverer, and as ready to find fault as others were to praise. "Who is this Columbus?" they asked, "and what has he done? Is he not a pauper pilot from Italy? And could not any other seaman sail across the ocean just as he has done?"

One day Columbus was at a dinner which a Spanish gentleman had given in his honor, and several of these persons were present. They were proud, conceited fellows, and they very soon began to try to make Columbus uncomfortable.

"You have discovered strange lands beyond the sea," they said. "But what of that? We do not see why there should be so much said about it. Anybody can sail across the ocean; and anybody can coast along the islands on the other side, just as you have done. It is the simplest thing in the world."

Columbus made no answer; but after a while he took an egg from a dish and said to the company, "Who among you, gentlemen, can make this egg stand on end?"

One by one those at the table tried the experiment. When the egg had gone entirely around and none had succeeded, all said that it could not be done.

Then Columbus took the egg and struck its small end gently upon the table so as to break the shell a little. After that there was no trouble in making it stand upright.

"Gentlemen," said he, "what is easier than to do this which you said was impossible? It is the simplest thing in the world. Anybody can do it—after he has been shown how."

Day 166

1. Read the story, *Eureka*.
2. What was he wearing when he made and announced his great discovery? (Answers)

THERE was once a king of Syracuse whose name was Hiero. The country over which he ruled was quite small, but for that very reason he wanted to wear the biggest crown in the world. So he called in a famous goldsmith, who was skillful in all kinds of fine work, and gave him ten pounds of pure gold.

"Take this," he said, "and fashion it into a crown that shall make every other king want it for his own. Be sure that you put into it every grain of the gold I give you, and do not mix any other metal with it."

"It shall be as you wish," said the goldsmith. "Here I receive from you ten pounds of pure gold; within ninety days I will return to you the finished crown which shall be of exactly the same weight."

Ninety days later, true to his word, the goldsmith brought the crown. It was a beautiful piece of work, and all who saw it said that it had not its equal in the world. When King Hiero put it on his head it felt very uncomfortable, but he did not mind that—he was sure that no other king had so fine a headpiece. After he had admired it from this side and from that, he weighed it on his own scales. It was exactly as heavy as he had ordered.

"You deserve great praise," he said to the goldsmith. "You have wrought very skillfully and you have not lost a grain of my gold."

There was in the king's court a very wise man whose name was Archimedes. When he was called in to admire the king's crown he turned it over many times and examined it very closely.

"Well, what do you think of it?" asked Hiero.

"The workmanship is indeed very beautiful," answered Archimedes, "but—but the gold—"

"The gold is all there," cried the king. "I weighed it on my own scales."

"True," said Archimedes, "but it does not appear to have the same rich red color that it had in the lump. It is not red at all, but a brilliant yellow, as you can plainly see."

"Most gold is yellow," said Hiero; "but now that you speak of it I do remember that when this was in the lump it had a much richer color."

"What if the goldsmith has kept out a pound or two of the gold and made up the weight by adding brass or silver?" asked Archimedes.

"Oh, he could not do that," said Hiero; "the gold has merely changed its color in the working." But the more he thought of the matter the less pleased he was with the crown. At last he said to Archimedes, "Is there any way to find out whether that goldsmith really cheated me, or whether he honestly gave me back my gold?"

"I know of no way," was the answer.

But Archimedes was not the man to say that anything was impossible. He took great delight in working out hard problems, and when any question puzzled him he would keep studying until he found some sort of answer to it. And so, day after day, he thought about the gold and tried to find some way by which it could be tested without doing harm to the crown.

One morning he was thinking of this question while he was getting ready for a bath. The great bowl or tub was full to the very edge, and as he stepped into it a quantity of water flowed out upon the stone floor. A similar thing had happened a hundred times before, but this was the first time that Archimedes had thought about it.

"How much water did I displace by getting into the tub?" he asked himself. "Anybody can see that I displaced a bulk of water equal to the bulk of my body. A man half my size would displace half as much.

"Now suppose, instead of putting myself into the tub, I had put Hiero's crown into it, it would have displaced a bulk of water equal to its own bulk. All, let me see! Gold is much heavier than silver. Ten pounds of pure gold will not make so great a bulk as say seven pounds of gold mixed with three pounds of silver. If Hiero's crown is pure gold it will displace the same bulk of water as any other ten pounds of pure gold. But if it is part gold and part silver it will displace a larger bulk. I have it at last! Eureka! Eureka!"

Forgetful of everything else he leaped from the bath. Without stopping to dress himself, he ran through the streets to the king's palace shouting, "Eureka! Eureka! Eureka!" which in English means, "I have found it! I have found it! I have found it!"

The crown was tested. It was found to displace much more water than ten pounds of pure gold displaced. The guilt of the goldsmith was proved beyond a doubt. But whether he was punished or not, I do not know, neither does it matter.

The simple discovery which Archimedes made in his bath tub was worth far more to the world than Hiero's crown. Can you tell why?

Day 167

1.   Read the story, *The Fountain of Youth*.

AMONG the Spaniards who flocked to America in the hope of finding gold, there was a certain officer whose name was Juan Ponce de Leon. He had distinguished himself in the Spanish army and was very rich. He also had much influence with the king—so much, in fact, that he was soon appointed governor of all the eastern part of Haiti.

While attending to his duties in Haiti, he learned that at some distance farther eastward there was a rich island abounding in gold and other precious metals. The Indians called this island Borinquen; it was the same land which Columbus had discovered a few years before and called Porto Rico.

Ponce de Leon was so much pleased by the reports which were brought to him of the great wealth of Porto Rico that he at once made up his mind to get that wealth for himself. The king of Spain was very willing to please him and to have a share of the profits, and therefore appointed him governor of Porto Rico. Ponce was not a man to waste time in any undertaking. With eight stanch ships and several hundred men, he at once set sail for his new province and in due time landed upon the island.

The natives were kind and gentle. They welcomed the white men to their pleasant country and tried to help them in such ways as they could. Ponce de Leon repaid them as the Spaniards at that time usually repaid a kindness,—he robbed them of all they had and made slaves of as many as he could. Then at length the harassed savages turned against their oppressors and tried to drive them from the island; but what could they do against enemies so cunning and strong?

Ponce was as heartless and unfeeling as any wild beast. Soon the once happy island was filled with distress and terror. The Indians were hunted from their homes. Thousands of them were killed, and the rest became the slaves of their conquerors.

Ponce began to form a settlement at a place now called Pueblo Viejo; but he soon changed his plans and removed to a fine harbor on the north shore of the island. There he laid out the city of San Juan. He built for himself, near the mouth of the harbor, a grand house which he called Casa Blanca, or the White Castle; and there he made his home for some time.

But, with all his wealth, Ponce was not happy. He had lived so carelessly and wildly that his youth went from him early. At fifty years of age he was a miserable old man. There was no more joy in the world for him.

One day as he was sitting unhappy in the White Castle, a thing occurred that kindled a spark of hope in his despairing mind. He overheard an Indian slave say, "In Bimini no one grows old."

"Bimini! What is Bimini?" he asked.

"It is a beautiful island that lies far, far to the north of us," was the answer.

"Tell me about it."

"There is a fountain there, a spring of clear water, the most wonderful in the world. Every one that bathes in it becomes as young and strong as he was in his best days. No one grows old in Bimini."

"Have you ever been there?"

"Ah, no. It is too far away for any of our people to make the voyage. But we have heard talk of the fountain all our lives."

Ponce asked other Indians about Bimini and its magic fountain. All had heard of it. It. was a land fragrant with flowers. It lay far to the northwest—too far for frail canoes to venture. But the great ships of the white men could easily make the voyage in a few days.

Ponce made up his mind to discover the fountain. He first got the king's permission to conquer Bimini, wherever it might be. Then with three ships and a number of followers he sailed toward the northwest. He passed through the great group of islands known as the Bahamas; and, wherever there were natives living, he stopped and made inquiries.

"Where is Bimini? Where is the magic fountain of youth?"

They pointed to the northwest. It was always a little farther and a little farther. No one had ever seen the fountain, but Ponce understood that every one had heard of it.

At length, after leaving the Bahamas far behind them, the Spaniards discovered a strange coast where the land seemed to be covered with flowers. Was this Bimini?

Nobody could tell. The coast stretched so far northward and southward that Ponce felt sure it was no island but the mainland of a continent. The day was Easter Sunday, which in Spain is called Pascua de Flores, or the Feast of Flowers. For this reason, and also because of the abundance of flowers, the Spaniards named the land Florida.

Ponce de Leon went on shore at many places and sought for the wonderful fountain. He drank from every clear spring. He bathed in many a limpid stream. But his lost youth did not come back to him.

He sailed southward and around to the western coast of Florida, asking everywhere,—

"Is this Bimini? And where is the fountain of youth?"

But the Indians who lived there had never heard of Bimini, and they knew of no fountain of youth. And so, at last, the search was given up, and Ponce returned disappointed to Porto Rico.

Nine years passed, and then he sailed again for Florida. This time he took a number of men with him in order to conquer the country and seize upon whatever treasures he might find there. More than this, he expected to explore its woods and rivers and seek again for the mysterious fountain of youth.

The Florida Indians did not have any treasures; but they were brave and loved their homes. They would not be conquered and enslaved without a struggle. They therefore fell upon the Spaniards when they landed, and drove them back to their ships.

Ponce de Leon was struck by an arrow. He was wounded in the thigh.

"Take me back to Spain," said he, "for I shall never find the fountain of youth."

His ship carried him to Cuba; but no skill could heal his wound. He lingered in pain for a long time, and then died, bewailing his lost youth.

Day 168

1. Read the story, *Galileo and the Lamps*.

IN Italy about three hundred years ago there lived a young man whose name was Galileo. Like Archimedes he was always thinking and always asking the reasons for things. He invented the thermometer and simple forms of the telescope and the microscope. He made many important discoveries in science.

One evening when he was only eighteen years old he was in the cathedral at Pisa at about the time the lamps were lighted. The lamps—which burned only oil in those days—were hung by long rods from the ceiling. When the lamplighter knocked against them, or the wind blew through the cathedral, they would swing back and forth like pendulums. Galileo noticed this. Then he began to study them more closely.

He saw that those which were hung on rods of the same length swung back and forth, or vibrated, in the same length of time. Those that were on the shorter rods vibrated much faster than those on the longer rods. As Galileo watched them swinging to and fro he became much interested. Millions of people had seen lamps moving in this same way, but not one had ever thought of discovering any useful fact connected with the phenomenon.

When Galileo went to his room he began to experiment. He took a number of cords of different lengths and hung them from the ceiling. To the free end of each cord he fastened a weight. Then he set all to swinging back and forth, like the lamps in the cathedral. Each cord was a pendulum, just as each rod had been.

He found after long study that when a cord was 39 1/10 inches long, it vibrated just sixty times in a minute. A cord one fourth as long vibrated just twice as fast, or once every half second. To vibrate three times as fast, or once in every third part of a second, the cord had to be only one ninth of 39 1/10 inches in length. By experimenting in various ways Galileo at last discovered how to attach pendulums to timepieces as we have them now.

Thus, to the swinging lamps in the cathedral, and to Galileo's habit of thinking and inquiring, the world owes one of the commonest and most useful of inventions,—the pendulum clock.

You can make a pendulum for yourself with a cord and a weight of any kind. You can experiment with it if you wish; and perhaps you can find out how long a pendulum must be to vibrate once in two seconds.

Day 169

1. Read the story of *Sir Isaac Newtown and the Apple.*

SIR ISAAC NEWTON was a great thinker. No other man of his time knew so much about the laws of nature; no other man understood the reasons of things so well as he. He learned by looking closely at things and by hard study. He was always thinking, thinking.

Although he was one of the wisest men that ever lived, yet he felt that he knew but very little. The more he learned, the better he saw how much there was still to be learned.

When he was a very old man he one day said: "I seem to have been only like a boy playing on the seashore. I have amused myself by now and then finding a smooth pebble or a pretty shell, but the great ocean of truth still lies before me unknown and unexplored."

It is only the very ignorant who think themselves very wise.

One day in autumn Sir Isaac was lying on the grass under an apple tree and thinking, thinking, thinking. Suddenly an apple that had grown ripe on its branch fell to the ground by his side.

"What made that apple fall?" he asked himself.

"It fell because its stem would no longer hold it to its branch," was his first thought.

But Sir Isaac was not satisfied with this answer. "Why did it fall toward the ground? Why should it not fall some other way just as well?" he asked.

"All heavy things fall to the ground—but why do they? Because they are heavy. That is not a good reason. For then we may ask why is anything heavy? Why is one thing heavier than another?"

When he had once begun to think about this he did not stop until he had reasoned it all out.

Millions and millions of people had seen apples fall, but it was left for Sir Isaac Newton to ask why they fall. He explained it in this way:—

"Every object draws every other object toward it.

"The more matter an object contains the harder it draws.

"The nearer an object is to another the harder it draws.

"The harder an object draws other objects, the heavier it is said to be.

"The earth is many millions of times heavier than an apple; so it draws the apple toward it millions and millions of times harder than the apple can draw the other way.

"The earth is millions of times heavier than any object near to or upon its surface; so it draws every such object toward it.

"This is why things fall, as we say, toward the earth.

"While we know that every object draws every other object, we cannot know why it does so. We can only give a name to the force that causes this.

"We call that force GRAVITATION.

"It is gravitation that causes the apple to fall.

"It is gravitation that makes things have weight.

"It is gravitation that keeps all things in their proper places."

Suppose there was no such force as gravitation, would an apple fall to the ground? Suppose that gravitation did not draw objects toward the earth, what would happen?

To you who, like Sir Isaac Newton, are always asking "Why?" and "How?" these questions will give something to think about.

Day 170

1. Read the story of *The First Printer*. Read the first section.

I. ONE evening in midsummer, nearly five hundred years ago, a stranger arrived in the quaint old town of Haarlem, in the Netherlands. The people eyed him curiously as he trudged down the main street, and there were many guesses as to who he might be. A traveler in those days was a rarity in Haarlem—a thing to be looked at and talked about. This traveler was certainly a man of no great consequence. He was dressed poorly, and had neither servant nor horse. He carried his knapsack on his shoulder, and was covered with dust, as though he had walked far.

He stopped at a little inn close by the market place, and asked for lodging. The landlord was pleased with his looks. He was a young man, bright of eye and quick of movement. He might have the best room in the house.

"My name," he said, "is John Gutenberg, and my home is in Mayence."

"Ah, in Mayence, is it?" exclaimed the landlord; "and pray why do you leave that place and come to our good Haarlem?"

"I am a traveler," answered Gutenberg.

"A traveler! And why do you travel?" inquired the landlord.

"I am traveling to learn," was the answer. "I am trying to gain knowledge by seeing the world. I have been to Genoa and Venice and Rome."

"Ah, have you been so far? Surely, you must have seen great things," said the landlord.

"Yes," said Gutenberg; "I have walked through Switzerland and Germany, and now I am on my way to France."

"How wonderful!" exclaimed the landlord. "And now, while your supper is being cooked, pray tell me what is the strangest thing you have seen while traveling."

"The strangest thing? Well, I have seen towering mountains and the great sea; I have seen savage beasts and famous men; but nowhere have I seen anything stranger than the ignorance of the common people. Why, they know but little more than their cattle. They know nothing about the country in which they live; and they have scarcely heard of other lands. Indeed, they are ignorant of everything that has happened in the world."

"I guess you are right," said the landlord; "but what difference does it make whether they know much or little?"

"It makes a great difference," answered Gutenberg. "So long as the common people are thus ignorant they are made the dupes of the rich and powerful who know more. They are kept poor and degraded in order that their lords and masters may live in wealth and splendor. Now, if there were only some way to make books plentiful and cheap, the poorest man might learn to read and thus gain such knowledge as would help him to better his condition. But, as things are, it is only the rich who can buy books. Every volume must be written carefully by hand, and the cost of making it is greater than the earnings of any common man for a lifetime."

"Well," said the landlord, "we have a man here in Haarlem who makes books. I don't know how he makes them, but people say that he sells them very cheap. I've heard that he can make as many as ten in the time it would take a rapid scribe to write one. He calls it printing, I think."

"Who is this man? Tell me where I can find him," cried Gutenberg, now much excited.

"His name is Laurence—Laurence Jaonssen," answered the landlord. "He has been the coster, or sexton, of our church for these forty years, and for that reason everybody calls him Laurence Coster."

"Where does he live? Can I see him?"

"Why, the big house that you see just across the market place is his. You can find him at home at any time; for, since he got into this queer business of making books, he never goes out."

Day 171

1. Read the second part of the story about the first printer.

II. The young traveler lost no time in making the acquaintance of Laurence Coster. The old man was delighted to meet with one who was interested in his work. He showed him the books he had printed. He showed him the types and the rude little press that he used. The types were made of pieces of wood that Coster had whittled out with his penknife.

"It took a long time to make them," he said; "but see how quickly I can print a page with them."

He placed a small sheet of paper upon some types which had been properly arranged. With great care he adjusted them all in his press. Then he threw the weight of his body upon a long lever that operated the crude machine.

"See now the printed page," he cried, as he carefully drew the sheet out. "It would have taken hours to write it with a pen. I have printed it in as many minutes."

Gutenberg was delighted.

"It was by accident that I discovered it," said old Laurence. "I went out into the woods one afternoon with my grandchildren. There were some beech trees there, and the little fellows wanted me to carve their names on the smooth bark. I did so, for I was always handy with a penknife. Then, while they were running around, I split off some fine pieces of bark and cut the letters of the alphabet upon them—one letter on each piece. I thought they would amuse the baby of the family, and perhaps help him to remember his letters. So I wrapped them in a piece of soft paper and carried them home. When I came to undo the package I was surprised to see the forms of some of the letters distinctly printed on the white paper. It set me to thinking, and at last I thought out this whole plan of printing books."

"And a great plan it is!" cried Gutenberg. "Ever since I was a boy at school I have been trying to invent some such thing."

He asked Laurence Coster a thousand questions, and the old man kindly told him all that he knew.

"Now, indeed, knowledge will fly to the ends of the earth," said the delighted young traveler as he hastened back to his inn. He could scarcely wait to be gone.

The next morning he was off for Strasburg.

At Strasburg young Gutenberg shut himself up in a hired room and began to make sets of type like those which Laurence Coster had shown him. He arranged them in words and sentences. He experimented with them until he was able to print much faster than old Laurence had done.

Finally, he tried types of soft metal and found them better than those of wood. He learned to mix ink so it would not spread when pressed by the type. He made brushes and rollers for applying it evenly and smoothly. He improved this thing and that until, at last, he was able to do that which he had so long desired—make a book so quickly and cheaply that even a poor man could afford to buy it.

And thus the art of printing was discovered.

Day 172

1. Read the story *John Gutenberg and the Voices.*

ONE night John Gutenberg worked until very late at his press. He was printing a large folio edition of the Bible in Latin. For weeks he had given all his thoughts to this great work, and now he was completing the last sheets. He was worn out with fatigue, but proud of that which he had accomplished. He leaned his head upon the framework of his press, and gave himself up to thought.

Suddenly from among the types two voices were heard. They were speaking in low but earnest tones, and seemed to be talking about Gutenberg and his invention.

"Suddenly from among the types two voices were heard."

"Happy, happy man!" said the first voice, which was gentle and sweet and full of encouragement. "Let him go on with the work he has begun. Books will now be plentiful and cheap. The poorest man can buy them. Every child will learn to read. The words of the wise and the good will be printed on thousands of sheets and carried all over the world. They will be read in every household. The age of ignorance will be at an end. Men will learn to think and know and act for themselves.

They will no longer be the slaves of kings. And the name of John Gutenberg, inventor of printing, will be remembered to the end of time."

Then the other voice spoke. It was a stern, strong voice, although not unpleasant, and it spoke in tones of warning. "Let John Gutenberg beware of what he is doing. His invention will prove to be a curse rather than a blessing. It is true that books will be plentiful and cheap, but they will not all be good books. The words of the vulgar and the vile will also be printed. They will be carried into millions of households to poison the minds of children and to make men and women doubt the truth and despise virtue. Let John Gutenberg beware lest he be remembered as one who brought evil into the world rather than good."

And so the two voices went on, one claiming that the printing press would bless all mankind, the other saying that it would surely prove to be a curse. John Gutenberg felt much distressed. He did not know what to do. He thought of the great harm that might be done through the printing of bad books—how they would corrupt the minds of the innocent, how they would stir up the passions of the wicked.

Suddenly he seized a heavy hammer and began to break his press in pieces. "It shall not be said of me that I helped to make the world worse," he cried.

But as he was madly destroying that which had cost him so much pains to build, he heard a third voice. It seemed to come from the press itself, and it spoke in tones of sweet persuasion.

"Think still again," it said, "and do not act rashly. The best of God's gifts may be abused, and yet they are all good. The art of printing will enlighten the world. Its power for blessing mankind will be a thousand times greater than its power for doing harm. Hold your hand, John Gutenberg, and remember that you are helping to make men better and not worse."

The upraised hammer dropped from his hands. The sound of its striking the floor aroused him. He rubbed his eyes and looked around. He wondered if he had been dreaming.

Day 173

1. Read the story about James Watt.
2. What did he do when his experiments failed? (Answers)

A LITTLE Scotch boy was sitting in his grandmother's kitchen. He was watching the red flames in the wide open fireplace and quietly wondering about the causes of things. Indeed, he was always wondering and always wanting to know.

"Grandma," he presently asked, "what makes the fire burn?"

This was not the first time he had puzzled his grandmother with questions that she could not answer. So she went on with her preparations for supper and paid no heed to his query.

Above the fire an old-fashioned teakettle was hanging. The water within it was beginning to bubble. A thin cloud of steam was rising from the spout. Soon the lid began to rattle and shake. The hot vapor puffed out at a furious rate. Yet when the lad peeped under the lid he could see nothing.

"Grandma, what is in the teakettle?" he asked.

"Water, my child—nothing but water."

"But I know there is something else. There is something in there that lifts the lid and makes it rattle."

The grandmother laughed. "Oh, that is only steam," she said. "You can see it coming out of the spout and puffing up under the lid."

"But you said there was nothing but water in the kettle. How did the steam get under the lid?"

"Why, my dear, it comes out of the hot water. The hot water makes it." The grandmother was beginning to feel puzzled.

The lad lifted the lid and peeped inside again. He could see nothing but the bubbling water. The steam was not visible until after it was fairly out of the kettle.

"How queer!" he said. "The steam must be very strong to lift the heavy iron lid. Grandma, how much water did you put into the kettle?"

"About a quart, Jamie."

"Well, if the steam from so little water is so strong, why would not the steam from a great deal of water be a great deal stronger? Why couldn't it be made to lift a much greater weight? Why couldn't it be made to turn wheels?"

The grandmother made no reply. These questions of Jamie's were more puzzling than profitable, she thought. She went about her work silently, and Jamie sat still in his place and studied the teakettle.

How to understand the power that is in steam, and how to make it do other things than rattle the lids of teakettles—that was the problem which James Watt, the inquisitive Scotch boy, set himself to solve. Day after day he thought about it, and evening after evening he sat by his grandmother's fireside and watched the thin, white vapor come out of the teakettle and lose itself in the yawning black throat of the chimney. The idea grew with him as he grew into manhood, and by long study he began to reason upon it to some purpose.

"There is a wonderful power in steam," he said to himself. "There was never a giant who had so much strength. If we only knew how to harness that power, there is no end to the things it might do for us. It would not only lift weights, but it would turn all kinds of machinery. It would draw our wagons, it would push our ships, it would plow and sow, it would spin and weave. For thousands of years men have been working alongside of this power, never dreaming that it might be made their servant. But how can this be done? That is the question."

He tried one experiment after another. He failed again and again, but from each failure he learned something new. Men laughed at him. "How ridiculous," they said, "to think that steam can be made to run machinery!"

But James Watt persevered, and in the end was able to give to the world the first successful form of the steam engine. Thus, from the study of so simple a thing as a common teakettle, the most useful of all modern inventions was finally produced.

Day 174

   1. Read the story of *Webster and the Woodchuck.* (Part 1)

ON a farm among the hills of New Hampshire there once lived a little boy whose name was Daniel Webster. He was a tiny fellow for one of his age. His hair was jet black, and his eyes were so dark and wonderful that nobody who once saw them could ever forget them.

He was not strong enough to help much on the farm; and so he spent much of his time in playing in the woods and fields. Unlike many farmers' boys, he had a very gentle heart. He loved the trees and flowers and the harmless wild creatures that made their homes among them.

But he did not play all the time. Long before he was old enough to go to school, he learned to read; and he read so well that everybody liked to hear him and never grew tired of listening. The neighbors, when driving past his father's house, would stop their horses and call for Dannie Webster to come out and read to them.

At that time there were no children's books such as you have now. Indeed, there were but very few books of any kind in the homes of the New Hampshire farmers. But Daniel read such books as he could get; and he read them over and over again till he knew all that was in them. In this way he learned a great deal of the Bible so well that he could repeat verse after verse without making a mistake; and these verses he remembered as long as he lived.

Daniel's father was not only a farmer, but he was a judge in the county court. He had a great love for the law, and he hoped that Daniel when he became a man would be a lawyer.

It happened one summer that a woodchuck made its burrow in the side of a hill near Mr. Webster's house. On warm, dark nights it would come down into the garden and eat the tender leaves of the cabbages and other plants that were growing there. Nobody knew how much harm it might do in the end.

Daniel and his elder brother Ezekiel made up their minds to catch the little thief. They tried this thing and that, but for a long time he was too cunning for them. Then they built a strong trap where the woodchuck would be sure to walk into it; and the next morning, there he was.

"We have him at last!" cried Ezekiel. "Now, Mr. Woodchuck, you've done mischief enough, and I'm going to kill you."

But Daniel pitied the little animal. "No, don't hurt him," he said. "Let us carry him over the hills, far into the woods, and let him go."

Ezekiel, however, would not agree to this. His heart was not so tender as his little brother's. He was bent on killing the woodchuck, and laughed at the thought of letting it go.

"Let us ask father about it," said Daniel.

"All right," said Ezekiel; "I know what the judge will decide."

Day 175

1. Read the story of *Webster and the Woodchuck.* (Part 2)

They carried the trap, with the woodchuck in it, to their father, and asked what they should do.

"Well, boys," said Mr. Webster, "we will settle the question in this way. We will hold a court right here. I will be the judge, and you shall be the lawyers: You shall each plead your case, for or against the prisoner, and I will decide what his punishment shall be."

Ezekiel, as the prosecutor, made the first speech. He told about the mischief that had been done. He showed that all woodchucks are bad and cannot be trusted. He spoke of the time and labor that had been spent in trying to catch the thief, and declared that if they should now set him free he would be a worse thief than before.

"A woodchuck's skin," he said, "may perhaps be sold for ten cents. Small as that sum is, it will go a little way toward paying for the cabbage he has eaten. But, if we set him free, how shall we ever recover even a penny of what we have lost? Clearly, he is of more value dead than alive, and therefore he ought to be put out of the way at once."

Ezekiel's speech was a good one, and it pleased the judge very much. What he said was true and to the point, and it would be hard for Daniel to make any answer to it.

Daniel began by pleading for the poor animal's life. He looked up into the judge's face, and said:—

"God made the woodchuck. He made him to live in the bright sunlight and the pure air. He made him to enjoy the free fields and the green woods. The woodchuck has a right to his life, for God gave it to him.

"God gives us our food. He gives us all that we have. And shall we refuse to share a little of it with this poor dumb creature who has as much right to God's gifts as we have?

"The woodchuck is not a fierce animal like the wolf or the fox. He lives in quiet and peace. A hole in the side of a hill, and a little food, is all he wants. He has harmed nothing but a few plants, which he ate to keep himself alive. He has a right to life, to food, to liberty; and we have no right to say he shall not have them.

"Look at his soft, pleading eyes. See him tremble with fear. He cannot speak for himself, and this is the only way in which he can plead for the life that is so sweet to him. Shall we be so cruel as to kill him? Shall we be so selfish as to take from him the life that God gave him?"

The judge's eyes were filled with tears as he listened. His heart was stirred. He felt that God had given him a son whose name would some day be known to the world.

He did not wait for Daniel to finish his speech. He sprang to his feet, and as he wiped the tear from his eyes, he cried out, "Ezekiel, let the woodchuck go!"

Day 176

1. Read about *Why Alexander Wept.*
2. Why did he cry? (Answers)

ALEXANDER with his little army overran all the western part of Asia.

"The world is my kingdom," he said.

He conquered Persia, which was then the greatest and richest country known. He burned the mighty city of Tyre. He made himself the master of Egypt. He built, near the mouth of the Nile River, a splendid new city which he called, after his own name, Alexandria.

"What lies west of Egypt?" he asked.

"Only the great desert," was the answer. "To the farthest bounds of the earth there is nothing but sand, sand, burning sand."

So Alexander led his army back into Asia. He overran the country beyond the great river Euphrates. He crossed the grassy plains that lie along the shores of the Caspian Sea. He climbed the snowy mountains that seem to overlook the world. He gazed northward upon a desolate land.

"What lies beyond?" he asked.

"Only frozen marshes," was the answer. "Mile after mile, mile after mile, to the farthest bounds of the earth there is nothing but fields of snow and seas of ice."

So Alexander led his army back toward the south. He overran a large part of India. He subdued one rich city after another. At last he came to a mighty river called the Ganges. He would have crossed the river, but his soldiers would not follow him.

"We go no farther," they said.

"What lies to the east of this wonderful stream?" asked Alexander.

"Only tangled forests," was the answer. "Mile after mile, mile after mile, to the farthest bounds of the earth there is nothing else."

So Alexander caused ships to be built. He launched them on another river called the Indus, and with his army floated down to the sea.

"What lies farther on?" he asked.

"Only trackless waters," was the answer. "Mile after mile, mile after mile, to the farthest bounds of the earth there is nothing but the deep sea."

"Truly, then," said Alexander, "all the inhabited world is mine. West, north, east, south, there is nothing more for me to conquer. But, after all, how small a kingdom it is!"

Then he sat down and wept because there were not other worlds for him to conquer.

Day 177

1. Read the story of the sleepy goatherd. (A goatherd is like a shepherd, except they watch goats of course.)

I. IN the village of Sittendorf in Germany there dwelt, a long time ago, a poor but worthy man whose name was Peter Klaus. All the people for miles around knew Peter. He was not fond of hard work. He could not have been persuaded for all the money in the world to spend his days in a shop tinkering at a trade. He liked to be out of doors. He liked to wander at his ease in the fields and the woods, enjoying the sunlight and the flowers and the songs of the birds.

Since he could not be induced to follow any occupation in the village, his neighbors sometimes hired him to take care of their goats. Every morning he drove a great flock of

Billies and Nannies out upon the slopes of the Kyffhäuser Mountain; and while they browsed upon the grass, he wandered around in the groves and glens or went to sleep on the sunny slope of some great rock. In the evening he got the goats together and drove them slowly back to the village. This was just the kind of life that he liked, and he wished no grander title than that of "Peter Klaus the goatherd."

One morning, soon after reaching the pasture, Peter missed the prettiest Nanny goat in the flock. He hunted for her among the rocks and in the thickets of underbrush; he called her; he climbed to the top of the hill whence he could see all over the country for miles around. But no stray goat could he find.

When evening came and it was time to go home, he was in great despair. Should he go home and say that he had lost one of his flock? Such a thing had never happened before. But what was his surprise upon rounding up the flock, to see the lost Nanny in its midst!

The same thing happened for several days. Every morning Nanny would disappear and nothing could be seen of her until late in the evening, when she would suddenly join her fellows and run, frisking and playing, back to the village.

Peter was much puzzled, for, do what he could he was unable to find out what the frolicking creature did with herself during the day. At length he made up his mind not to take his eyes off her during the whole day. He watched her closely and saw that, when the flock passed the corner of an old broken-down wall at the foot of a hill, she quietly dropped behind and was out of sight in a moment.

Peter examined the wall. He had seen it many a time before. People said that it was part of the ruins of an old castle. As he looked closely he saw that, just behind a hawthorn bush, there was a hole large enough for a goat, or even a man on all-fours, to pass through. This, then, was the place where Nanny disappeared so strangely; indeed, she had worn quite a path beneath the hawthorn, and the only wonder was that her master had not discovered it before.

Day 178

1. Continue the story.

The next day Peter watched her as before, and when she ran slyly through the wall he followed her. After creeping on his hands and knees for some distance he found himself in a long and lofty cavern. The sunlight streamed through some crevices in the rocks and made the place look quite light and cheerful. At the farther end he saw Nanny busily picking up some oats that were scattered on the floor. How did the oats come there? The plump grains were constantly trickling down from above, and the goat had nothing to do but stand and eat.

Peter could not understand it. But as he came nearer he heard the stamping of heavy feet overhead and the whinnying of horses.

"Oh, somebody has a stable up there," he said to himself; "but how can that be? I have been all over these hills, and have never seen even the sign of a house."

As he was looking about him, a door in the side of the cavern suddenly opened and a queer little fellow with a big head and saucer eyes came in.

"Good morning to you, sir," said Peter, thinking it was the stable man. "I beg you will pardon me for coming in without any invitation. Is there anything I can do to serve you?"

The little man made no answer, but looked at Peter funnily with those great eyes, and beckoned him to follow.

Peter was too good-natured to refuse, and besides this he was curious to learn all about the strange place. So he followed his queer guide through the door and up a long flight of stairs until he again felt the warm sun on his cheeks and saw the green; grass beneath his feet.

He saw that he was now in a square courtyard surrounded by stone walls and shaded by tall trees. His guide led him through another broad cavern and then out upon a green lawn that was fenced in on every side by tall cliffs and rocky heights. Near one end of the lawn were twelve old-fashioned knights playing at ninepins. The knights were dressed in a very queer way. They wore long hose and silver-buckled shoes. Their snow-white hair and beards reached almost to their knees.

They scarcely noticed Peter, so busy were they at their game, and not one of them spoke a word. The guide motioned to Peter to pick up the nine-pins and return the bowls to the bowlers. Peter was so badly frightened by the strangeness of everything that he dared not disobey. Trembling in every limb, he hastened to serve the knights as he was bidden.

He noticed as the bowls were rolled over the lawn that they made a noise like thunder rumbling among the hills, and this frightened him still more. By and by, however, he began to gain courage. As the players were never in a hurry, he learned to humor himself and to do his work as slowly as he pleased. Looking around him, he saw a pitcher of wine and twelve golden goblets on a table at the end of the lawn. He did not stop to think that the goblets were for the knights and that there was none for him; he was very thirsty, and he drank right out of the pitcher.

The wine made him very brave. He felt that he would rather pick up ninepins than mind his neighbors' goats; and every time one of the bowls rolled toward the table he would run and take another sip from the pitcher. At last, however, his head began to feel heavy; and while he was in the act of picking up the ninepins, he fell gently over upon the grass and went to sleep.

Day 179

    1. Continue the story.

II. When Peter Klaus awoke he found himself lying on the grass where he had been in the habit of feeding his goats. He sat up and looked around. There were the same rocks upon which he had sat a hundred times; there were the same hills among which he had so often wandered; and there was the same noisy brook along which he had walked a thousand times with so much delight. But the trees and shrubs seemed strange to him—they were much larger than when he had seen them before, and there were many new ones that he did not remember.

He looked for his goats, but they were nowhere in sight. He called, but not one of them came to him. He started out to seek them, but was surprised to see that all the well-known paths among the hills were overgrown with tall grass. He rubbed his eyes to make sure that he was awake. "Strange! strange!" he muttered. "I will go back to the village and see if the beasts are there."

His legs were so stiff that walking was a hard task. He stumbled along slowly, wondering why the rheumatism should trouble him so much. After a while he came to a spot from which he could see the village spread out before him at the bottom of the valley. It was the same pretty village of Sittendorf; he could not see that it had changed. He hurried along to the main road, hoping to find his flock there. But not a goat could he see.

Before reaching the village he met a number of people; but they were all strangers to him, and they looked at him so queerly that he did not dare to ask any questions. In the village the women and children stood in their doorways and stared at him as he passed. All were strangers to him. He noticed that some of them stroked their chins and laughed; and without thinking much about it, he put his hand to his own chin. What was his surprise to find that he had a beard more than a foot long!

"Ah, me!" thought he. "Am I mad, and has all the world gone mad too? Where am I?"

But he knew that the village was Sittendorf—for there were the church and the long street which he knew so well, and towering above them was the great Kyffhäuser Mountain looking just as it did when he was a child.

He went on until he came to his own house. It was greatly altered. The roof was beginning to fall in; the door was off its hinges; the rooms were empty and bare. He called his wife and children by their names; but no one answered him. A strange dog came round the corner and snarled at him. A strange man in the next dooryard looked over the fence and told him to go away.

Soon a crowd of idlers and women and children gathered around him. They were laughing at his long beard and his tattered clothes. A woman who seemed more thoughtful than the rest asked him what he wanted.

"I don't know what I want," he answered. "I came here to find my goats and I find everything and everybody lost. Does anybody know—"

He was about to inquire for his wife and children; but he thought how odd that would seem, and stopped short. He was silent for a moment; then he looked around at the circle of strange faces and asked, "Where is Kurt Steffen, the blacksmith?"

The crowd stared at him, but no one spoke. Then an old woman who had hobbled across the street to look at him answered, "Kurt Steffen! Why, Kurt Steffen went to the wars years and years ago. Nobody has heard from him since."

Day 180

1. Finish the story.

Poor Peter Klaus looked around him, more dazed than ever. His lips quivered pitifully as he asked, "Then where is Valentine Meyer, the shoemaker?"

"Ah, me!" answered another old woman. "Valentine has been lying for nearly twenty years in a house that he will never leave."

Peter thought that he had seen both of the old women before—but as he remembered them they were young and handsome and of about his own age. He was about to ask another question when he saw a sprightly young mother, who looked very much like his wife, coming down the street. She was leading a little girl about four years of age, and on her arm was a year-old baby. He staggered and rubbed his eyes, and leaned against the wall for support.

"Does anybody know Peter Klaus, the goat-herd?" he stammered.

"Peter Klaus!" cried the young mother. "Why, that was my father's name. It is now twenty years since he was lost. His flock came home without him one evening, and all the village searched night and day among the hills and on the mountain, but could not find him. I was then only four years old."

"And are you little Maria?" asked Peter, trembling harder than ever.

"My name is Maria," was the answer, "but I am no longer little Maria."

"And I am your father!" cried Peter. "I am Peter Klaus who was lost. Don't any of you know Peter Klaus?"

All who heard him were filled with astonishment; and Maria, with her two children, rushed into his arms crying, "Welcome, father! Welcome home again! I felt sure it was you as soon as I saw you."

And soon all the old people in the village came to greet him. "Peter Klaus? Yes, yes, it seems only yesterday that you drove our goats to the pasture. How time does fly! Welcome, old neighbor! Welcome home after being away twenty years."

Congratulations on finishing the EP Second Reader!

Answers

Day 1

    2. No

Day 2

    2. Sleeping

    3. Wants to play

    4. Clean face and ready hands

Day 3

    3. She's not telling the truth. She's pulling your leg.

Day 4

    2. Under a hill

    3. A big crow scared them

Day 5

    2. When she's not with anyone else

Day 6

    2. Nothing to do

    3. Butcher shop

    4. Can't stand it

Day 7

    2. If he's good, his grandma will give him a piece of the cake she keeps in a locked cupboard.

    3. He's peeking out from behind a blind.

    4. She has all she needs.

Day 9

    4. Claws/paws, sky/high, deep/sleep, set/yet

    5. Mouse and cricket

Day 11

    4. It's late in fall.

    5. He loves that time of year!

    6. O, it's then's the times a feller is a-feelin' at his best, They's something kindo' harty-like about the atmusfere (There is something kind of hearty-like about the atmosphere), But the air's so appetizin', O, it sets my hart (heart) a-clickin' like the tickin' of a clock, I don't know how to tell it — but ef (if) sich (such) a thing could be, As the Angles wantin' boardin', and they'd call around on me – I'd want to 'commodate 'em — all the whole-indurin' flock — (This says that all the angels would want to come and stay with him after the harvest and there is abundant food and the women have made cider and goodies. He says he would "accommodate them — all the whole enduring flock" of angels.)

Day 12

2. She's describing keeping warm on a cold, winter day.

3. In the snow and in the sand

4. The snow will melt and the flowers will be there, but flowers don't grow in sand because there is no water or nutrition in the sand.

6. Some boys came and crushed their eggs and ruined their nest.

Day 13

2. She says in winter she's not sure who is better off, but she says in the spring, when "trees burst out in leaf" (or when leaves grow on trees again), everyone knows the bird in the tree is luckier. She says, "Who could doubt?"

3. You need sun and rain to make a rainbow.

4. It means they smell sweet.

Day 14

3. Creates sparks of fire

4. Flowers

9. She likes the nightingale's song. When you are doing something you like, the time seems to go quickly. When you are doing something you don't like, the time seems to go slowly. Since the time is going by quickly for her (the night seems short), we can figure out that she likes listening to the nightingale.

Day 15

2. A caterpillar eating, spinning a cocoon and turning into a butterfly.

4. That it is going to take *forever* to finish her work

5. She's happy that she got the work done little by little and then she can play!

6. Say/day, new/do

Day 16

2. It teaches time measurements.

3. It teaches how much money is worth.

1. (vocabulary) Pounds are worth the most, then shillings, pence, then farthings.

Day 19

2. A boat that takes passengers (and today cars) back and forth across a river or small body of water

3. A penny

4. The milk is from the cows, and it must be time to milk them when the cows come back to the barn from the pasture (grassy area).

6. A bird

7. Winter

8. Summer

9. The bird is migrating, flying to a warm place for winter and returning for the summer.

Day 20

2. Cloud

3. Rainbow

4. The rose is the prettiest flower.

5. Don't hurt living creatures.

Day 21

2. They didn't have enough money. The animals earned money for the zoo.

3. He was liked by all the animals.

Day 25

1.   A

2.   H

3.   K

4.   D

5.   E

6.   I

7.   C

8.   G

9.   F

10. B

11. J

Day 27

2. He is trying to figure out why Mr. Toad was in a hurry.

3. He is going to go to the Smiling Pool to see what Mr. Toad is doing there.

Day 28

2. They don't know! They can't find him.

Day 29

2. Sing

Day 30

2. His throat swells. It's his "music bag."

Day 32

2. Hooty the Owl

Day 33

2. Grandfather Frog

Day 34

2. Grew a new tail

Day 36

1. (vocabulary) to be jealous of

Day 37

    2. It catches bugs; it's sticky; it's really long; it's fast.

    3. It isn't attached at the back by the throat; it's attached at the front of his mouth.

Day 40

    2. Down the crooked little path

    3. Underground, he sinks into the sand

Day 41

    2. He's worried he'll be eaten by Mr. Blacksnake.

Day 42

    2. Mr. Blacksnake

Day 43

    2. Jimmy Skunk

Day 44

    3. (vocabulary) Mr. Toad

Day 47

    2. To not be proud

Day 61

    3. Peter Rabbit, Reddy Fox, Sammy Jay, Jimmy Skunk

Day 62

    3. "It never remembers other people."

    4. It remembers other people.

Day 63

    2. He thought he had killed Jimmy Skunk.

Day 64

    2. Reddy Fox

    3. Sprayed him

Day 66

    2. The yellow jackets had just stung him. It means that he hurt all over.

Day 67

    2. Sammy Jay suspects that Peter knew Jimmy was in the barrel and tricked Reddy into rolling it on purpose.

Day 70

    2. He thought there might be a back door, and he tried to find it.

    3. He told Peter that he would be waiting for him at nightfall and that he might play a joke on Peter.

Day 71

    2. Jimmy Skunk kept his word by doing what he said he would do. He told Peter that he would come back and he did.

Day 73

2. Prickly Porky, the porcupine

3. (vocabulary) It means that they don't attack people with their spray or pokes; they only use them to stop attackers.

Day 74

2. They are good to eat; they hatch cute babies.

Day 75

2. Eating eggs

Day 76

2. Uncle Billy knows Jimmy sprays his scent in the front, so just in case, he wants to be behind him.

3. Jimmy wants Uncle Billy to go first in case there is a trap.

Day 77

2. A china egg is not a real egg. It's a decoration. The Browns were using them to show the hens that they could lay eggs there.

Day 78

2. They had bad tempers because they were disappointed that they didn't get any eggs.

Day 79

2. Jimmy Skunk isn't afraid of Farmer Brown's boy because he knows the boy is afraid of getting sprayed by him.

Day 81

4. (Vocabulary) A trifle is something unimportant. Farmer Brown's boy was saying it's not worth getting upset over things that aren't important. And Uncle Billy hadn't thought it was important that he kick or not kick the egg, but now it made it so that he was caught by Farmer Brown's boy and the hiding place was going to be boarded up.

Day 82

2. Uncle Billy pretended to be dead.

3. No, Farmer Brown's boy knew he was pretending.

Day 83

2. Farmer Brown's boy tickled Uncle Billy's nose with a piece of straw until he sneezed.

Day 91

3. England

4. They were fighting the Danes.

5. Woodcutter's house

6. Forgot to keep the cakes from burning

7. She scolded him.

Day 106

    2. America

Day 107

    2. She threw herself over him so that the Indians from her tribe wouldn't kill him by beating them with their clubs.

Day 108

    2. He chopped down his father's cherry tree. He told the truth about what he had done.

Day 109

    2. She went out in the storm with her father to save some shipwrecked men.

Day 110

    2. He had to shoot an arrow through an apple on top of his son's head.

Day 111

    2. A horse rang the bell; No, he was just hungry.

    3. His master left him cold and starving and it was ordered that half his master's gold be used to care for the horse.

Day 112

    2. Impossible

Day 113

    2. He was wise and just.

Day 114

    2. Her sons

Day 115

    2. He pulled a thorn out of his paw.

    3. The slave had run away and was captured and was to be fed to a lion. But the lion turned out to be his friend that he had helped.

Day 116

    2. He defended the bridge so that the Etruscans couldn't enter the Roman city.

Day 117

    2. Rome

Day 118

    2. Damocles realizes that rich people are always worried and so are not as happy as they seem.

Day 119

    3. He let them both go free.

Day 120

    2. A short answer–using as few words as possible

Day 121

    2. The soldier

Day 122

    3. The father spoke scornfully, like he thought, "Alexander is nothing special. Why would he be able to tame the horse if no one else can?"

Day 124

    2. The hawk knocked the cup out of his hand because a poisonous snake was in the water he was going to drink from.

Day 126

    2. Money

    3. All the money he had at home

Day 127

    2. The kingdom of heaven

Day 128

    2. One locust went into the granary and took out a grain of sand. Another locust went into the granary and took out a grain of sand. Another locust…

Day 129

    2. They had each felt a different part of the elephant: the trunk, the leg, the ear…and so each thought an elephant looked like what he had felt. They didn't realize that it was all different parts of the elephant.

Day 130

    2. Crack a whip (snap a whip so fast that it makes a loud sound)

    3. Two pieces (one before he goes and one when he gets back)

Day 131

    2. He put a buoy, something that floats, with a bell on it to mark the spot so ships could avoid it.

    3. They cut off the bell and cut loose the buoy.

    4. The robbers crashed into it.

Day 132

    3. A penny

    4. His cat

Day 133

    2. The king

Day 134

    2. Butter

Day 135

    2. Napoleon's wife

Day 136

    2. Freddie and Flossie and Bert and Nan

    3. Bert and Nan are older and Freddie and Flossie are younger.

    4. Their dog

Day 137

    3. Horses have runaway

    4. Danny is another kid and a bully. Bert does not like him.

    5. Nan and some other girls

    6. There is no right answer. You don't have to be right, but you do have to think and give an answer.

Day 138

    2. Sledding

Day 139

    2. Snowballs

Day 140

    2. Someone put a giant snowball on the school steps and it froze and blocked the door.

Day 141

    2. Bert

    3. I don't think he did it because he says he can explain how he knows he didn't leave his knife there.

Day 142

    2. Danny Rugg

Day 144

    2. Mr. Carford

    3. We don't know yet, but he had some kind of trouble there. He's saying if Snow Lodge had burned down, then he wouldn't have been there for whatever trouble occurred.

    4. You can't know. You aren't supposed to be right. You are supposed to think.

Day 145

    2. Mr. Carford

    3. His nephew, his sister's son He raised him as a son when his sister died.

    4. He left Snow Lodge after Henry left.

Day 146

    2. The keys to Snow Lodge

Day 149

    2. Danny Rugg

Day 151

2. Their cousins

Day 160

2. Snap, their dog

Day 166

2. He was naked because he had been taking a bath.

Day 173

2. He persevered.

Day 176

2. There were no more worlds to conquer.

PLEASE consider contacting us at allinonehomeschool@gmail.com about passing this book along to a family in need when your family has finished with it.

ABOUT THE EASY PEASY ALL-IN-ONE HOMESCHOOL

The Easy Peasy All-in-One Homeschool is a free, complete online homeschool. There are 180 days of ready-to-go assignments for every level and every subject. It's created for your children to work as independently as you want them to. Preschool through high school is available and courses ranging from English, math, science and history to art, music, computer, thinking, physical education and health. A daily Bible lesson is offered as well. The mission of Easy Peasy is to enable those to homeschool who otherwise thought they couldn't.

Look for other books in the EP Reader Series and for more offline materials to come.

Made in the USA
Lexington, KY
06 September 2017